# THE
# GREAT CITIES
# IN HISTORY

EDITED BY

# John Julius Norwich

# THE
# GREAT CITIES
# IN HISTORY

*51 illustrations*

Thames & Hudson

*For Mollie – who did much of the work*

*The Great Cities in History* © 2009 Thames & Hudson Ltd,
London, save for the articles listed on page 356

First published in the United States of America in 2009
by Thames & Hudson Inc., 500 Fifth Avenue, New York,
New York 10110

www.thamesandhudsonusa.com

This compact paperback edition first published in 2019

Library of Congress Control Number 2018945504

ISBN 978-0-500-29251-8

Printed and bound by CPI Group (UK) Ltd, Croydon, CRO 4YY

To find out about all our publications, please visit
**www.thamesandhudson.com.**
There you can subscribe to our e-newsletter, browse or download
our current catalogue, and buy any titles that are in print.

# CONTENTS

# FROM MESOPOTAMIA TO MEGALOPOLIS

JOHN JULIUS NORWICH

It is one of the great paradoxes of history that towns and cities could be said to be born of agriculture. Before man learnt to till the fields, he was a hunter; and the early hunters were nomads – they had to keep on the move, following their prey wherever it might lead them. Even when prey was plentiful, it made sense that one family of hunters should not live too close to the next. Agriculture, on the other hand, calls for settled habitation in more durable structures, and for cooperation. With the advent of farming, in 8000 BC or thereabouts, architecture was born; people built themselves houses in groups near the land they cultivated. Then, gradually over the centuries, as larger communities came together and greater investment was made in individual buildings, a multiplicity of functions emerged within settlements: there were temples in which to sacrifice to the gods; a palace from which a ruling elite governed; storerooms for the accumulated agricultural produce; baths and open spaces where people could gather and refresh themselves after their labours; and walls for defence. Demand for prestige goods would stimulate trade and exchange, though that in turn would probably depend on the proximity of the sea or a great river. And so the village became the town, and the town – if large and important enough – eventually became the city.

The greatest of these cities form the subject of this book. The first section deals with those of the ancient world, extending to AD 100 or thereabouts. Of the very earliest – Uruk in Mesopotamia, for example, which can be claimed as the first true city in the world, or Mohenjo-daro in the Indus Valley – relatively little is left above ground. Some fragmentary texts may survive; otherwise we have to rely for our knowledge on the archaeologist's spade alone. The civilization of ancient Egypt, represented here by Memphis and Thebes, is the oldest culture of which, thanks to its surviving monuments, paintings, carvings and inscriptions, we can begin to form a distinct idea in our minds. Of Athens and imperial Rome, too, there is fortunately enough still standing – together with a considerable body of superb literature – to enable us to build up an even clearer picture of what these cities looked like, and of the sort of life that was lived by their inhabitants. Jerusalem is, I think, a special case. It possesses no majestic architecture of the classical period on the scale of Greece or Rome, but its primary position in both the Jewish and Christian (and later also Islamic) religions and the wealth of great literature that they have left behind have given it – despite its unhappy history – an aura possessed by no other city in the world.

Next we pass on to the cities that had their finest flowering during the first millennium of the Christian era. Here we can extend our gaze to a larger world. Two of our great cities – Tikal and Teotihuacan – are in Central America. Another is Chinese: Chang'an, the capital of the dazzling Tang dynasty. No fewer than four are Islamic – throwing into sharp relief the superiority of the Arab-Moorish civilizations during those centuries that in northern Europe are not surprisingly known as the dark ages. Christianity is represented by one city only: Constantinople. It appears late on the historical scene, having been founded by the emperor Constantine the Great as recently as AD 330; but from the moment of its foundation it was the capital of the Roman empire, and it dominated the eastern Mediterranean for the best part of a thousand years – until the catastrophe of the Fourth Crusade in 1204.

In the medieval period – which, for the purposes of this book, spans the years from around AD 1000 to 1500 – our net is cast wider still. It spreads north to Lübeck and the cities of the Hanseatic League; south to Cairo and Palermo, Benin and Timbuktu; east to Kraków, Samarkand and Angkor; and west to two more great cities of pre-Columbian America, Aztec

Tenochtitlan – later buried beneath present-day Mexico City – and Cuzco, the 2-mile-high capital of the extraordinary Inca people. It is impossible to compare these cities with each other, if only because of the immense distances – both geographical and cultural – which extended between them. The world in the Middle Ages seemed of unimaginable size, with most of it still shrouded in mystery. Journeys were slow, long-distance communications almost non-existent, navigation rudimentary, since longitude was still incalculable. Outside Europe, few of the cities on our list would ever even have heard of one another.

The very end of the 15th century, however, marks a sudden and spectacular leap forward. In 1492 Christopher Columbus discovered – or perhaps rediscovered – the New World; and only a year or two later Vasco da Gama was to open up the Cape Route to the Indies from Europe. Henceforth a ship could be loaded in London or the Hanseatic ports and unloaded at its final destination in Bombay or the Spice Islands; no longer was it necessary to risk valuable cargoes in the pirate-ridden Red Sea or Persian Gulf, nor yet to entrust them to the shambling camel caravans that might take three or four years to cross the steppes of Central Asia. If this was bad news for the Mediterranean, which now seemed fated to become little more than a backwater, it was worse news still for Venice and the other great commercial ports of the Middle Sea, which had already been rocked by the fall of Constantinople to the Ottoman Turks in 1453. Spain and Portugal, on the other hand, rejoiced – particularly after the Borgia Pope Alexander VI had, by the Treaty of Tordesillas, drawn a line on the map and divided up the new-found South American continent between them.

The Early Modern World was consequently a world very different from its predecessor. Its horizons were far broader, its shipbuilding and navigational skills far more highly developed. And its potential by comparison seems virtually unlimited. New empires were taking shape. The Byzantine was replaced by the Ottoman; Vienna became the centre of Habsburg power; Russia coalesced, with Peter the Great moving his capital to St Petersburg at the beginning of the 18th century; and, further east, new capitals appeared in Isfahan, Agra, Beijing and Kyoto. The Spanish empire in the New World is represented by Mexico City, successor to the Aztec Tenochtitlan. There was also the spiritual empire, represented – not always, it must be said, very spiritually – by the Papacy, centred on that magnificent if occasionally monstrous phenomenon, Renaissance Rome. Now, too, London enters the lists for the first time – as does Edinburgh, scene of that astonishing 18th-century artistic and cultural explosion that we know as the Scottish Enlightenment.

And so we reach the Age of the Modern City. It opens – for the purposes of this book – around 1800, though all the cities are hard to confine within a chronological compartment, spreading across centuries, defying our attempts to arrange them neatly into sections. By now, the industrial revolution was well under way, resulting in mass immigration from the countryside to the towns and the appearance of the megalopolis. London and Paris are here for the second time, since both were undergoing a dramatic change: London with its tremendous population explosion – made possible largely by improvements in sanitation – and Paris with the radical surgery of Napoleon III and Baron Haussmann. North America – which has not up to this moment put in an appearance – now looms large: in Canada we look at Montreal, in the United States at New York and Washington, Chicago and Los Angeles. Here too we witness another astonishing innovation – the skyscraper, which in turn owes its existence to the invention of the electric elevator. South of the isthmus of Panama, we cast an eye on Buenos Aires and São Paulo. Europe – apart from London and Paris – is represented by Barcelona, Berlin and Budapest; Asia by New Delhi and Singapore, Shanghai and Tokyo: and Australasia by Sydney.

The selection of all these cities was, needless to say, extremely difficult and we are braced for objections: are we really trying to argue that Timbuktu is more important than Toronto, or Meroë than Melbourne? The answer lies, of course, in those two words of the title, 'in history'. Timbuktu in the

13th and 14th centuries may have been little known in the western world, but it was the key city of three successive empires, and when considered in this light it surely deserves its place in the medieval spectrum.

This book can indeed be seen as a work of history, for those who prefer to read it in such a light; but it is also about art and architecture, about trade and commerce, about travel and exploration, about economics and planning. Above all it is about people: how they work and play, how they worship; and how, over the centuries, they have tackled that greatest of all social problems: how to live together in close proximity, yet also in harmony and concord.

# THE ANCIENT WORLD

I well remember, perhaps half a century ago, flying over Egypt and being struck by how the country beneath looked exactly like a map of itself. There below me flowed the Nile, a thin line of water flanked by broad strips of brilliant green; and beyond these strips, nothing but yellow sand, disappearing to the horizon. That was the day when I first consciously realized that, for the peoples of desert lands where rainfall is scarce, rivers are everything. In the days of antiquity they provided not only water to irrigate the fields, but also the principal means of communication. Roads were virtually non-existent; the only effective method of transport was by water, which had the added advantage of being able to support immense weights immovable by any other means. Uruk – the earliest civilization of those described in this book – had a broad and magnificent river, the Euphrates, to support it; it was the water, rather than any wealth of natural resources, that made life possible. The same can be said of Meroë and of Mohenjo-daro, of Nineveh and Babylon, and of the two great cities of ancient Egypt, Memphis and Thebes. Without the Tigris, the Euphrates and the Nile, the world of early antiquity would have been a desolate place indeed.

The only successful civilizations without great rivers to rely on were those which enjoyed an adequate rainfall and were centred on or near the coast. Athens and Carthage are the obvious examples. But the sea is a good deal harder to navigate than a river, and there were few, if any, even moderately seaworthy ships before around 1500 BC. (Odysseus, sailing in around 1200 BC, took ten years – if we are to believe Homer – to get from Troy to Ithaca: surely, even in his day, something of a record.) River cities, therefore, were able to grow up long before maritime cities; when Athens was born, Uruk was probably over three thousand years old.

Athens, however, was a city of the Mediterranean; and for the Athenians, as well as for the other peoples dwelling around its shores, the

Mediterranean had – long before the 6th century BC – become less of a barrier than a bridge. There were close links between the Athenians and the Alexandrians, and rather less friendly relations between the Romans and the Carthaginians, for whom their thriving colony of Cartagena in Spain was, by the time of the Punic Wars in the 3rd century BC, almost as important as the mother city itself. Jerusalem too, though a mountain city rather than a maritime one, was within easy reach of the sea; we read in the First Book of Kings how the Phoenician, Hiram, King of Tyre, sent Solomon timber and skilled craftsmen for the building of his temple. And after the conquest of Palestine by Pompey in 63 BC Jerusalem could be said to be part of the Roman – and hence of the Mediterranean – world.

Of all the cities in this section, those of the Warring States of China from the 5th to the 3rd centuries BC are perhaps the most astonishing, not only for their sheer size and organization – they were probably the largest cities in the world at that time – but for another reason too. If a city is to prosper, we normally see peace as one its principal requirements; here it was war that provided the stimulus they needed. Another city based on military might was the rocky stronghold that the Hittites built at Hattusas.

What, apart from their antiquity, did all these peoples have in common? Very little, perhaps, except that in their day the world was young. For the earliest of them, there were no written records; they could take nothing for granted; they had to discover everything for themselves. Agriculture they understood, up to a point; they were fascinated, too, by astronomy, which helped them in their first tentative efforts at navigation. Having had their origins in the Bronze Age, all except the very earliest experienced the slow but vitally important transition to the Age of Iron. But all of them, without exception, could pride themselves on one thing: they had created a city. In those days, it was no small achievement.

# URUK

## The World's First City

MARGARETE VAN ESS

*Climb Uruk's wall and walk back and forth! Survey its foundations,*
*examine its brickwork! ... Did the Seven Sages not lay its*
*foundations? A square mile is the city, a square mile date-grove ...*
*half a square mile the temple of Ishtar: three square miles*
*and a half is Uruk's expanse.*

EPIC OF GILGAMESH, 3RD MILLENNIUM BC

At the beginning of the 3rd millennium BC, Uruk was a thriving city of some 30,000 to 50,000 inhabitants, standing on the river Euphrates on the northern shore of the delta with the Tigris, some 300 km (186 miles) south of modern Baghdad. Enclosing an area of 5.3 sq. km (2 sq. miles) within its great city wall, it was the largest metropolis of its day and maintained political and commercial relations with other nations and cities both near and far. Its brilliantly organized urban administration and its achievements in monumental architecture were well known, and were commemorated in several epics, notably that of Gilgamesh, one of the earliest of all literary works.

Although King Gilgamesh of Uruk may have been a historical ruler of the 27th–26th centuries BC, the heroic deeds narrated in that epic reflect events from earlier periods as well, and suggest that by his day the kingdom had attained a remarkably high degree of sophistication. Uruk in the time of Gilgamesh could already look back on around fifteen hundred years of history, during which it had successfully adapted to the harsh living conditions of southern Mesopotamia. While older permanent human settlements existed elsewhere in the region, the flat, alluvial and often marshy land between the Euphrates and the Tigris had been inhabited only since the 6th millennium BC; the climate was too hot and the river waters, which flooded the flat lands, too difficult to tame.

Secure life in this difficult region depended on a highly developed system of control. Such a system demands agreements, first with neighbouring and then with more distant settlements; and as more villages and fields become involved, these agreements call for specialized negotiators. Archaeological evidence shows that by 3500 BC Uruk had become a large urban centre, with an efficient administration, organized religion and impressive public architecture – all hallmarks of a true city. There were farmers to ensure food supply, artisans organized in the mass production of clothes, pottery and tools, as well as artists to create beautiful works of art for the city's adornment.

Southern Mesopotamia has few natural resources, and consequently a considerable import trade developed – in wood and metals from the Taurus, Zagros and Lebanon ranges, as well as semiprecious stones and lapis lazuli from as far away as Afghanistan. As the social hierarchy became more complex, the number of professions grew: to the administrators and soldiers were added priests, scientists and astronomers who made observations of the natural world. Then, around 3200 BC, came the earliest form of writing, which was created initially for the purposes of administration.

In Uruk's early days its public buildings, raised up on artificial hills, impressed by their sheer size and by the splendour of their decoration. Visible from far away, they left onlookers in no doubt as to the city's wealth and power. But then, around 3000 BC, the entire centre was remodelled on a completely new design. At its heart, on a terrace, stood a single temple, dedicated to Ishtar, goddess of love and war; surrounding this were other, humbler buildings with spacious courtyards that were given over to the temple administration.

As the city prospered, its area steadily increased; and finally, probably in the time of Gilgamesh, it was enclosed by its celebrated wall, 8.7 km (5½ miles) long, reinforced by 900 buttresses. Construction of the wall meant that the rivers providing the city with water had to be canalized, and the resulting network of large and small channels facilitated the movement of traffic around and within the city. The sheer scale and sophistication of these monumental works ensured Uruk's renown for the next 2,500 years.

The urban core continued to be inhabited until the 4th century AD, and both as a city and as a religious centre, Uruk retained a certain importance, but it never recovered its former political power. Its ruins now lie isolated in the deserts of Iraq.

# MOHENJO-DARO

## Mysteries of the Indus Civilization

ROBIN CONINGHAM

*Rarely has it been granted to archaeologists, like Schliemann
in Tiryns and Mycenae or Stein in the deserts of Turkmenistan,
to reveal to the world the remains of a long-forgotten civilization.
Nevertheless, we are now apparently on the very brink of such
a revolutionary discovery in the Indus Valley.*

SIR JOHN MARSHALL, 1924

In the 2nd century AD, Buddhist devotees constructing a monastery beside
the Indus river reused bricks from earlier structures that they had found at
the site. Abandoned within four centuries, the ruins of this monastery, now
in modern Pakistan, became known as Mohenjo-daro, or the 'Mound of the
Dead'. When R. D. Banerjee, the first archaeologist to excavate at the site,
began work there in 1921, he believed that all the mounds were historical
in age, but quickly recognized that its seals bore the same indecipherable
script discovered the previous year at Harappa. The British archaeologist
Sir John Marshall soon resolved the issue when he announced that the
similarity of the two sites, 400 km (250 miles) apart, confirmed the presence of a previously unknown Bronze Age civilization in the Indus valley.

Mohenjo-daro is both the best-preserved city of this civilization – which
spread over an area of half a million sq. km (193,000 sq. miles) between
2500 and 1900 BC – and also its largest, covering 200 ha (494 acres), of
which only a small fraction has been excavated. The site was first occupied
around 3500 BC as hill farmers and herders settled on the river floodplain,
but these levels are now metres below the water table. Enveloping its

predecessor, Bronze Age Mohenjo-daro was pre-planned, and although only the final phases of its 600-year life are now exposed, the streets still echo this first blueprint. A work of some 4 million days of communal labour, the city was formed by erecting two enormous silt platforms stabilized by facings of mud brick.

The larger of the two platforms, the Lower Town was divided by a grid of wide streets into city blocks, each with access to wells for water close by. Side streets and lanes provided entry to individual courtyard houses. Mostly extremely regular, a few of these compounds were larger than average and perhaps had a non-residential function. One block of simple structures may have housed slaves or renounceants. Evidence indicates that the majority of households were engaged in making shell, stone, ceramic or metal objects. A further unifying feature was the widespread provision of bathing platforms, emptying through a network of drains leading into lanes and through silt traps into the city's thoroughfares. A vast investment, it is thought that these baths performed a ritual role, as well as coping with bathwater and the little rain that fell each year.

If the Lower Town is characterized by uniformity, its neighbour to the west, the 'Citadel', is distinguished by its unique monuments. Its most exceptional structure is the Great Bath, a basin measuring 12 m by 7 m (39 ft by 23 ft) and 2.4 m (8 ft) deep, made waterproof by setting brick in bitumen and surrounded by a colonnaded courtyard. Narrow entrances to the Great Bath on minor streets suggest that access to it was restricted. A second monument to its west comprised rows of mud-brick podiums. It was first identified as a hypocaust for underfloor heating, but the archaeologist Sir Mortimer Wheeler later interpreted it as the state granary; analogies with a similar structure at the site of Lothal (in India) suggest it indeed had a storage function. At the southern end of the mound is a hall measuring 900 sq. m (3,000 sq. ft), formed by four rows of five rectangular brick piers. This vast space was the largest permanently covered area in the city. Despite these grand monuments, the absence of anything resembling palaces, temples or royal tombs is puzzling, suggesting that the civilization's rigid uniformity was guided by less overtly hierarchical values than its Mesopotamian neighbours.

Ever since Mohenjo-daro's discovery, scholars have tried to ascertain why the city fell into ruin almost four thousand years ago. One theory saw invasions from outside the region as the main culprit, while another pointed to natural catastrophes. It is likely, however, that the end came gradually, with the inhabitants moving back to the countryside as the river shifted its course away from the city, and the annual inundation on which its farmers relied became unpredictable. Mohenjo-daro was a unique experiment in urban planning and it was to be another thousand years before urban communities were re-established in the region – though never again in such a regimented style.

# MEMPHIS

## The Balance of the Two Lands

IAN SHAW

*Then, when this first king Menes had made what he thus
cut off to be dry land, he first founded in it that city
which is now called Memphis.*

HERODOTUS, 5TH CENTURY BC

Memphis is a city unusually overshadowed by its cemeteries. The Great Pyramid at Giza, the Step Pyramid at Saqqara, and the catacombs of the Sacred Animal Necropolis and the Serapeum are all better preserved and better known than the streets, houses, temples, palaces and markets of the city of Memphis. Yet this was the capital and governmental heartbeat of Egypt for the best part of three and a half millennia, from the beginning of the pharaonic period (c. 3000 BC) until the Arab conquest (AD 641), only to be eventually replaced by Cairo itself (p. 120). Like many other ancient Egyptian towns and cities, it has neither survived so well as the cemeteries, nor received the same level of attention from archaeologists. The site of Memphis as a whole now covers almost 4 sq. km (1½ sq. miles), but the residential sections are mostly either destroyed or buried beneath such modern villages as Mit Rahina and el-Badrashein.

The city's location at the apex of the Delta made it well suited for the control of both this and the Nile valley, so that it was sometimes also known as the 'balance of the two lands'. The earliest recorded name for the city is Ineb-hedj, meaning 'white walls' or 'white fortress', probably referring to the dazzling appearance of the fortified palace of one of the earliest kings. It has been suggested that this original town may have been situated near the modern village of Abusir and that the settlement gradually shifted southwards.

The remains of Memphis have suffered from their proximity to the suburbs of medieval and modern Cairo, but archaeologists from the early 1800s to the present day have gradually pieced together parts of the network of temples, palaces and private houses, including a large temple complex dedicated to the local god Ptah. The city's gradual expansion seems to have been influenced primarily by the locations of the series of royal pyramids built in the Saqqara necropolis, which stretched along its western side. As construction began on each new pyramid, so the geographical focus of the town slowly shifted. By the late Old Kingdom, Ineb-hedj seems to have been eclipsed in importance by a set of suburbs further to the south, centring on Djed-isut, the town and palace associated with the pyramid of the 6th dynasty King Teti. But it was Men-nefer (meaning 'established and beautiful'), the part of the city associated with the pyramid of Pepi I (c. 2321–2287 BC), that provided the basis for the name Memphis, by which the whole city was known for the rest of its history.

Later accounts claimed that the city was named after its supposed founder, the semi-mythical 1st dynasty ruler Menes. According to the Egyptian historian Manetho (c. 305–285 BC), Menes was responsible for the unification of the 'Two Lands' and was thus the founder of the Egyptian state. Many scholars believe that the legendary Menes is the same person as the better-documented King Narmer, but we know virtually nothing of his reign. The Greek writer Herodotus credits him with draining the plain of Memphis as well as founding the city. It has recently been suggested that his name may mean 'the Memphite', thus commemorating both the founding of Memphis as the capital city and also the unification of Egypt. To the ancient Egyptians he was the first human ruler, in contrast to his predecessors on the throne who were regarded as demi-gods.

From at least the New Kingdom onwards, a vast temple dedicated to the god Ptah lay at the centre of Memphis. Little of this has survived, particularly when we compare it with the temple of Amun at Karnak, in the heart of Thebes (p. 25), which it must once have rivalled. Ptah formed a divine triad with his consort the lioness goddess Sekhmet and the lotus god Nefertem. Ptah himself was usually portrayed as a mummified man, with his hands protruding from his linen wrappings and his head shaven and covered by a tight-fitting skull cap. One of Ptah's Memphite shrines was called Hwt-ka-Ptah, which was possibly corrupted by the Greeks to become Aiguptos, and hence the origin of the modern name Egypt.

Part of the New Kingdom temple is built out of Old Kingdom pyramid casing blocks, perhaps brought from Saqqara, and other reused elements, including a lintel of the Middle Kingdom ruler Amenemhat III (c. 1855–1808 BC), have been found there, indicating that older monuments are yet to be discovered at Memphis.

In modern times a fallen colossus of the great New Kingdom ruler Ramesses II (c. 1279–1213 BC) and an 'alabaster' sphinx are the features of the ancient city most commonly visited, since the site of the temple itself is often flooded. Remains of a palace of King Merenptah (c. 1213–1203 BC), successor to Ramesses II, along with a smaller Ptah temple, are found in the Kom Qala area of the site. Throughout the pharaonic period the houses and temples gradually spread southwards and eastwards as the course of the Nile retreated eastwards towards its modern location. The remains of large parts of early Memphis must therefore lie beneath thick deposits of Nile alluvium, and much is below the water table.

An embalming house for the Apis bull, the living manifestation of the god Ptah, was built at Memphis by Sheshonq I (c. 945–924 BC) of the 22nd dynasty, probably replacing an earlier structure, and traces of this, including enormous travertine embalming tables, are still visible. At the death of each Apis bull there was national mourning, and its corpse was embalmed and carried in procession along the sacred way for burial in a huge granite sarcophagus in a set of underground catacombs known as the Serapeum.

North of the precinct of Ptah is an enclosure of the Late Period, best known for the 26th dynasty palace of King Apries (589–570 BC). All that survives of Apries' once impressive palace is a massive mud-brick platform surmounted by the limestone bases of columns. The fourth ruler of the 26th dynasty, Apries is known in the Bible as Hophra. His reign was dominated by military campaigns, primarily defending Egypt's northeastern frontier against Cyprus, Palestine and Phoenicia. It was shortly after a defeat by Nebuchadnezzar II of Babylon that he was deposed by his own former general, Amasis, who replaced him as king. Apries fled the country and probably died in battle in 567 BC, when he attempted to regain his throne by force with the help of a Babylonian army (Herodotus suggests that he was captured and later strangled). From his palace, Apries would have had a clear view of the Saqqara necropolis, which was a source of inspiration for an artistic revival during the 26th dynasty.

In Ptolemaic times the once great city of Memphis dwindled in importance, losing out to the new sea-port at Alexandria (p. 51). After the Arab conquest in the 7th century AD, the founding of the nearby town of Fustat (out of which Cairo grew) dealt the final blow to Memphis. Its remains were still clearly visible in the 12th century AD, but over the centuries the stone blocks of its temples and palaces have been quarried and reused, while the mud bricks from many of its houses have been spread over the fields as fertilizer.

# THEBES

## Heart of Egypt's Golden Age

BILL MANLEY

*'My name is Ozymandias, king of kings: Look on my works,*
*ye Mighty, and despair!' Nothing beside remains: round*
*the decay of that colossal wreck, boundless and bare,*
*The lone and level sands stretch far away.*

PERCY BYSSHE SHELLEY, 1818

At Thebes, the ancient Egyptians created a city at the limit of human under-standing; a city outside time where, paradoxically, immortal pharaohs were born and then later buried. The nation's craftsmen cleared a 'sacred land' of gold and painted stone, where the *akhu* ('illuminated spirits') of the long-departed are forever present. Here the Creator, Amun ('the hidden one'), and 'his son of his belly', the Pharaoh, would 'sweeten their hearts'. The city's temples, palaces, cemeteries and avenues, as we know them today in modern Luxor, took two thousand years to imagine and build. Spelled out, still, in giant hieroglyphs across massive walls of limestone and granite is the irreducible story of how Amun's will revealed itself in human affairs. For unknown reasons, classical writers called this city after 'seven-gated Thebes' in Greece, but the Egyptian name was Wāse ('place of authority'), while its inhabitants simply called it Nō, 'the City'. At its height, during the 13th century BC, one poet sang 'Wāse is the pattern for every city', which is why 'all others are called after her true name'.

Thebes entered history late in the 3rd millennium BC, as the capital of the fourth district of Upper Egypt. The great chief of nearby Edfu sailed a hostile fleet there around 2100 BC, and reported an unexceptional scatter of farms, forts and tombs. In population, Thebes was already dwarfed by the national capital at Memphis (p. 21), nearly 700 km (400 miles) to the north, and even at its height probably numbered no more than 30,000 inhabitants in a nation of up to 3 million.

The rise to national prominence took place amid civil war, when the city's governors installed themselves as the 11th dynasty of pharaohs, in opposition to the established monarchy at Memphis. Their reasons are unclear and to their enemies they were usurpers, but they portrayed themselves as defenders of the nation's values during a century of chaos and confusion – Theban martial bravado was usually laced with self-righteousness and calls for Egyptian ethnic purity. One of their number, Montjuhotep II (c. 2010–1960 BC), prosecuted this war to a bloody final victory and, for the next fifteen hundred years Theban values, Theban gods and, indeed, Thebans themselves were at the heart of Egyptian life.

The tombs of the 11th dynasty kings are clustered on the West Bank of the Nile around a natural amphitheatre at Deir el-Bahri, directly across the river from Amun's great temple at Karnak. These two sites mark one of two axes that defined the extent of ancient Thebes: from sunrise behind Karnak to sunset beyond Deir el-Bahri. Hidden even in the warmth and illumination of the Egyptian sun, Amun was worshipped at Karnak inside a darkened shrine called Ipe Isu, 'most special of places'.

Throughout two thousand years the estate of Amun at Karnak alone would grow to cover at least 100 ha (250 acres – more than twice the size of the Vatican State), including temples for Amun's consort, Mut, their son, Khons, and other gods. Once each year, during the Dry-season, the little wooden statue of Amun left Ipe Isu and sailed to Deir el-Bahri to spend the dark night in one of the shrines made for each of the kings who had gone before, and there celebrate the fusion of the god's immortal spirit with the king's mortal body. This was the Perfect Festival of the Valley, when Theban families would trek to their own forefathers' tombs to feast and make offerings.

The counterpoint to the Valley Festival was the Festival of Ope, held over many days during the Flood-season. Bright-painted statues of Amun and statues of former kings sailed southwards on the river or were carried along a festival avenue from Ipe Isu in the north for 5 km (3 miles) along the second defining axis of Thebes: a festival avenue from Ipe Isu in the north to the southern edge of the city. At the south was Luxor temple, or Ope Rasi ('the southern harim'), which by the 14th century BC, had become as grand as Karnak. Food and beer were distributed to crowds gathered around the processional route, while folk vied to place a question before the god's statue in the hope of a response, positive or negative (indicated by the statue approaching or walking away from the questioner). Such oracles became a typical means of resolving matters as mundane as property disputes. At the crux of the festival, the king proceeded alone to the shrine to be with Amun, who spoke to him 'in the way that a father talks to his son'.

Thebes' heyday was the New Kingdom (c. 1539–1069 BC), when the city was at the centre of a world of Egyptian ideas, and Amun was venerated from the *gebels* of Nubia and the shores of Punt to the mountains of Lebanon. The burial of Pharaoh was the emotional heart of the entire nation's faith and, from the reign of Thutmose III (c. 1479–1425 BC), almost every New Kingdom pharaoh was laid to rest in a vast gash in the desert beyond Deir el-Bahri, known to us as the Valley of the Kings. The royal tomb walls still carry epic scenes of the soul's journey through darkness and void to attain *duat*, 'the state of adoration'. The vivid colours and delicate reliefs belie the painstaking skill with which generations of Thebans cut these enduring visions of spiritual awakening into the local fractured, shaley limestone.

Such commitment was the work not of slaves but of prosperous, educated craftsmen. Most of what lay beyond the estates and temples of Amun has now disappeared beneath modern Luxor, but the village of the royal tomb builders at Deir el-Medina was situated in the desert and hastily abandoned when the Valley of the Kings was eventually closed. As a result, streets and houses still stand, while letters and documents were left behind in such numbers that they record the best understood community in the ancient world. In the 13th century BC, there were up to 80 extended households in the village, with dozens more in the vicinity, and the palace supplied all their food and textile needs from the temple-stores. The first room in each house had a shrine for the family's ancestors, which could then be screened to accommodate the birth of the next generation.

One evening at dusk, in the Flood-season around 1111 BC, the governor of Thebes, Paser, was confronted in the street by a rowdy crowd of workmen, chanting because they had just been vindicated of charges of tomb-robbery. 'Would you gloat over me at the door of my own house?', he barked at them, 'What you have made today is not just chanting, it is your downfall you have made.' Oh, but they said, the tombs in the Valley are safe, to which the governor is reported to have replied, 'What you have done is far from what you have said.' So began a drawn out and ignominious final act in the Valley's story. The last king was laid to rest there at the end of the 11th century BC and the final curtain fell around 961 BC when the Priests of Amun shut the whole Valley down and removed the bodies of Thutmose III and his successors to a secret tomb at Deir el-Bahri, where they lay hidden until modern times. Later pharaohs were buried far from Thebes, and without these royal burials the city lost some of its lustre and wealth, although not its spiritual authority within Egypt. The festivals went on, the tombs of the local magnates grew ever larger, and the city was still run by priests enacting Amun's oracles.

Likewise, kings and governors throughout Egypt and Nubia still vied to have their daughters chosen as the God's Wife of Amun – an office that continued to bring prosperity and influence in this life and the next, so that by the 9th century BC Thebes had become a playground for the ambitions of kings from elsewhere. Then, in a brutal moment, the city's greatness all but ended as it had begun – in violence. In 664 BC Ashurbanipal of Assyria and his armies sought to lay low the whole Egyptian nation by ripping out its heart and sacking Thebes. Afterwards, the Old Testament prophet Nahum used the event to warn his own people: 'Art thou better than populous Nō … her young children also were dashed in pieces at the top of all the streets: and they cast lots for her honourable men, and all her great men were bound in chains.'

Building on the colossal scale of the pharaohs continued for centuries more in the estates of Amun at Thebes, but usually now on behalf of rulers from Persia, Macedon or Rome. Luxor temple eventually became a Roman military headquarters, and the West Bank of the Nile here was a magnet for tourists already in classical times. Occasionally, Thebes did become a focus for uprisings against foreign rule, and the worship of Amun survived the groundswell of Christianity much longer in his own city than in the countryside around. In time local monks and priests came to reuse the pagan shrines as Christian foundations; as well as people like Franke who, around AD 650–700, ran a factory for religious writing in the tomb of Amenope, a Theban who had been a vizier of Egypt some two thousand years earlier.

Even today the grandeur of Thebes echoes in the Arabic name, Luxor, or 'the Palaces', while a vestige of the Festival of Ope persists in the feast of the Muslim holy man, Abu el-Hajjaj, during which model boats 'sail' from Luxor temple. Nevertheless, when the day came for archaeology, Thebes lay buried under 2 m (6½ ft) of Nile mud. In AD 1862 one early explorer of the city, Alexander Rhind, noted wistfully that, 'rich harvests now wave over its buried wreck'.

# HATTUSA

## Stronghold of the Hittite Empire

TREVOR BRYCE

*On its site I sowed weeds. May the Storm God strike down
anyone who becomes king after me and resettles Hattusa!*
FROM THE INSCRIPTION OF ANITTA

Hattusa was the royal capital of the Late Bronze Age kingdom of the Hittites. The history of this kingdom, called the Land of Hatti in ancient texts, spanned almost five centuries, from the 17th to the early 12th centuries BC. At its height, the Hittite empire extended across Anatolia and northern Syria to the Euphrates river and the western fringes of Mesopotamia. Hattusa, the heart of this empire, lay in north-central Anatolia, 160 km (100 miles) east of the modern Turkish capital Ankara, next to the village of Boghazköy (Boghazkale). Covering an area of more than 185 ha (457 acres) at the peak of its development, Hattusa became one of the greatest urban centres of the ancient Near East.

An earlier settlement on the site had been destroyed in the middle of the 18th century BC by a king called Anitta, who had declared the place accursed. In defiance of the curse, however, Hattusili, one of the first Hittite kings, refounded the city and built a palace on its acropolis. This natural outcrop of rock flanked by deep gorges, now called Büyükkale, was virtually impregnable from the north. But the new city lacked adequate defences in the south, and was to remain vulnerable to enemy attack until a wall, 8 m (26 ft) thick, was built around it two centuries later. Even then, it survived only a few decades before it was stormed, plundered and put to the torch by hostile forces who had launched attacks from all directions on the Hittites' homeland territories. In what scholars refer to as the 'concentric invasions', the kingdom itself was brought to the brink of annihilation some time during the first half of the 14th century.

Eventually, the occupation forces were driven from the land, thanks mainly to the military genius of a certain Suppiluliuma, at that time still a prince but later to become one of the greatest of all Hittite kings (r. c. 1350–1322). The task of rebuilding the capital now began, and was to continue until the final collapse of the Hittite kingdom almost two centuries later. The city was massively expanded to the south, more than doubling its original size. New fortifications were built, extending over a distance of 5 km (3 miles), their main feature a great casemate wall erected on top of an earth rampart to a height of 10 m (33 ft) and punctuated by towers at 20-m (66-ft) intervals along its length. Before it was a second curtain wall – also with towers, which were built in the intervals between those of the main wall. Access to the city was provided by a number of gateways, the most impressive being decorated with monumental relief sculptures, which have since given them their evocative names: the Sphinx, Lion and Warrior-God (or King's) gates.

The original city, containing the royal acropolis and an enormous temple of the Storm God was redeveloped and refortified, and is now commonly known as the Lower City. Archaeologists refer to the later extension to its south as the Upper City. Excavations of the latter have brought to light the foundations of 26 temples, a substantial addition to the five previously known, with perhaps more yet to be discovered. The 'new temples' make it clear, according to their excavator Peter Neve, that Hattusa had the character of a sacred and ceremonial city. In fact the layout of the whole city can be seen as symbolizing the cosmic world-form of the Hittites, with the palace as the earthly world, the temple-city as the godly world, and the cult district lying in between providing the passage from the transient to the eternal. Subsequent excavations conducted by Neve's successor, Jürgen Seeher, have revealed large complexes of grain silos, and five reservoirs, which for a short time (before they silted up) supplied much of the city's water.

Tens of thousands of fragments of clay tablets, from Hattusa's palace and temple archives, provide our chief source of written information on the history and civilization of the Hittite world, including matters of cult, law and relations with the other great empires of the age, especially Egypt. An intact bronze tablet unearthed near the Sphinx Gate with 352 lines of text throws important light on both the political geography and the history of the kingdom in the last decades of its existence. And an archive containing over 3,500 seal impressions has provided significant details about the genealogy of members of the Hittite royal family.

It was long believed that Hattusa's end was abrupt and violent, but recent excavations have dispelled that impression. While there is certainly evidence of violent destruction, it seems that this may have occurred only after the city had already been partly abandoned. The remains of the last period of Hattusa's existence in the early 12th century indicate that most of the city's valuable possessions had been systematically removed before the city fell, suggesting that the king and his court escaped to a safe place of refuge, taking their most important items, including official records, with them. Presumably they were accompanied by a large military escort – but the rest of the population may well have been left to fend for themselves. When the city finally succumbed to marauding external forces, it may already have been in an advanced state of decay.

# BABYLON

## Nebuchadnezzar and
## the Hanging Gardens

JOAN OATES

*Babylon the Great, the Mother of Harlots and of the Abominations
of the Earth.... What city is like unto this great city!*
BOOK OF REVELATIONS, 17:5; 18:18

Babylon is one of the best-known cities of the ancient world. In the West
its iniquitous reputation is largely derived from its biblical condemnation
as 'the Mother of Harlots and of the Abominations of the Earth', though
that reference alludes not to Babylon but to Rome. Classical descriptions,
especially that of Herodotus, of the great city and its 'hanging gardens' are
familiar but difficult to substantiate. In ancient times Babylon was widely
admired for its culture and learning; indeed, when the city first fell to the
Assyrians in around 1225 BC, the conquerors removed large numbers of
cuneiform tablets to their homeland, apparently yearning for Babylonian
culture. Babylon reached the pinnacle of its fame under the 7th-century
BC dynasty of Nebuchadnezzar, and its capture was one of Alexander's
greatest triumphs – he chose to make it his eastern capital and was to die
there in the royal palace.

While Babylon was undoubtedly the most impressive city of its time,
especially under the 'Neo-Babylonian' kings (625–539 BC), it was not an
ancient one, at least in Mesopotamian terms. Its name is not to be found
among the cities of the distant past diligently recorded by Babylonian
scribes. First mentioned late in the 3rd millennium BC, it was only in the
early 2nd millennium BC that the small village rose to power, perhaps as a

result of land salination and the loss of maritime trade routes in southern Mesopotamia. Babylon lay within that small area where the Tigris and Euphrates approach closest to each other, a position that controlled two of the most famous roads in the ancient world – the main overland route later known as the Royal Road that ran from Susa in southeastern Iran to Sardis in western Anatolia, and the Khorasan Road to the east, later part of the great Silk Road. Within this small area lay a succession of six great capitals of the ancient world.

The first king to exploit this geographical advantage was Hammurabi (r. 1792–1750 BC), noted for his 'Law Code'. Although he failed to establish an enduring national state, by uniting the country – if only briefly – under Babylon, he did achieve a political result that was to affect the history of Mesopotamia for the next two millennia. Babylon became, almost overnight, the established seat of kingship, a position it was to maintain unchallenged for almost fifteen hundred years. Hammurabi's dynasty fell in c. 1595 BC, when the Hittites swept down the Euphrates and destroyed the city. They returned equally quickly to their homeland in Anatolia, and Babylon was eventually taken over by Kassites, a people from the east whose origins and language remain little understood. Like many other intruders, however, the Kassites adopted local language, customs and even religion. They ruled Babylonia for over four centuries, far longer than any native dynasty, but fell eventually to Elamites from southwestern Iran, who carried away to Susa many Babylonian trophies including Hammurabi's Law Code stela, now in the Louvre.

In the 1st millennium BC Babylon was ruled by a number of native dynasties, with occasional intrusions from Assyria. In the 8th century BC a Chaldaean tribal sheikh claimed the throne, and with the accession of Nabonassar (747 BC) we enter a new, precisely dated era in the history of Babylon, whose rulers and enemies are now recorded in both biblical and classical sources. The Nabonassar era was recognized as a turning point in the history of astronomy, and the very term Chaldaean came to signify 'astronomer'. In 625 another Chaldaean sheikh, Nabopolassar, seized power, not only defeating the threatening Assyrians but also establishing a new dynasty under which Babylon achieved its greatest fame.

Nabopolassar's son Nebuchadnezzar (604–562 BC) needs no introduction. The Babylon of Herodotus was largely the work of his architects, and this is the city the visitor still sees today, its ruins extending over some 850 ha (2,100 acres), the largest ancient settlement in Mesopotamia. German excavators worked there between 1899 and 1917; since 1958 Iraqi archaeologists have carried out further excavation and considerable restoration.

A visitor to the city notices first its great surrounding double walls. To the north is the Summer Palace, so-called because of its ventilation shafts, of a type still known in the region today. Here the name Babil has survived from ancient times. Next is an inner city, surrounded by another set of massive double walls enclosing the major public buildings, including over 40 temples. Most impressive is the 'Processional Way', leading from Babylon's main temple (Esagila), past the great ziggurat – the 'Tower of Babel' – and Nebuchadnezzar's vast palace, and through the famous Ishtar Gate (now reconstructed in the Vorderasiatisches Museum, Berlin), passing the earliest known museum, founded by Nebuchadnezzar, en route to the temple of the New Year Festival.

Much debate surrounds a structure at the northeast corner of the palace – an underground 'crypt' consisting of a series of 14 vaulted rooms built to support some enormous weight and containing wells with a unique hydraulic system. This combination of features has led to its identification as the Hanging Gardens, one of the Seven Wonders of the World. One tradition associates these fabled gardens with the queen Semiramis, while another credits them to Nebuchadnezzar. He is said to have built them for his wife, Amyitis, who was homesick for the trees and mountains of her native Persia. Lists of rations for the Jewish exiles from Jerusalem were found here, however, and it seems more likely that this structure served as a warehouse and administrative unit.

Many buildings continued in use in Persian and Greek times. Darius (521–486 BC) added a new palace with a columned hall for his son Xerxes, who was responsible for the destruction of the city in 482 BC. Greek influence is clearly evident in the now restored theatre. Nearby stood the remains of the funeral pyre ordered by Alexander for Hephaestion, his childhood friend and trusted general, as well as a great mound of brick rubble – debris removed by Alexander when he decided to rebuild the ziggurat destroyed by Xerxes.

Alexander chose Babylon for his eastern capital, but following his early death (323 BC), his general Seleucus founded a new city nearby (Seleucia-on-the-Tigris), marking the end of Babylon's civil power. Yet Seleucus' successor rebuilt the temple of Esagila, where Babylonian scholars maintained its great library and where the Babylonian priest Berossus dedicated his history of Babylonia to Antiochus. Babylon's last known document is dated AD 75. In AD 116 the Roman emperor Trajan wintered in Babylon, and offered a sacrifice in the room where Alexander died.

Babylon was much restored in the late 20th century. Saddam Hussein built himself a palace, for which he created a high artificial mound overlooking the palace belonging to Nebuchadnezzar, a splendid example of a ruler's attempt to manipulate the past for his own aggrandizement. This was built on the ancient river bed, causing relatively little damage , but the site has not fared so well in recent conflicts. A large area was flattened for 'hard standing' for heavy vehicles and helicopters, which themselves caused considerable damage both to the underlying site structure and to some standing buildings. A helicopter landing zone led to the destruction and removal of the ziggurat debris left by Alexander's troops and Hephaestion's funeral pyre, both of immense archaeological importance. Tanks and heavy vehicles were driven along the Processional Way, destroying forever the well-preserved street surface on which Nebuchadnezzar, Darius and Alexander had once walked and whose bricks preserved their names.

# NINEVEH

## Palaces and Temples of the Assyrian Kings

JULIAN READE

*Now the word of the Lord came unto Jonah the son of Amittai,
saying, Arise, go to Nineveh, that great city, and cry
against it; for their wickedness is come up before me.*

JONAH, 1:1–2

The name of Nineveh, for anyone familiar with the Bible, once suggested visions of limitless wealth and debauchery set in an exotic oriental landscape. Very little was positively known about the city, leaving all the more room for the imagination. The poet Lord Byron wrote a play about the effeminate Sardanapalus, supposedly last king of Nineveh, while painters including Eugène Delacroix and John Martin illustrated the dramatic fall of the city.

The real, rather than imaginary, Nineveh, as revealed by archaeologists, now largely consists of massive mounds of earth overlooking the crowded suburbs of Mosul in northern Iraq. Near one side of the city wall flows the Tigris river; rafts formerly carried merchandise past Mosul down this river, from Turkey towards the Persian Gulf. To the north and east of Nineveh, a rolling plain dotted with agricultural villages stretches towards the mountains of Kurdistan. To the west, low hills flank the Mesopotamian desert, traditionally the home of pastoral Arab tribes rich in camels and sheep. Nineveh owed its importance to its geographical position, as a natural crossroads where people from many regions met to exchange goods and gossip.

The earliest settlement on the site dates back before 6000 BC, and the town expanded around its great temple of Ishtar, the Assyrian equivalent of

Aphrodite, goddess of love, war and irrational emotion. Ishtar of Nineveh was worshipped in many parts of the Near East, and about 1750 BC the king Shamshi-Adad I, after conquering the city, built her a new temple in the fashionable Babylonian style. The temple walls, like those of nearly all Assyrian public buildings, were made of sun-dried mud brick, which requires regular maintenance to remain in good condition. Nonetheless, this impressive building stood for over a thousand years.

Despite the wide fame of its goddess, the city of Nineveh was not always the capital of Assyria. It was Sennacherib (r. 704–681 BC), on becoming Assyrian king, who decided to build himself a metropolis that would reflect the extent and variety of what was by then the greatest empire yet known in the Middle East. This empire controlled, directly or indirectly, an area reaching from central Turkey to the Persian Gulf and from central Iran to Cyprus and the borders of Egypt. Not long afterwards Assyrian armies would reach the Nile valley, capturing statues of Nubian kings for public display at Nineveh. The streets of the city were filled with a great variety of people – bearded soldiers and sleek eunuchs associated with the royal court, merchants and mercenaries, farmers and slaves, many of them coming from distant lands and speaking any number of languages.

Sennacherib enclosed Nineveh with a massive defensive wall 12 km (over 7 miles) long, incorporating 18 gates, and divided the city into three parts. The main public buildings, including royal palaces and the temple of Ishtar, occupied a fortified citadel now called Kuyunjik. Another fortified area held the army base and arsenal: this is where today a medieval mosque, once a church, covers the supposed tomb of Jonah, the biblical prophet swallowed by a whale, who urged Nineveh to repent. The remainder of the city included residential and industrial quarters, with a system of roads that were protected against any attempt at encroachment by severe penalties. Nineveh was also at the heart of an ambitious network of canals, based on those which the Assyrians had seen while campaigning in ancient Armenia (Urartu). Nineveh's canals brought water 50 km (30 miles) from the Zagros mountains to irrigate the royal gardens and the orchards and farmland of the citizens. A stone aqueduct, part of which still survives, was depicted in a stone wall-panel decorating one of the palaces on Kuyunjik.

Sennacherib's palace, located beside the temple of Ishtar, dominated the city and was known as Incomparable Palace: there had never been anything like it, at least in Assyria. Some 500 m (1,640 ft) long and up to 250 m (820 ft) wide, it was not only a royal residence but also contained government offices. Its principal rooms and courtyards were decorated with stone wall-panels displaying Sennacherib's achievements, both his victories in foreign lands and the manufacture and transport of colossal human-headed winged stone bulls as magical guardians, to protect against enemies, sickness and ill fortune. One wing of the palace contained tall cedar pillars; another was specifically built for the queen. Sennacherib described her as 'perfect above all women' and expressed the hope that she and he would live together in health and happiness, an unusual sentiment to find in one of the Assyrian royal inscriptions, which were mainly devoted to accounts of war.

A. H. Layard, the English archaeologist who explored part of this palace during 1847–51, reckoned that he had found 71 rooms, with nearly 2 miles of carved wall-panels and 27 doors guarded by colossal bulls or sphinxes. Among his finds were thousands of clay cuneiform tablets. Sennacherib's grandson, Ashurbanipal (r. 668–631 BC), had attempted to create a library containing all the traditional science and literature of Babylonia and Assyria, an endeavour anticipating the great libraries of Alexandria and the modern world. This same Ashurbanipal built for himself another palace on Kuyunjik: carved wall-panels there included naturalistic scenes of a royal picnic and lion-hunt unlike anything seen before.

This great cosmopolitan city flourished for less than a century. The Assyrian royal family, like so many others, was repeatedly divided against itself, and the whole imperial structure became vulnerable to internal and external enemies. In 612 BC, after several years of warfare, an alliance of

Medes from Iran, Babylonians and doubtless others combined to capture Nineveh. The bodies of soldiers who died in the fighting are still to be found within the city's gates. The palaces and the temple of Ishtar, with their monuments of Assyrian conquest, were torched. Survivors who sheltered inside the ruined buildings left only modest traces of their presence, and by 400 BC the Greek soldier Xenophon, passing by, described the city as desolate.

Nineveh later recovered its importance as a market-town, but was eventually superseded by Mosul, which lies on the opposite, western bank of the Tigris. The name of Nineveh was never lost, but it was only in the mid-19th century AD that European travellers and archaeologists recognized how much of the ancient city survived beneath the surface. In the 20th century Iraqi archaeologists worked to restore some of its major monuments, and the walls of the city can still be seen from space, though once again it finds itself in a conflict zone.

# CARTHAGE

## Phoenician and Roman Cities

HENRY HURST

*Carthage must be destroyed*
CATO THE ELDER, C. 150 BC

Twice in its history Carthage was one of the world's greatest cities. Both times it was seen as a threat to what might be called the West: first to the growing power of Rome, then, five centuries later, to the religion which the ageing Roman world had, misguidedly in Gibbon's view, clasped to its bosom.

The first Carthage was slightly older than Rome, being founded traditionally in 814 BC by colonists from Tyre. Culturally it was thus a hybrid of eastern Mediterranean and North African influences; its inhabitants spoke Phoenician. Overlooking the passage between the east and west Mediterranean seas, Carthage rose to commercial prominence, exercising control over all trade in the western sea, including the vital metals supply from Spain. In the 3rd century BC, faced with the rising power of Rome, a territorial empire was established under one of Carthage's leading families, the Barcids, in Spain. This included Cartagena – 'New Carthage' – from which the family's most famous son, Hannibal, set out to crush Rome in the second of the three Punic Wars. Hannibal nearly succeeded, but was finally defeated at the battle of Zama in 202 BC. The third Punic War saw the fulfilment of Cato's wish, the destruction of Carthage, in 146 BC.

The second Carthage was a Roman imperial city, exemplar of the 'concord' of Augustus – whose (re)foundation is celebrated in the story of Dido and Aeneas in Virgil's *Aeneid*, Book 4. Though it stood on the same spot as the first Carthage, it was developed over a century after 146 BC and was thus physically a different city. Yet the cultural continuities were powerful. In the early 5th century AD, St Augustine's outrage at the licence and popularity of the cult of Caelestis indicates that behind the material veneer of Roman Carthage the city's pre-Roman spiritual core – the worship of Caelestis/Tanit, their variant of the Phoenician goddess Astarte – was intact.

The two Carthages also show intriguing conceptual similarities, over and above their delicious setting at the side of the Gulf of Tunis. Characteristic of both was an ordered and technologically advanced urbanism. Both cities had gridded street layouts with rectangular city blocks. Punic Carthage was disposed radially around the acropolis on the Byrsa hill, but the Roman plan took order to extremes, with the whole city laid out on a single grid that paid no respect to natural variations in elevation. Four centuries later, the city authorities were still adding blocks of exactly the correct size and alignment, where necessary effacing misaligned buildings. The entry for Carthage in a 4th-century World Geography – the *Anonymi Orbis descriptio* – shows that the orderliness of the city plan was also noteworthy to contemporaries.

The same love of the abstract in planning can be found in the naval arsenal of the Punic city. This was an inner harbour made by digging out flat coastland in the shape of a circle, leaving a concentric circle of undug island at its centre. It was celebrated in the *Aeneid*, while its name, *cothon*, became a generic name for a dug-out harbour and it was imitated in Trajan's hexagonal basin at Rome's imperial harbour of Portus.

Little sympathetic writing survives about the people of Carthage. *Punica fides* – not unike 'perfidious Albion' – was the Roman catchphrase in dealings with pre-Roman Carthaginians, and revulsion was expressed at their cruel religion. Turbulent and still in thrall to unspeakable religious practices is how Christian writers saw their Roman successors. But their city belies that. The last word goes to one of the first 'discoverers' of the defunct city, El Bekri, writing in the 11th century AD: 'If someone was to go to Carthage every day of his life and occupy himself only with looking at it, every day he would find a new marvel which he had not noticed previously.'

# ATHENS

## Birthplace of Democracy

BETTANY HUGHES

*The magnitude of our city draws the produce of the world into our harbour, so that to the Athenian the fruits of other countries are as familiar a luxury as those of his own.*

THUCYDIDES, LATE 5TH CENTURY BC

Skulls are a surprise in a public park. Yet the storeroom of the Agora Museum in Athens hides drawers full of them. Today, the Agora is a butterfly-filled haven in the heart of 'Athena's City'. We amble through the Stoa of Attalos, past the stumpy remains of the 5th- and 4th-century BC law courts, around the solid temple of Hephaistos – drinking in the triumphs of Athens' classical Golden Age. We crane our necks to catch the columns of the Parthenon and the polished-bare rocks of the Areopagus (*Areios Pagos* – 'massive hill'), where Athens' council of wise men sat. But as we stroll and marvel it can be easy to forget we are walking on the ghosts of a multi-layered past. In the case of the Agora, physically – this teeming hub, this engine of democracy, of high art, of the 'Greek Miracle', was once a graveyard.

There have been Greeks in Athens for over 3,500 years, human habitation for over 8,000. The Bronze Age Mycenaean Greeks buttressed the Acropolis and today their fortifications are still visible, their arrowheads and perfume bottles, their skeletons still unearthed by the excavator's trowel. Then came the Greek 'Dark Ages' (a misnomer if ever there was one), when tribes, tyrants, despots and oligarchs tussled over who should hold the reins of power in this well-placed settlement. The Agora's flesh and blood remains remind us not to read ancient Athens as a romance. This was a visceral

43

place. A city capable of mesmerizing beauty, of the most inspirational and high-minded thoughts, but also a seat of torment, of trial and tribulation.

Geography gave Athens a kick-start. The story goes that the goddess of wisdom Athena and the sea-god Poseidon fought over the city. Surrounded by defensive mountains and lands rich in the raw materials of culture – marble, limestone, clay and silver – Athens is also a kingfisher's whisper from the sea. Athenians have always benefited from maritime trade, but have little to fear from pirates. So Poseidon was rejected and wise Athena won out: the goddess was welcomed as a long-term resident of that great lump of red-veined Late Cretaceous limestone that we call the 'High City': the Acropolis.

In 507 BC the Acropolis witnessed something rather extraordinary. Sheltering a Spartan king – ally of bullish Athenian aristocrat Isagoras – it was suddenly, violently, inhabited by the common crowd, *hoi polloi*, 'the people', who, for the first time in recorded history, acted as one, as a political agent. For an entire territory to erupt requires something seismic and in Athens there had already been popular stirrings. Sick of the filibustering power of a family of aristocrats, the law-giver Solon instituted a series of reforms (*c.* 594/593 BC). He reduced the power of those who 'pushed through to glut yourselves with many good things'. He broadened Athens' powerbase. Political reforms in Athens in the 6th and the 5th centuries, founded as they were on a philosophical bedrock of justice and wisdom, paved the way for Athena's city to become unique. Here the solidarity and self-determination of the world's first true democracy – enacted before the word *demos-kratia* was invented – was made flesh.

And in 479 BC, the beating back of the vast and powerful Persian empire, the bully-boy of the eastern Mediterranean, further electrified the city. Suddenly it seemed that there was nothing this fledgling democracy could not do. Citizens strode through the newly constructed Stoa of Zeus Eleutherios, 'Zeus the Liberator'. In democracy's name Athenians gathered together an empire. The *strategos* – the elected general – Perikles, urged Athenians to treat their violet-crowned city 'like a lover'. High-fliers nominated their sons 'Demokrates'. Come the 4th century BC, Demokratia was worshipped as a goddess.

Throbbing with the energy of the newly empowered, Athens now became the economic centre of the Greek world. In the assembly, bootmakers sat alongside aristocrats; one year in two these new democrats voted for war. The resident population more than doubled. Rows of modest homes – some little more than shacks – were erected. Plato might have quipped that the Greeks lived like 'frogs around a pond' – but those frogs were all jostling to spring on to Athens' gilded lily-pad.

The Agora was no longer the home of the dead, but of life. A place where fountains were untapped, where musical recitals were held, where soldiers drilled, where offerings were made to immortals at fragrant altars and where administrators met to standardize the business of democratic living. During the 6th and 5th centuries the market here developed, slaves were sold alongside pyramids of figs and opiates, fresh fish, woven cloth straight off the loom, and aromatic oils from the east. The tang of newly excavated minerals, newly minted silver coins would have been in the air, the taste of exotically seasoned stews, cooked on outdoor stoves, on the tongue.

We think of Athens as a city of marble and stone yet at its height there was something distinctly floral about the place. Men and women flooded in from the hills and plains of Attica, the craftsmen, stonemasons and painters – whether consciously or not – brought *rus in urbe*. Lilies unfurled on masonry, on vases olive trees were shaken, and architraves were shaded with a canopy of carved green. The lost rivers – the Eridanos and the Illyssos (today blocked underground) – flowed free. At rituals across the city and during the Mysteries of Eleusis, maidens wreathed in laurel and vines or carrying pungent, flaming pine-torches, adored and honoured the turn of the seasons. In the Agora protecting rows of plane trees were planted. All around the city forests of stelas (carved stone blocks) sprang up, inscribed with the workings and decisions of the democratic assembly.

And of course the imperial influence brought with it seeds of intellect. Scientists from the west coast of Asia Minor, rhetoricians from Sicily, philosophers from Thessaly and Macedonia. Just imagine the hubbub – the Athenians had a name for it even – the *thorubos* – the buzz of opinion and dissent in the streets, the council chambers, the assembly, the Agora, and at those famous symposia that Plato, Aristophanes et al. have immortalized, where wit and wine flowed, where poetry was sung and schemes of self-advancement were hatched.

Visual matched verbal delights. Current excavations are beginning to show us just what a gaudy, glittering place classical Athens would have been: statues painted fairground-jaunty; dinner services gleaming bright; semiprecious stones glinting from the eyes of gods and demi-gods in shrines and on street corners, saffron-veiled prostitutes leaning in the doorways of their 'knocking-shops'.

While some Athenians debauched themselves in the many (and obligingly varied) brothel districts, others, notably Perikles, were famously austere. This Olympian's kicks, it seems, were satisfied by the philosophical conversation of Anaxagoras and Sokrates, by drama (as a young man he produced Aeschylus), and by his clever courtesan Aspasia. His energies were dedicated to raising monumental structures on the Athenian skyline: the Propylaia, perhaps too the Erectheion, the Temple of Athena Nike. And above all Athena's Parthenon, decorated green, blue, gold – dazzling like a peacock.

Travelling around Athens today it is still hard to escape the Parthenon. Gleaming at dawn, shadowing at twilight, it is always there, a double exposure on an old-fashioned photograph. Plutarch, writing 500 years after the Periklean building programme, marvels: 'though built in a short time they have lasted for a very long time ... in its perfection, each looks even at the present time as if it were fresh and newly built. ... It is as if some ever-flowering life and un-ageing spirit had been infused into the creation of these works'.

But then flame burnt back the crops of democracy and empire. In 404 BC the Spartans, sometime allies but long-term enemies of the Athenians, toppled Athens' famous city walls, took the Acropolis, and flute-girls, we are told, danced in the embers of an empire.

There were shoots of regrowth. Orators such as Demosthenes ensured that Athens was a centre of excellence once more. Democracy was briefly restored. But with hindsight, these were just spasms in the Golden Age's slow, lingering death. Perikles himself thought that Athens would be remembered because the city 'ruled more Greeks than any other Greek state'. The Athenians weren't consciously providing us with a robust, benign, egalitarian basis for our own modern democracies. Their inspiring, experimental society was volatile, often unforgiving, paradoxical. All qualities that enhance, rather than diminish, their achievements.

We do Athens best service if we remember the sweat and grime as well as the scent of violets; if we admit the struggle to create and maintain democratic politics, the graft in realizing the world-class art. This was not a utopia. In all its complex delight and terror, in its sensuality and soulful philosophy, its rise and its fall, Golden Age Athens reminds us what it is to be human.

# LINZI

## Cities of Warring States China

W. J. F. JENNER

*There are five reasons for a city to fall. The first is long walls and too few people. The second is the walls being too small and overcrowded. The third is not enough food. The fourth is the market being too far from the walls. The fifth is livestock and supplies outside [the walls] and the rich living in the suburbs.*

MO ZI, 5TH CENTURY BC

The great cities of China from the 5th to the 3rd centuries BC were built of wood and dirt. Little remains of these except for some city walls and palace foundations of pounded earth, but they set the pattern for urban China's whole future course.

This era, aptly known as the Warring States, was one of total war. Since the fall of the Western Zhou monarchy in 771 BC there had been no effective central authority over the whole Chinese world. Zhou's former fiefdoms devoured each other. Some became large, independent states that created substantial walled cities. The Warring States powers had to be able to use all their resources in order to survive, and the capitals of the seven leading powers were fortresses to frustrate and exhaust an invading army. In these cities rulers encouraged bureaucratic government through which they could register all the people of the state, tax them and conscript them for labour or military service. They did not allow the people any part in government.

The great Warring States capitals dwarfed earlier Chinese cities. The measurable walls of three of them enclosed 15 to 18 sq. km (6–7 sq. miles): Linzi, the capital of Qi, in today's Shandong; Handan, the capital of Zhao some 320 km (200 miles) to the west; and Ying, the capital of Chu, the great power of the middle and lower Yangtze, 900 km (560 miles) to the southwest. The biggest walled city of the period, the Yan capital Yan Xiadu (southwest of Beijing), was at least 20 times the size of Yan's earlier capital when it had been a Zhou fief, and twice as big as Linzi. Most had both inner and outer walls, the inner being vital. Each probably had a population of one hundred thousand or more. In each state there were also many smaller but still substantial walled cities. Revolutions in agriculture and commerce made such big cities possible. Cast-iron tools enabled farmers to produce far more food, which led in turn to more people and rapid economic growth.

In the great capitals the most important structures apart from the city walls and gates were the palace complexes of the rulers, which were walled off from the rest of the city. Close by were the central government offices, where armies of officials and clerks kept the records and issued the orders through which the country was run. All capitals would also have housed large garrisons of some of the state's best troops. Civilians lived in walled wards.

In times of foreign invasion the whole urban population was organized for the city's defence. A siege was terrible for both attackers and defenders. For the author of *Sun zi's Art of War*, attacking a walled city was to be avoided if at all possible. It took three months to prepare the siege engines and another three months to build the earth ramps from which to storm the wall. If an impatient commander sent his troops swarming into the attack like ants he would lose a third of them – and the city still might not fall.

One class who had everything to lose from war were the artisans who had to make military equipment as unpaid labour service. Many joined the Mohists, an anti-establishment political party that followed the teachings of Mo zi, a 5th-century BC thinker who wanted to end the extravagance of rulers at the common people's expense, and opposed aggressive war. Mohists became specialists in counter-siege warfare and were sent to defend cities facing attack. The book *Mo zi* gives detailed instructions on how to organize a defence, covering methods of mobilizing the city-dwellers and also military technology, including the use of counter-mining and poison gas weapons.

Most Warring States political thinkers and freelance strategists sought an audience with a king in order to pitch him a plan that would make him secure and his country strong, so winning themselves a lucrative job. Some kings encouraged thinkers of many schools to come to their capitals. In Linzi, the Qi capital, for instance, there was an academy where they could stay. Out of the ferment of ideas in Warring States cities came the principles and practices of bureaucratic authoritarian rule that were to govern China for the next 2,000 years and more.

Merchants and trade were essential to the prosperity of the great cities and were closely regulated by state-controlled markets. Some traders developed business theories to match the military thinking of Sun zi and others. Each capital was linked with hundreds of other cities by a dense network of trade routes. The twin cities that made up the powerless Zhou dynasty's capital at Luoyang had lost all political importance, but flourished as a commercial metropolis. Having no great state behind them, Luoyang people had to live on their wits, and they traded across the Chinese world.

Walls did not always provide security. In line with an aristocratic tomb just south of Yan Xiadu are 14 pits filled with some 30,000 human skulls, nearly all belonging to men aged between 18 and 35: no doubt soldiers of a losing side in Yan's civil wars and foreign invasions of the late 4th century who were sacrificed to the tomb owner, an earlier victim of the troubles.

A strategist trying to talk up the city of Linzi at about this time paints a more lively picture of urban life. He estimates that each of its 70,000 households had three men capable of bearing arms.

> *Linzi enjoys great and solid prosperity. All its people play pipes, zithers and lutes; they enjoy cockfights, dog racing, board games and kickball. In the streets of Linzi the carts scrape hubs and people jostle past each other. They are crowded so close together that their clothes are like a hanging screen. If they lift their sleeves they form a canopy and when they shake off their sweat it falls like rain.*

# ALEXANDRIA

## Greek Capital of Egypt

ALAN B. LLOYD

*The city contains most beautiful public precincts and also the royal palaces ... for just as each of the kings, from love of splendour, was wont to add some adornment to the public monuments, so he would also invest himself at his own expense with a residence ... so that now, to quote the words of the poet, 'there is building upon building'.*

STRABO, 1ST CENTURY BC/AD

Alexandria was founded by Alexander the Great in 331 BC and quickly became one of the major cities of the Mediterranean world, a position it maintained for more than nine hundred years. At one level it was a memorial to Alexander's conquest of Egypt, but he had more in mind than that. The city's economic advantages were great – it was well connected to the hinterland of Egypt and beyond, and excellently placed to exploit the commerce of both the Mediterranean and Red Sea. But there was also another, less obvious motive: its location reflected a line of vision directed firmly northwards to the traditional centres of Greek cultural and political life in the eastern Mediterranean, Asia Minor and the Aegean. Alexander merely had time to signal his intended perspective before continuing his expedition against the Persian empire, but it became central to the self-perception of his successors in Egypt. The principal focus of their attention was the same regions to the north, and this strongly Mediterranean dimension to the city has remained with it ever since.

Alexandria became the capital of Egypt in the reign of Ptolemy I, one of Alexander's generals, who formally became king of Egypt and the adjacent territories in 306 BC, following the division of Alexander's vast empire. The Ptolemaic dynasty he inaugurated survived until the death of the gifted Cleopatra VII in 30 BC. The city remained the seat of the country's administration until the Arab conquest in AD 641; this initiated a gradual decline in its fortunes not reversed until the 19th century.

Designed with a grid plan of streets, Alexandria stood on a narrow strip of land with the Mediterranean to the north and Lake Mareotis to the south, thereby benefiting from harbours on both sides. Westwards, outside the city wall, lay a necropolis area replete with splendid gardens. East of that was Rhakotis, the Egyptian quarter, and beyond that stood the city's heart, the royal or Greek quarter, containing a concentration of spectacular buildings. Finally to the east came the Jewish quarter. These ethnic divisions were a major institutional weakness of the city and gave rise to much dissension, which sometimes boiled over into savage conflict.

Offshore, Pharos Island was linked to the city centre by an artificial causeway (the Heptastadium) which created two harbours (the Great Harbour to the east and Eunostos to the west). The east side of the Great Harbour boasted numerous palaces on the island of Antirrhodos and the coast opposite, including that of Cleopatra. By ancient standards Alexandria's population was very large, amounting in the 1st century AD to 180,000 male citizens, which meant that the true, total population was considerably greater.

The early Ptolemies developed their capital into a showplace for projecting an image of the dynasty's wealth, power and exoticism, surpassing anything in the Greek world. As such it became a grand theatre in which spectacular royal festivals such as the Ptolemaieia could be performed to focus attention on the glories of the Ptolemaic empire. The fleet based in its harbours was renowned for its large, state-of-the-art warships, which were not only considerable military assets but also instruments for announcing Ptolemaic power throughout the Mediterranean. This role as a naval base Alexandria has never lost, and warships are still a striking feature of its harbour, but it was Alexandria's buildings which made the deepest impression on visitors. Although the palace area has now disappeared beneath the sea, the result of earthquakes and subsidence, substantial underwater remains survive, revealing a mixture of Greek and Egyptian styles, which reflects the Ptolemaic concern to exploit the exotic allure of Egypt.

The royal necropolis in the centre of the city was impressive in its own right, but acquired even greater glamour by including the tomb of Alexander himself, his body hijacked by Ptolemy on its journey back to the intended burial in Macedonia. The complex containing the Museum and its associated Library stood close by. Together, these institutions became the major powerhouse of learning, literary endeavour and scientific enquiry in the Greco-Roman world – often imitated, but never equalled by any other dynasty or state. Under the Ptolemies they nurtured such towering figures as the polymath Eratosthenes, the writers Callimachus of Cyrene (who did much to define the highly influential Alexandrian school of literature) and Apollonius of Rhodes, the astronomer Aristarchus and the grammarian and critic Aristophanes of Byzantium.

Through the achievements of such men these institutions also served as yet another means of enhancing the prestige of the city and of the Ptolemaic dynasty. They continued to function as great centres of learning under Roman rule, through, among others, the brilliant experimental scientist Heron, the neoplatonist philosopher Plotinus, and the renowned Claudius Ptolemaeus (Ptolemy), whose work in geography, astronomy and astrology exercised an enormous influence on the late classical and medieval worlds.

The advent of Christianity did nothing to diminish the city's academic status. It was one of the four original Patriarchates of the early Church and it quickly evolved into a major focus of Christian teaching and theological debate through the work of international figures such as Clement and Origen. It also played a major role in the debates which bedevilled the early years of Christianity. The Jewish community too made significant contributions to the city's reputation as a scholarly centre, not least through the produ in the mid-2nd century BC of a Greek translation of the Old Testament (the Septuagint) and the writings of Philo Judaeus.

Great buildings were not confined to the royal quarter. The Egyptian quarter could boast the Serapeum, a magnificent temple dedicated to the city's patron god, Serapis, constructed on a height which made it visible from far out to sea. It suffered disastrously from the advent of Christianity that led to the closure, recycling and even destruction of many pagan temples, which were rapidly replaced by ecclesiastical foundations.

The jewel of the city, however, was the Pharos lighthouse, one of the Seven Wonders of the World, erected near the eastern end of Pharos Island in the reign of Ptolemy I and dedicated, around 283 BC, in that of Ptolemy II. This not only had practical value for sailors, but also served as yet another vehicle of Ptolemaic image-projection to all those entering the city from the north. Such structures made Alexandria in its heyday a city of unsurpassed splendour; but in the last analysis it is the city's role as a cultural and scientific centre that constitutes its greatest achievement and its strongest claim to the gratitude of posterity.

# MEROË

## Royal City of Nubia

ROBERT MORKOT

*South of Elephantine the country is inhabited by Ethiopians.... After [the] forty days' journey on land one takes another boat and in twelve days reaches a big city named Meroë, said to be the capital city of the Ethiopians. There is an oracle of Zeus there, and they make war according to its pronouncements.*

HERODOTUS, 5TH CENTURY BC

Meroë was a place of romance for the Greeks and Romans, a remote and exotic land lying just beyond their world but still within direct contact. Although in 1772 the traveller James Bruce noted some ruins in passing, guessing correctly that it was Meroë, it was not until the early 19th century that the extensive pyramid cemeteries were brought to the attention of the western world through the publications of travellers and scholars.

The ancient city lies on the east bank of the Nile, near modern Shendi, some way south of the confluence of the Nile and Atbara rivers. To the east, the land between the two rivers was, in ancient times, wooded savannah, with elephant, giraffe and other wild animals found today only much further south. Still within the rain-belt, this region was used for pasturing cattle; Meroite society was based partly on cattle herding – rather like the Masai and Dinka of today – and settled agriculture. The culture was a complex mix of indigenous 'Kushite' and strong Egyptian influences, particularly at the high official level in religion and architecture.

Meroë acted as an important entrepot for 'exotica' from near and further afield, supplying Egypt under the Persians and the Ptolemaic dynasty, and then the Roman empire. The major commodities traded were ivory, ebony, incense and slaves. Herodotus records the 'Ethiopian' (Kushite) soldiers who were sent to the Persian king Xerxes and were part of his vast army in his expedition against Greece. It is these connections with the Mediterranean world of classical antiquity that placed Meroë in the western tradition.

Although Meroë's origins are certainly much older, the earliest remains so far excavated date from early in the 1st millennium BC. By the 8th and 7th centuries BC it was a major centre for the rapidly expanding kingdom of Kush. Elite cemeteries with pyramid tombs were constructed on the hilly ridges to the east of the town, and minor members of the Kushite royal family were buried there. Royal inscriptions reveal that by the 5th century BC it was the major royal residence city, but it did not become the kings' burial place (which at that time was further north near the city of Napata, at the 4th Cataract of the Nile) until about 300 BC. The pyramid cemeteries continued to grow until the mid-4th century AD.

Reconstructing the appearance of the ancient city of Meroë is difficult, in part because of the relatively small amount of excavation that has taken place, but it must have been a sprawling, low-level settlement, with mixed types of housing – some regular mud-brick buildings, some large conical grass huts. Excavations at the site have concentrated on the 'Royal City', a large rectangle enclosed by a massive stone wall, with palace and temple structures, and an extraordinary building dubbed by the archaeologists 'the Roman Bath', but now thought to be a Nymphaeum (a fountain house).

This Royal City originally stood on an island in the river, but over time the eastern river channel dried up or was diverted. Next to the enclosure wall was an enormous temple to the Egyptian ram-headed god Amun, one of the state deities of Meroë. Constructed in typical Egyptian style, the large stone towers of the temple's pylon, or entrance, opened on to a colonnaded court, columned hall and inner sanctuaries. A processional way leading to the temple entrance was flanked by avenues of rams, as well as other, smaller, shrines.

Within the Royal City were streets with large palatial residences constructed on at least two storeys. A small temple there contained fragments of painted plaster depicting the Kandake (Meroitic queen) with foreign captives. Beneath the temple floor an over-lifesize bronze head of a statue of the emperor Augustus was discovered. The statue was the prize taken by the Meroitic armies that stormed across the frontier and seized Aswan – a military conflict recorded by the Greek geographer and historian Strabo. Following a peace treaty in 23 BC, enormous trade flowed between Rome and Meroë, ushering in one of the city's most splendid periods. A series of new temples was constructed in Meroë itself and in other towns of the kingdom.

The decline of Meroë coincided with – and was related to – the economic and political problems faced by the Roman empire in the 3rd century AD. Its end seems to have been brought about by invasions of the Noba peoples (from Nubia) and the rising power of the kingdom of Aksum in the Ethiopian highlands.

# JERUSALEM

## City Founded on Faith

### MARTIN GOODMAN

*Beyond Idumaea and Samaria stretches the wide expanse of Judaea divided into ten toparchies [including] Orine, where Jerusalem was formerly situated, by far the most famous city of the East.*

PLINY THE ELDER, AD 70S

The Italian polymath Pliny wrote these words in the AD 70s, shortly after the reduction of Jerusalem to rubble by Roman forces led by the future emperor Titus. An oriental city, in which Aramaic and Hebrew were the predominant languages, Jerusalem had been accustomed to the influence of Western powers since the conquests of Alexander the Great in 330 BC. The population consisted almost entirely of Jews, a nation whose historical memory, preserved in the Hebrew Bible, stretched far back, but in these centuries, especially after the siege of the city by Pompey the Great in 63 BC, their fortunes were increasingly enmeshed with those of Rome.

The biblical texts enjoined Jews to treat Jerusalem as the unique place on earth where God wished to be worshipped through sacrifices, libations and incense. In the late 1st century BC the Jewish king Herod, appointed ruler of Judaea in 40 BC by the Roman state, rebuilt and enlarged the existing Temple on a scale of astonishing size and grandeur. Almost all that remains today is the Western Wall, part of the platform on which the Temple stood, but this still impresses.

The Temple dominated the city. It was here that crowds gathered and movements like the early Christians met and gained supporters. From dawn to sunset each day a select group of the hereditary caste of priests performed the fixed sacrifices on behalf of the nation, together with a constant stream of private offerings. In the surrounding porticoes throngs of worshippers bought the sacrificial animals and changed their coins into Tyrian shekels for the payment of sacred donations. This daily rhythm of worship was disrupted three times a year when the Temple and the city were invaded by huge crowds of pilgrims at the festivals of Passover, Pentecost and Tabernacles. At these times there was a truly international flavour to the place, as it played host to what St Luke describes in the Acts of the Apostles as 'devout Jews from every nation under heaven'. Such religious festivals were also occasions for political volatility.

In AD 66 the revolt which led to the destruction of Jerusalem four years later began at the time of Passover. Some 36 years earlier, Jesus of Nazareth had been executed by the Roman governor Pontius Pilate during the same festival season. But the religious excitement and enthusiasm that led to such disturbances also enabled the city to prosper to such a remarkable extent: Jerusalem enjoyed no exceptional natural resources and lay astride no natural trade route, so the wealth of the city was founded entirely on the influx of funds from elsewhere, brought there out of pious devotion.

By the mid-1st century AD a building boom fuelled by this international pilgrimage had transformed much of Jerusalem into an impressive display of Hellenistic and Roman architecture. New aqueducts enabled the settled population to expand into the large new suburb of Bezetha to the north. The hilly site on which the city had been founded some thousand years before discouraged a clear urban layout, but amid the narrow streets were town houses with mosaics and frescoes reminiscent of those in contemporary Pompeii. The Pax Romana which facilitated pilgrimage also encouraged international trade. Jerusalem, in the years before its downfall, appeared to be a flourishing and integrated part of the Roman empire.

Such appearances were deceptive, however. When Herod had tried around 30 BC to import into Jerusalem modern entertainments such as competitions of athletes, stage artists and charioteers (on the Greek model), and wild beast hunts (on the Roman), his attempts were roundly rejected by unenthusiastic locals, who argued that such activities were against ancestral custom. Public attitudes were puritanical, and there was a widespread belief that physical purity could be a powerful metaphor for spiritual purity – ritual baths are a striking characteristic of the archaeology of Jerusalem at this time.

The zealous attachment of Jews to their religious customs was well known to outsiders: that was why Pompey had attacked Jerusalem on the Sabbath. While Jewish interpretations of their law varied widely, with quite contrary views espoused by groups such as the Pharisees and Sadducees, and different ideas again held by the authors of some of the Dead Sea Scrolls found at Qumran, a few miles away to the east, it was their complete devotion to that law which encouraged many of the defenders of Jerusalem to fight to the end in August AD 70 as the Roman siege drew to its terrible close.

For much of the 1st century up to AD 70, Jerusalem was ruled by Rome through an elite class led by High Priests selected by the governor or (through authority delegated by Rome) by a descendant of Herod. The Roman state in Judaea was represented by only a very small military force. Any serious unrest had to be suppressed by legions stationed far to the north in Syria. In AD 66 a series of events escalated into war. Jerusalem was the epicentre of the revolt, and in the following years Vespasian, the obscure general sent from Syria by the emperor Nero in AD 67 to suppress the rebellion, encircled the city.

Following Nero's death by suicide in late AD 68, and the proclamation of Vespasian himself as emperor by his troops in June AD 69, victory over Jerusalem took on new significance as a means to win prestige in Roman society. Just before Passover in AD 70, Vespasian's son Titus began a prolonged assault on the city. The contemporary Jewish priest Josephus recorded the dire consequences: 'The city was so completely levelled to the ground as to leave future visitors no ground for believing that it had ever been inhabited.'

But even destroyed, Jerusalem was to linger in people's imaginations. Among Jews, hope for the restoration of the Temple continued powerfully for many years, until rabbinic Jews evolved a new theology in which prayer and good deeds might partially compensate for the sacrifices which could no longer be offered. Among Christians, the destruction of the city took on a special significance as a mark of divine retribution for those who had rejected the message of Christ; they, like the Jews, watched and waited for the New Jerusalem to arise at the end of days.

# ROME

## Augustus' City of Stone

NIGEL POLLARD

*Aware that the city was architecturally unworthy of her position as capital of the Roman Empire, besides being vulnerable to fire and river floods, Augustus so improved her appearance that he could justifiably boast: 'I found Rome built of bricks; I leave her clothed in marble.'*

SUETONIUS, EARLY 2ND CENTURY AD

When the former warlord Octavian received the title Augustus ('Revered One') in 27 BC, becoming the first of the autocratic rulers we term emperors, Rome was already the capital of an empire stretching from the English Channel to Aswan in Egypt. The city had been in existence, according to legend, for over 700 years, and even in Augustus' day there were sites associated with its founder, Romulus, preserved on the Palatine Hill. Rome's wealth and power drew people from all over the empire – immigrants, traders, tourists and slaves – creating a total population of nearly 1 million, one of the largest urban populations in the pre-industrial world. Yet the physical appearance of the city belied the military and political might of its ruling class.

Rome was an urban sprawl that had grown without central or long-term planning, the product of a Republican political system in which individuals held power for a year at a time. The city spread over the hills (traditionally seven, though there were more, and even in antiquity there was argument over which the seven were) that formed its site, outstripping the great 'Servian' city walls that had stopped Hannibal's army 200 years earlier.

While there were public buildings in Rome with pretensions to grandeur – most of them temples and many of them built from profits of military success – they were largely constructed of dull local tufa stone coated with plaster, and were nothing compared to the marble temples and sanctuaries of the Greek world. Permanent theatres, long a feature of Greek cities, were a recent innovation among the Romans, who claimed to fear the erosion of traditional morality that they represented. The first such building in Rome, the Theatre of Pompey, had been completed just two decades earlier. Even gladiatorial games and wild beast hunts, public spectacles that are to us so quintessentially Roman, took place in the Forum and other public spaces, surrounded by temporary wooden stands. The Colosseum would not be constructed for another century. When Augustus came to power, the city of Pompeii had possessed an amphitheatre for 50 years, but not Rome. Of Rome's major sporting venues, only the Circus Maximus, for chariot races, already existed in developed form – its track and seating arrangement echoing the contours of a natural valley.

The Roman Forum, the civic centre of the greatest city in the world, was likewise an accretion of centuries of building rather than the product of unified planning. It lay in a low valley in the shadow of the Capitoline Hill, with its temple to Jupiter the Best and Greatest, the central temple of the Roman world. A roughly rectangular piazza, the Forum was flanked by basilicas (halls for judicial business), political buildings and more temples.

The wealthy political elite of the city were well housed in grand and elaborately decorated houses on the Palatine Hill, but the dense urban population was crowded into dirty and dangerous tenement buildings, built of shoddy materials. The Augustan architectural writer Vitruvius bemoans the use of wattle-and-daub (wood and timber) construction, with its vulnerability to fire and collapse. Fire, the bane of life in pre-industrial cities, regularly destroyed large parts of Rome. There was no proper civic fire service, and wealthy citizens with private fire brigades might buy your burning apartment block on the cheap before putting the fire out. Aqueducts had long brought clean water into the city – the Aqua Marcia, over a century old, was a marvel of engineering that carried water from 24 km (38 miles) away, piping it to the top of the Capitoline Hill. At the same time, however, the Tiber still flooded regularly, inundating low-lying parts of the city like the Campus Martius (Field of Mars).

Rome had long outstripped the agricultural capacity of its hinterland, and its population depended on grain imported from Sicily and North Africa. Piracy, civil war and bad weather all conspired to interrupt supplies, and rioting often ensued. Violence was a regular feature of Roman life. The civil wars that had filled the previous century had seen regular street fighting between rival political factions, but violence was also a means of settling private scores and a way of life for criminals, while slaves were tortured publicly, with judicial sanction. Beyond the *pomerium* (the sacred boundary of the city), the tombs of aristocratic families jostled for prominence along the major roads, smoke rose from the funeral pyres of ordinary citizens, the bodies of executed slaves hung from crosses before their corpses, like those of the destitute free-born, were dumped into mass graves.

Rome was not transformed overnight when Augustus came to power, but it began a gradual development into a city worthy of a world empire. The new emperor both beautified the city and attended to its public services. He was helped in this process by the enduring nature of his power (he was emperor for 45 years, 31 BC–AD 14), by the fact that he was, despite his claims, an autocrat, and by his control of vast private and public wealth. All of this meant that, unlike his Republican predecessors who served for only a year or so, he could plan for the long term; and unlike his assassinated adoptive father, Julius Caesar, he lived long enough to bring those long-term plans to fruition. Augustus' impact on the urban fabric of Rome was so important that he advertised it prominently, alongside his military conquests, in his autobiographical funerary inscription, the *Res Gestae*, displayed on an Augustan building, his great concrete mausoleum at the north end of the Campus Martius.

Religious revival was a central theme of Augustus' domestic policy, echoed in his restoration of temples (82 in 28 BC alone) and construction of new ones. While the policy of religious revival was, superficially, conservative, the architecture was anything but. Even an old temple such as that of Castor (dedicated back in the 5th century BC to the Greek twins Castor and Pollux) was rebuilt in gleaming white marble from the recently exploited quarries at Carrara (Luni) in Tuscany. The temple would have appeared like a forest of tall columns (three survive today) set on a high podium, each capped with a capital of the lavish Corinthian order, imitating in carved decoration the leaves of the acanthus plant.

This innovative, soaring architectural grandeur was true of new temples too, including that to Augustus' patron deity, Apollo, on the Palatine Hill, and that of Mars Ultor ('The Avenger'), vowed by the emperor for the god's aid in avenging the assassination of Julius Caesar. The latter temple formed part of a planned architectural complex, the Forum of Augustus, contrasting with the piecemeal development of the old Roman Forum. In addition to providing extra space for economic and judicial activities, Augustus' forum provided visitors with an elaborate sculptural display reminding them of Rome's past glories and the role of Augustus' Julian ancestors (all the way back to the legendary Trojan hero Aeneas, and so to his mother Venus) in the past.

The old Roman Forum now reflected Augustus' political and dynastic ambitions, as well as a new, more orderly sense of space. A new speaker's platform was established at its north end, on-axis with a new temple, that of the deified Julius Caesar, built on the site of his funeral pyre, to the south. Augustus also erected a new Senate House, but the diminishing importance of the old Republican political buildings reflected the contemporary reality of the imperial autocracy. Instead, new monuments (basilicas and victory arches) presented the message of Augustus' power and political values. In the Campus Martius were more new monuments dedicated to Augustus' incipient dynasty – not just the Mausoleum, but also a complex comprising the Altar of Augustan Peace (*Ara Pacis Augustae*) and a giant sundial, its pointer an obelisk looted from Egypt, symbolic of Augustus' conquest of Cleopatra and her kingdom.

Nor did Augustus neglect his citizens' more basic needs. After centuries without permanent structures for entertainment, Rome received two new theatres, one dedicated to Augustus' son-in-law Marcellus and the other by his general Balbus. These theatres served Rome for the rest of its history – no others were ever built. Romans could view gladiatorial games and wild beast hunts in the city's first stone amphitheatre, dedicated by Augustus' general Statilius Taurus, until it burnt down in the fire of AD 64 (and, ultimately, was replaced by the Colosseum). Even the long-established Circus Maximus received adornment and elaboration. And Augustus paid for festivals and spectacles too. His biographer Suetonius notes that the number, diversity and extravagance of his public shows were unprecedented, recording theatrical performances, gladiatorial contests, wild beast hunts, athletic competitions and even a mock naval battle held in an artificial lake. Augustus himself mentions the participation of 10,000 men in eight gladiatorial spectacles, and the slaughter of 3,500 wild animals in 26 shows.

On a less spectacular level, Augustus improved public services. He divided Rome into 14 administrative districts with their own local magistrates. He set up a lasting structure for imperial supervision of crucial services such as food supply, roads and maintenance of the banks of the Tiber. He also established a permanent fire service, its commander appointed by the emperor himself. The relatively new material of concrete, advocated by Vitruvius as a safer alternative to wattle and daub, became more widely used for a variety of buildings, including great multistorey apartment blocks. Augustus' trusted subordinate Agrippa overhauled the city's drains, famously sailing through the sewers in a boat to inspect them. Agrippa also built a grand bath building, fed by a new aqueduct, the Aqua Virgo; he bequeathed this facility to the public in his will, providing a model for the great imperial baths of Augustus' successors.

Some things did not change immediately. Riots, floods and fires still occurred regularly, and for many Romans, life remained dirty, dangerous and violent. Nevertheless, the city was gradually transformed into one more fitting as a world capital. Augustus set a precedent that emperors were responsible for the city and its people, and many of his successors followed his example. Augustus' impact on Rome endured, even as it was transformed into a Christian capital, the capital of a reunified Italy and a Fascist capital, and his legacy is still visible today.

# THE FIRST
# MILLENNIUM AD

Of the eight great cities in this section that flourished during the first thousand years of the Christian era, only one was Christian. Constantinople is the only candidate, for what other candidates could there be? Certainly not Rome, which in these centuries was little more than a fever-ridden swamp, its popes – with very few exceptions, such as Leo the Great in the 5th century and Gregory the Great in the 6th – for the most part nonentities or even worse; they were followed in the 9th and 10th centuries by a whole succession known as the Papal Pornocracy.

Such goings-on would have been unthinkable on the Bosphorus. In 330, the city of Constantinople had been formally dedicated by its founder Constantine the Great to the Virgin. All succeeding emperors for the next eleven centuries were Equals of the Apostles, standing halfway to heaven; and daily life, for themselves and all their subjects, was permeated by their religion. While western Europe was being overrun by the barbarians, and the lights of learning had – except for a few fitful monastic flickers – been all but extinguished, in Byzantium they blazed; and much of the Greek and Latin literature that has come down to us we owe to the scholars, scribes and copyists of Constantinople. Finally, the empire of Byzantium has left us with a priceless heritage of art and architecture. With his Great Church of St Sophia, in the space of five and a half years during the early 6th century, the emperor Justinian created what is still one of the greatest buildings in the world. In their mosaics, frescoes and icons, Byzantine artists were required to depict the spirit of God. It was a tall order, but one which, again and again, they triumphantly accomplished.

In the West, by contrast, these were indeed the 'dark ages'; and the deep mistrust felt by the Church for all things scientific or cultural made them darker still. Islam felt no such inhibitions. In mathematics, physics and medicine, in geography, astronomy and architecture, it was the Arabs who led the way. In the visual arts, they were restricted by the strictures placed by their religion on the representation of the human form; but in abstract design and, in particular, calligraphy, they were without compare. No fewer than four of the cities in this section are in consequence Islamic: Mecca, birthplace of the Prophet and Islam's holiest shrine; Damascus, capital of the Umayyad Caliphate – and consequently of the entire Muslim world until the Abbasid conquest in 750; Baghdad, where the Abbasid Caliphs set up their new administration, ruling for the next 500 years; and finally Córdoba, where the refugee Umayyad prince 'Abd al-Rahman built his great mosque, the Mezquita. On its completion towards the end of the 8th century it was the most sumptuous mosque in the world.

Our two cities of ancient Central America may find us on rather less familiar ground. The great Pyramids of the Sun and the Moon in Teotihuacan – 'where', according to a recent guidebook, 'the cardiectomies were performed' – are among the most astonishing sights in Mexico; we tend to forget, however, that this was not just a vast sacrificial site but also a teeming city – the largest in the Americas – for around four centuries. Tikal, in modern Guatemala, was smaller; on the other hand the Maya were, with the Inca, by far the most talented of all the pre-Columbian peoples, and the drama of their architecture – to say nothing of the beauty of their art and hieroglyphic inscriptions – still has the power to take away the breath.

But if Teotihuacan was the largest city in the Americas, Chang'an – with a population of more than 1 million – was the largest in the world. It is best known today under its later name of Xian; few visitors to the famous terracotta army of the emperor Qin Shi Huangdi realize that it was also the capital of Tang dynasty China, the country's golden age. Had one been born in the 7th century, that, surely, was the place to be.

# TEOTIHUACAN

## Where Time and Water Flow

SUSAN TOBY EVANS

*The gods had their beginning ... there in Teotihuacan.*
BERNARDINO DE SAHAGÚN, 1569

Teotihuacan was not only the birthplace of the gods but of time itself, according to legends recorded long after the great city's decline. In its heyday, roughly AD 100–500, Teotihuacan was revered by cultures as distant as the Maya, over 1,600 km (1,000 miles) to the east. The city itself was a cosmopolis in the literal and modern senses: an *axis mundi* where heavens and underworld converged, and a sophisticated multi-ethnic capital with enclaves of people from Monte Albán in Oaxaca, 350 km (some 220 miles) southeast, and from the Gulf lowlands 200 km (125 miles) to the east. The city's merchants carried goods to communities all over ancient Mexico and Central America, and its symbols became enduring emblems of power for rulers elsewhere.

Teotihuacan's size matched its influence. Extending over 20 sq. km (8 sq. miles) and with a population of perhaps 100,000 by AD 400, it was the largest city in the Americas until AD 1519 and the Aztec empire's capital, Tenochtitlan (p. 169). The orientation of Teotihuacan's major avenues and monuments and their precise dimensions and proportions reveal close attention to the site's placement in its natural environment and spiritual cosmos. In plan, the modernity of the gridded complex of pyramids and apartment compounds at Teotihuacan is strikingly unlike the convoluted streets characteristic of many other ancient cities of the Old and New Worlds. The grid is diagonal to the natural slope of the hill on which it lies, effectively channelling downslope rainfall runoff through the city to the spring line, where water from the heavens and that from the earth merged in a canal system sanctified by state-controlled water temples. Teotihuacan's urban development was enmeshed with the evolution of the city's religion, as civil engineering on a vast scale changed the city's physical and spiritual relationship to the essential resource in least abundance: water.

The mature city's rulers and architects may have planned and built an urban construct fit for deities, but the origins of settlement in this area, the Teotihuacan Valley, were late and modest, due to a challenging climate. A cold, dry region, about 40 km (25 miles) northeast of modern Mexico City (p. 222) and at an altitude of 2,240 m (7,306 ft), it has a long frost season and its low annual rainfall is delivered in torrential storms that gouge gullies out of the valley's slopes. Thus effective cultivation of maize, the staple food crop, required well-planned intensification. The Teotihuacan Valley was eventually settled by overflow population from more productive regions, such as the warmer and wetter southwestern sector now home to Mexico City. The largest centre there, Cuicuilco, was located in the shadow of great volcanoes. About 2,000 years ago it was buried so deeply by lava that its 20-m (66-ft) high pyramid could only be excavated, in modern times, with jackhammers.

After this, Teotihuacan's population exploded, and most scholars believe that Cuicuilco's refugees became Teotihuacan's workforce, and that the great pyramids rising at this time were built by these labourers, directed by the Teotihuacanos according to a plan aligned to landscape features and the heavens, and able to manage the flow of rainfall runoff. The great north–south axis of the 'Street of the Dead' (as a later culture called it) was orientated slightly east of north, perpendicular to a sightline to a western horizon marker from a cave under the Pyramid of the Sun. This may commemorate a celestial arrangement on 11 August 3113 BC, the beginning of the present universe as calculated by Teotihuacanos, Maya and other Mesoamericans.

The oldest of the city's monuments is the Pyramid of the Moon, dominating the Street of the Dead's northern portion. The Pyramid of the Sun dominated the centre. The final great monuments formed a southern complex straddling the street. The matched pair of huge enclosures covered about 0.5 km sq. (123 acres): on the east, the Pyramid of the Feathered Serpent was encompassed by the 'Ciudadela' (Citadel), and faced the Great Compound on the west. Through them, and perpendicular to the Street of the Dead, ran the axis of a straight avenue extending for miles to east and west.

Construction of the three great pyramid-temples took place over several centuries, with much of the population living in shacks. While the sheer volume of the pyramids and their surroundings is an obvious statement of high construction investment, this represents only a fraction of the effort required. Before development of the southern complex, the valley's largest river (now the Rio de San Juan) flowed across the building site. The river was re-routed for over 0.5 km (⅓ mile), with half of this distance conforming to the city's grid as the canalized river crosscut the Street of the Dead, hugging the northern edge of the southern complex before turning south and then west for half a kilometre. This east–west stretch gave travellers entering the city from the west a glittering sightline pointing directly towards the Pyramid of the Feathered Serpent's front façade, with a temple atop seven sculpted and painted levels of swimming feathered serpents, their bas-relief streams echoing the canalized river.

Teotihuacan's pyramids were funerary monuments, and this final pyramid in the city's history was particularly costly: hundreds of human sacrifices underlie the structure. But within decades, the façade was damaged and masked by a severely simple addition, as if to erase the memory of its iconographic programme and its expenditure of human lives. The Feathered Serpent remained important to the city, but broad changes involved new perspectives on spiritual and economic power.

The city's energies turned towards practical matters including housing the populace and organizing the civic and agricultural drainage systems.

About 2,000 walled apartment compounds were built, aligned according to the city's grid system. Overall, the compounds were square, averaging 60 m (about 200 ft) on a side, their windowless outer walls protecting an interior divided up into groups of single-storey rooms around open-air patios. Compounds varied considerably in quality of construction and affluence of material goods. The largest – the Street of the Dead Complex, probably the city's administrative palace – was over 300 m (985 ft) on a side. At the other end of the social spectrum were shabby aggregates of conjoined rooms around patios, such as Tlajinga, at the city's southern edge. Between them in size and quality were well-made mansions such as Zacuala, Tepantitla and Tetitla. Some compounds, such as Quetzalpapalotl and the Ciudadela compounds, may have housed priests.

Drainage systems ran around and through the compounds, evidence of sophisticated city planning. These not only contributed to the health of the citizenry, but also fed the irrigation system spreading out from the city's springs. Productivity there was consequently several times greater than that of upslope fields dependent on rainfall. These activities occurred at a critical juncture for the city's population, boosting its food supply.

Teotihuacan's art shifted its ideological emphasis away from the Feathered Serpent, associated with rain, towards jaguars, evoking water from springs as well as the power of rulers. These changes are evident in the murals painted in the apartment compounds, which depict many kinds of supernatural beings, as well as elaborately garbed officials of the state and cults. An example from the Tetitla compound depicts a jaguar dressed in accoutrements of power, and facing a water temple built over a spring. Both the jaguar's costume and the temple decorations artfully combine rare and costly materials that have iconographic significance across Mesoamerica. Jaguar skins covered rulers' thrones, and discs of jadeite were the most precious of all materials in ancient Mexico. Temple and jaguar are topped by panaches of the long green feathers of the rare tropical quetzal bird.

Jadeite, jaguar skins and quetzal feathers were all brought to Teotihuacan by long-distance traders in exchange for Teotihuacan products, such as green obsidian that was prized all over Mesoamerica. They also exported pottery vessels in Teotihuacan style; some were stuccoed and painted, abbreviated, small-scale versions of the murals. And the traders carried ideas about cycles of time, legitimacy of rulership and the ascendancy of important deities. Several major centres in the Maya lowlands – Tikal (p. 75) and Copán in particular – show direct influence by Teotihuacan before AD 400, possibly involving the installation of a Teotihuacan-related ruler. These dynastic interruptions were short-lived, but the Maya used symbols of power borrowed from Teotihuacan for hundreds of years after Teotihuacan's decline.

This decline occurred after a conflagration in the 6th century AD, ravaging monuments along the Street of the Dead. Whether caused by internal rebellion or external invasion, the event devastated the vital ceremonial core of the city. The population dropped precipitously and clustered into a few peripheral neighbourhoods. These settlements persisted for centuries, and are now the modern towns that surround the great World Heritage site of Teotihuacan.

# TIKAL

## Crucible of Maya Civilization

SIMON MARTIN

*Among the high hills which we passed over there is a variety of old buildings, excepting some in which I recognized apartments and though they were very high and my strength little I climbed up them (though with trouble). They were in the form of a convent, with the small cloisters and many living rooms all roofed over and ... whitened inside with plaster.*

ANDRÉS DE AVENDAÑO, 1696

Half-starved, thirsty and with only the vaguest notion of where he was, the Franciscan friar Andrés de Avendaño stumbled upon a great ruin in the Maya forest of 1696. Although the region Avendaño passed through contains the desolate remains of many fallen cities, his description quoted above best matches Tikal, and he was almost certainly the first European to lay eyes on it.

Today, Tikal, with its iconic architecture, has become the signature for ancient Maya culture. Images of its sharply inclined pyramids piercing the jungle canopy appear on everything from book covers to banknotes – their profiles so exotic that they were even used in the original Star Wars film. Tikal is a proud emblem of modern-day Guatemala, and increasingly a symbol for contemporary Maya people, who are now allowed to conduct rituals and make offerings there.

It was not until the 19th century that proper reports of Tikal appeared, and it was still largely unexplored when the University of Pennsylvania Museum began excavations there in 1955. Over some 14 field seasons the scale and complexity of the site became clear, as deep trenches cast light on its early history and a programme of mapping charted its outer limits. Subsequent projects, in particular those conducted by the Guatemalan government, have expanded and refined this picture. The map proved to be a particular revelation, shattering the long-standing view of 'ceremonial centres', in which a cluster of temples with few permanent residents stood isolated in the forest. It showed instead thousands of homes radiating out from the central core, establishing the model of low-density urbanism since identified throughout the Maya world. This sizeable population lived not in a dense jungle but in a cultivated landscape of maize, beans and squash, doubtless mixed with orchards and groves of useful trees.

Occupied for as much as 1,800 years, Tikal began life some time between 800 and 600 BC as two hamlets on elevated ridges, with a third lying along the perimeter of a swamp. It was only after about 300 BC that substantial structures developed on the ridge-tops – the large platforms and levelled plazas of the North Acropolis and the Lost World Complex – signalling Tikal as a place of importance. Even so, it was overshadowed by larger cities such as Nakbe, Tintal and El Mirador for centuries and did not come into its own until the beginning of the so-called Classic period in about AD 200. This marks a significant shift in Maya culture, as many major settlements were abandoned and a range of new features – especially monuments with historical texts – emerge at survivors such as Tikal.

The North Acropolis developed into a necropolis for Tikal's kings, and the Great Plaza in front of it became the central focus of the Classic-era city. The tall temple pyramids, some of them royal mortuary shrines, were erected during the 7th and 8th centuries, creating a more dramatic skyline. At the same time a series of broad causeways was constructed to connect the more distant elements of the city. On the south side of the Great Plaza lay the main royal palace, the Central Acropolis, a dense concentration of chambers and enclosed courtyards modified continually over time. It was joined by other grand complexes – probably the residences of noble families

– that formed a ring around the inner core. At a greater remove, the city was encircled by earthworks composed of a ditch backed by a rampart of the packed spoil, running to over some 25 km (15 miles) in length. Although the design is overtly defensive, there are many gaps and no line at all to the south. Evidently the system was started in a time of special need, but abandoned unfinished.

Inscriptions on carved limestone monuments and architectural features are common, but it was not until the 1970s and 1980s that they could be read to any real effect. Today, we can reconstruct the outlines of Tikal history and make important connections to the archaeological record. We can now trace the origins of the Classic-era dynasty of Tikal to some time around AD 100, when it was initiated by its founder, Yax Ehb Xook, a ruler who was celebrated by at least 28 royal successors. Little is known of the earliest kings, but during the reign of the 14th, Chak Tok Ich'aak, we see significant contacts with the distant power of Teotihuacan in Central Mexico (p. 70). Several inscriptions refer to a day in 378 and tell of the arrival of someone called Sihyaj K'ahk' and the death of Chak Tok Ich'aak. These events appear to represent the overthrow of the existing Tikal regime. A year later a new king took power under the aegis of Sihyaj K'ahk' and both lords are depicted in distinctive Central Mexican garb. It is at this same point that we find a surge of Teotihuacan-style art and artifacts. The father of this 15th Tikal king has a name with strong affinities to Teotihuacan and he might even have been a ruler of that great metropolis.

These events led to almost two centuries of prosperity and apparent regional dominance for Tikal. However, it was not without rivals, and in 562 the 21st king, Wak Chan K'awiil, suffered a major defeat. The main beneficiary and likely perpetrator was the mysterious kingdom of the 'Snake' – whose capital seems to have been at Dzibanche until the early 7th century, when it switched to Calakmul. There followed a long struggle as Tikal sought to restore its position, with success coming under the 26th king, Jasaw Chan K'awiil, who was victorious over Calakmul in 695. A new golden age followed, with Jasaw's son Yik'in Chan K'awiil defeating two of Calakmul's major allies: El Peru in 743 and Naranjo in 744 – apparently capturing both opposing kings.

Yet within a generation or two Tikal's position began to slip once again, although this time as part of a regional decline that reached crisis-point in the early 9th century. After this the population fell rapidly and all construction and monument erection ceased. Activity continued only at smaller, peripheral sites, whose lords put up stunted stelas and claimed the same royal titles as the Tikal line. After a long gap one last monument was dedicated in the Great Plaza of Tikal in 869, but by now the site was in terminal decline, and it was abandoned – save for a few families of squatters – by about 900.

Today Tikal lies within a small national park and is a magnet for regional tourism. Time will tell if visitors and the income they bring can save the wider tropical forest beyond it, but the signs are not good. Beset by logging and land clearance, the greater natural reserve of northern Guatemala – a haven for jaguars, tapirs, macaws and many other exotic species – is disappearing fast. The chainsaws may be too distant to hear, but when an untimely breeze catches the smoky haze of destruction it can blanket the site.

# CONSTANTINOPLE

## Christian Capital in the East

JOHN JULIUS NORWICH

*On foot … the emperor himself led the solemn procession
and directed the line which was traced as the boundary of
the destined capital; till the growing circumference was
observed with astonishment by the assistants.*

EDWARD GIBBON, 1776–81

At the end of the 1st millennium AD, Constantinople was not only the greatest
city in the world, it was also the most celebrated. To many, it was almost a
fairy tale. Relatively few western Europeans had seen it, but everyone had
heard of its fabulous wealth: the splendour of its churches and palaces, the
stateliness of its ceremonial, the majesty of its emperors – the equals, they
claimed, of the Apostles themselves.

It was not, by the standards of Rome or Milan, Alexandria or Antioch,
an old city. It had been founded by Constantine the Great as the new capital
of the Roman empire in AD 330, less than seven centuries before. Constantine
had always mistrusted Rome, whose republican and pagan traditions could
have no place in his burgeoning Christian empire and which was growing
increasingly out of touch with the new and progressive thinking of the
Hellenistic world. Instinctively he understood that the focus of civilization
had shifted irrevocably to the East. Italy had become a backwater.

The old Greek colony of Byzantium provided the perfect site. Standing
on the very threshold of Asia and occupying the easternmost tip of a broad,
triangular promontory, its south side washed by the Propontis – now called the

Sea of Marmara – and its northeast by that broad, deep and navigable inlet, some 8 km (5 miles) long, known as the Golden Horn, it had been moulded by nature into both a magnificent harbour and a well-nigh impregnable stronghold. Even a sea-borne attack was difficult, the Marmara itself being protected by two long and narrow straits, the Hellespont (or Dardanelles) leading down to the Mediterranean and the Bosphorus heading up northeast to the Black Sea. To counter any enemy ships that might nevertheless manage to penetrate these natural defences, a great chain was thrown across the neck of the Golden Horn, which could be raised or lowered at will.

Where Constantinople did need protection was along its landward side to the west; and here its tremendous walls first rose in the early 5th century. Running from the Marmara to the upper reaches of the Golden Horn, they are still by far the most impressive municipal defences in the world today, their huge russet-striped towers splintered and occasionally shattered, magnificent witnesses to the bludgeonings they have endured for 16 centuries. Only once, however, in 1453, were they ever breached – and that breach was to spell the end of the Byzantine empire.

From the moment that Constantine moved his capital, a curious process began: the Roman empire, transplanted into the Hellenistic world, gradually became Greek. In around 530 the emperor Justinian's recodification of Roman law had been in Latin, but already the language was dying on its feet; Justinian was probably the last emperor to speak it fluently. The old empire of Augustus and Hadrian lived on – the Byzantines continued to call themselves, and to think of themselves, as Romans – but it had become unrecognizable. Greek had always been the language of the people; soon it was to be the language of court and government as well. Constantinople was thus, well before the turn of the millennium, a completely Greek city. It was also a devoutly Christian one, its Church – although still paying lip service to the pope in Rome – following the Eastern, Orthodox rite.

The focus of imperial worship was the Great Church of St Sophia, dedicated not to a female saint but to the Holy Wisdom. It had been built by

ABOVE The Great Bath of Mohenjo-daro, filled by drawing water from a nearby well, is the largest surviving monumental structure from the Indus civilization and must have seemed miraculous in its semi-arid surrounds.

BELOW A carved relief wall-panel from Nineveh, carved for Ashburnipal's palace in 645 BC, shows a canal crossing an aqueduct to irrigate crops, in front of what may be a shrine housing the stela of his grandfather, Sennacherib.

TOP The Forum in Rome dates back as far as the 6th century BC, but this modern view reveals a palimpsest of buildings added and reconstructed through a thousand years of Roman history, as well as the effects of another thousand years of destruction, transformation and rediscovery.

ABOVE The Acropolis, crowned by the Parthenon, still forms the iconic image of Athens, but it was originally brightly painted. The complex emerged from Perikles' great building programme, begun after the Persian army had burned down the city in 480 BC only to be decisively driven from Greek soil the following year.

TOP  The Temple Mount and the Western Wall in Jerusalem, a site of Jewish pilgrimage since late antiquity. The dome of the Mosque of Omar, built many centuries later, rises approximately above the site of the Jewish Temple in Herod's day.

ABOVE  The pyramid field of Meroë was large and crowded, its monuments smaller and steeper-sided than those of the Egyptian Pharaohs, and owned by a wider section of society. The largest belonged to members of the royal family, however, and evidence suggests the dead were accompanied by food, jewelry, furniture and even animal and human sacrifices.

OPPOSITE The Pyramid of the Sun, Teotihuacan, as seen from the top of its lunar counterpart, echoes the mountains behind. By AD 225 it was 226 m (740 ft) wide and 75 m (246 ft) high, including a temple on top.

ABOVE Without water for our fields, we die; we worship the jaguar spirit who guards our springs. The stylistic conventions of Teotihuacan mural art challenge the modern eye, lacking that range of hue and intensity that help us focus.

RIGHT In the 1880s Alfred Percival Maudslay freed the great pyramids of Tikal from swathes of forest for the first time in a thousand years and was able to take this photograph of Temple 1.

BELOW Central Tikal today. Temple 1 covers the burial of the great king Jasaw Chan K'awiil, around AD 734, but the dynastic necropolis to the left originates as far back as 350 BC.

Le siege du grant turc auec ij deses principaulx conseilles
Le siege du capiteine general de la turquie

OPPOSITE A near-contemporary illustration of the conquest of Constantinople in 1453, after a siege of two months, from the *Voyage d'outremer*. It is not an accurate depiction of the city, but does show the Turkish soldiers dragging their ships overland (on the left) to avoid the barriers across the Golden Horn.

ABOVE Mecca thronged with pilgrims, with the mosque and the Ka'aba in the centre. Although ancient traditions are still followed, the city's many high-rise buildings make for a very different city compared to earlier times.

OVERLEAF The great mosque of Damascus overlooks a busy market in a scene redolent with history. This minaret was added in 1488 by a Mamluk sultan of Cairo, on a base of old Roman and Byzantine corner towers, while the arches were added in the 2nd century AD by Septimius Severus, a North African Emperor of Rome married to a Syrian princess.

Justinian after the blood-soaked riots of 532 which had left its predecessor, and indeed the whole centre of the city, a smouldering pile of ashes. Though undergoing a major restoration after the calamitous earthquake of 989, it was still – and would be, until the building of Seville Cathedral in the 15th century – the largest religious building in Christendom and one of the great architectural wonders of the world; its shallow saucer-dome, pierced by 40 windows around its rim, was infinitely broader and higher than any previously attempted. Next in importance was Justinian's equally beautiful St Eirene, the Holy Peace, a little to the northeast. Less significant – though the earliest chronologically and the model for S. Vitale in Ravenna – was SS Sergius and Bacchus, now the small mosque known as Küçük Aya Sofya Camii.

The importance of religion in Constantinople cannot be exaggerated. To every Byzantine it was the breath of life. 'If you ask a man for change,' wrote St Gregory of Nyssa, 'he will give you a piece of philosophy concerning the Begotten and the Unbegotten.' Theological disputation was incessant, everywhere; even the two factions of the Hippodrome, the Blues and the Greens, differed on the Single or Dual Nature of Christ. Usually, it was harmless enough; but it had led to disasters such as iconoclasm, which had accounted for the destruction of countless icons, frescoes and mosaics in the 8th and 9th centuries. And with every succeeding century the differences with Rome became more acute, until in 1054 the two Churches split irremediably.

Since Constantine's day, the Great Palace had occupied the southeast corner of the city, adjacent to St Sophia and the Hippodrome – essentially the same area, though considerably larger, as that occupied by its Ottoman successor, Topkapı Palace, today. Like Topkapı, it was more than just a palace – it was a vast compound, consisting of some 20 separate buildings, several churches, even its own small harbour. One of these buildings was the Palace of the Magnaura, where in the 9th century the emperor Theophilus had installed his famous mechanical toy – a golden plane tree, its branches full of jewelled birds which burst periodically into song. Another was the New Church (the Nea, now alas destroyed) built by Theophilus's second successor Basil I. Its cluster of gilded domes could be seen from far out to sea; within the central rotunda was a dazzling mosaic of Christ Pantocrator, the Ruler of All; the iconostasis was of gold and silver, studded with precious stones. A century later the Comnenus emperors were to build themselves a magnificent new palace at Blachernae, where the walls sweep down to the Horn; but in 1000 Basil II ('the Bulgar-Slayer') still kept his court on the ancient ground.

At least for the moderately well-to-do, life in Constantinople was probably more comfortable than in any other city in the world. Thanks to its wealth, and its position at the crossroads of world trade routes, there were few commodities not readily available in the shops and markets; the main streets were lit at night; and another luxury that always impressed visitors in the summer months was the unfailing supply of water. As early as 375, the emperor Valens had built a colossal aqueduct – of which a good half-kilometre remains, crossing what is now the Atatürk Boulevard – which provided the city with water for fifteen centuries. Once there, the water had to be stored; and the city possessed a number of superb cisterns for the purpose. The oldest is now known as the Binbirdirek – 'the cistern of 1,001 columns' – and dates from the days of Constantine; the most astonishing is Justinian's Yerebatansaray – 'the sunk-in-the-ground palace' – almost opposite St Sophia, still today one of the marvels of Istanbul.

In AD 1000, Basil II still had a quarter of a century to reign. Ugly, dirty, philistine, almost pathologically mean, caring nothing for the outward trappings of power, he was profoundly un-Byzantine; yet he dominated and directed every branch of Church and State. He was also one of the most brilliant generals that the empire had ever seen. He possessed no glamour, no charisma; nobody liked him much. A friendless bachelor, he cared only for the greatness and prosperity of his empire. No wonder that in his hands it reached its apogee.

# MECCA

## Sacred City of Islam

DORIS BEHRENS-ABOUSEIF

*Abraham said ... Lord, I have settled some of my*
*offspring in a barren valley near Your Sacred House,*
*so that they may observe true worship.*

THE KORAN, 14

Set in a high valley bordered by rugged mountains, Mecca has been the major city of the Arabian peninsula since early historical times. It owes its greatest fame and prestige to the fact that it was the birthplace of the Prophet Muhammad, but it has been a sacred city since antiquity; according to the Koran its shrine, the Ka'ba – the name means 'the Cube' – was constructed by the prophet Abraham. It is possible that the shrine antedates the city itself, but no archaeological evidence has been found to confirm this. Near the Ka'ba is the sacred well of Zamzam, which may be the origin of the sanctity of the site and would certainly have been welcome in such a hot and dry location.

The Ka'ba stands in the middle of the sanctuary or Haram – meaning 'holy' in Arabic – an enclosed space, open above, forming a mosque. An austere, windowless black cube, the Ka'ba is 15 m (almost 50 ft) high, with four unequal sides, varying between around 10 and 12 m (33 and 39 ft) in width, its corners oriented to the cardinal points, with the door on the northeastern side. It contains the black stone, a meteorite framed in a silver setting.

Mecca became a major commercial centre in the second half of the 6th century, its merchants trading with the caravans that journeyed between the Mediterranean and the Indian Ocean, via Syria, and to Abyssinia via South Arabia and Yemen. The city's society consisted of a confederation of tribes without a central government. From the 5th century the leading tribe was the Quraysh, to which the Prophet Muhammad belonged. Great merchants, they controlled the city and oversaw the shrine.

Muhammad was born in Mecca about 570 into a family of merchants. According to Islamic tradition, around 610 the Koran was revealed to him while he was working as an agent for a female merchant called Khadija, whom he later married. The new religion was not well received by all; some, fearful of political and social change, opposed it, and in 622 Muhammad fled with his followers to Medina, further north. This *hijra*, or migration, marks the beginning of the Islamic calendar. During his years in Medina, Muhammad fought against the Meccans, finally succeeding after the battle of Fath in conquering the city and converting it to Islam. Medina remained the capital of the new Muslim community, while Mecca, and more specifically its Ka'ba, became the *qibla* or the direction towards which Muslims pray. The pilgrimage to Mecca, the *hajj*, at least once in a lifetime, is one of the five tenets of Islam.

After Muhammad's death in 632, the four right-guided caliphs ruled the expanding Muslim community from Medina, but 'Umar and 'Uthman constructed barrages and dykes to protect Mecca from potentially devastating torrents. Between 661 and 750 Damascus was the capital of the Umayyad Caliphate (p. 94). Mu'awiya, the first Umayyad caliph, being from Mecca, took particular care of the city and its hinterland, as did his successors. His son, Yazid, however, did not enjoy the support of the Quraysh tribe and he was challenged by a rebel, Abd Allah Ibn al-Zubayr, who rallied support in Mecca and proclaimed himself caliph. He was eventually defeated by the caliph Abd al-Malik in 682. During the struggles a fire destroyed the Ka'ba and it had to be rebuilt.

In the early 8th century the caliph al-Walid built galleries around the open sanctuary, giving it the appearance it has maintained to the present.

Before modern radical transformations of the city, Mecca was characterized for centuries by dwellings and oratories abutting on the mosque's arcades. The Ka'ba is the only Islamic monument that has always been maintained and restored according to the original configuration it was believed to have had in the time of the Prophet. Every year during the pilgrimage season, the curtain covering the Ka'ba is replaced, following ancient tradition.

Having lost any real political role, the Meccan aristocracy in the Umayyad period began to enjoy the wealth of the expanding Muslim empire, leading a refined social life amid poets and musicians. The Abbasid caliphs, succeeded by Mamluks and later the Ottomans, generously sponsored Mecca, endowing the shrine to fulfil its role as pilgrimage site. Muslim rulers and patrons founded hospices, colleges and dwellings to accommodate those who wished to lead a life of devotion, and provided infrastructure and accommodation for pilgrims. The population of Mecca eventually became accustomed to living at the expense of the central government and developed little of their own economic activity, apart from the business related to the pilgrimage.

Although it has never been the seat of a caliphate or the capital of a nation, Mecca has, nevertheless, long enjoyed a unique status, and one which continues today.

# DAMASCUS

## Splendours of the Oasis City

BARNABY ROGERSON

*Damascus has seen all that ever occurred on earth and still she lives.*
*She has looked upon the dry bones of a thousand empires, and will*
*see the tombs of a thousand more before she dies.*

MARK TWAIN, 1869

Damascus sits below the slopes of a sacred mountain, Mount Kassion, looking out over the desert and watered by a near-miraculous torrent that comes gushing out of an otherwise arid mountain range. To the east of Damascus stretches the vast plateau of the Syrian desert, engraved by a hundred caravan trails that pick their way northeast to the cities along the Euphrates and the trade of Asia, while the routes to the south and east lead to Egypt, the Yemen and the ports for the Indies. It is the abundance of the Barada river (the Abana of antiquity), supplying the city with water and irrigating an oasis of orchards and scented gardens, that enables Damascus to exist on this strategic site.

To the Islamic pilgrim visitors who flocked to its shrines, Damascus was the city of 'the odour of Paradise'. The great Moorish traveller Ibn Jubayr wrote that, 'If Paradise be on earth, it is, without doubt, Damascus, but if it be in Heaven, Damascus is its counterpart on earth.' The Prophet Muhammad passed beside the city as a young man, but was content to look out over the gorgeous city rather than tempt himself with its pleasures.

The citizens of Damascus considered it to be the oldest city on earth, for Cain slew Abel on the slopes of Mount Kassion and Abraham was transfigured by a vision of his Lord here, just as in the 1st century AD the Christian-persecuting Saul was transformed into St Paul, the great co-founder of the early Church, on the road to Damascus. Their ancient shrines would be joined by such holy relics as the head of St John the Baptist, the tomb of the prophet Hud, the tombs of the Prophet's two daughters, Zaynab and Rukayyah, not to mention the shrines of the veiled three, the seven and the 40 sheikhs and the hidden shrine of El-Khidr, the immortal, ever-vigilant green knight of Islam. For over a thousand years the vast crowds associated with the *hajj* pilgrimage would annually assemble outside the walls of Damascus for the desert crossing to Mecca (the last such caravan departed in 1864, after which the sea journey down the Red Sea to Jeddah took over). Excavations among the ancient palace libraries of Ebla, Amarna and Mari confirm Damascus's breathless antiquity. For whether written in the script of Egypt or Mesopotamia, the city's name appears just as it does today in Arabic – Dimashq – while the slang form of al-Shams, 'the sun', is probably just as old.

From the first, Damascus learnt to bend with the prevailing political wind, the better to concentrate on trade, culture, living and religion. The city's real relationships were not with the great powers of the ancient world, but with the other ancient trading cities of the Levant, such as Petra, Beirut, Dura Europos, Emesa, Baalbek, Palmyra and Apamea – though few of these had quite the same gift for continuity and survival.

The city occupies an irregular rectangle framed by nine gates. Like many Syrian cities, a single great processional avenue cut through its length, known in the Gospels as 'straight Street', by Romans as Via Recta and by Arabs as Souk al-Tawil. The western entrance gate (Bab al-Jabiye), once dedicated to Jupiter, led due east to Bab Sharqui, the old gate of the Sun. To the north, a second great processional avenue marched towards the sacred enclosure in the heart of the city. Here an ancient shrine dedicated to the god Baal Hadad had evolved into an ever more magnificent complex associated by the Greeks with Zeus and with Jupiter by the Romans. In the late 2nd century AD, the Roman emperor Septimius Severus (married to a formidably intelligent princess descended from an ancient dynasty of Syrian high priests) had lovingly rebuilt the colonnades, walkways and sacred temenos enclosure around the shrine. His work still survives, though the emperor Theodosius in the late 4th century tore down the temple and replaced it with a basilica dedicated to St John the Baptist.

Despite the endless series of frontier wars between the Zoroastrian Sasanid empire of Persia and the Christian Orthodox empire of Byzantium, Syria yet prospered in the early medieval period, as the extraordinary density of stone-built towns that still surround the cities of Bosra, Hama and Aleppo testify. The savage wars fought between the two empires during the reigns of Heraclius and Chosroes II in the late 6th and early 7th centuries would be followed by a tectonic shift in power, ushering in an entirely new phase in the history of Damascus.

Cavalry armies forged from a confederation of Arab tribes of central Arabia burst upon the Middle East in AD 634. They were united by a shared devotion to the teachings of the Prophet Muhammad and a desire for plunder. The city of Damascus, well aware of the events in the Arabian desert through its involvement in the caravan trade, was among the first of the Syrian cities to welcome these new conquerors. The annihilation of the entire Byzantine field army just two years later, destroyed during a midsummer sandstorm at the three-day battle of Yarmuk (636) just south of Damascus, confirmed the wisdom of this decision.

When a new frontier was created along the line of the Taurus mountains (roughly following the modern borders between Syria and Turkey), Damascus's new eminence was confirmed. For not only did it command the direct route across the desert to the Islamic cities of Mecca and Medina, but it was also both secure enough and yet close enough to the new frontier to become the central headquarters of the Arabs. Damascus was also excellently placed to watch over the desert plateau of northern Syria, where the best cavalry horses in the world could be found. The old centres of power in the region were quickly overshadowed.

Damascus prospered under the rule of Mu'awiya, who had been handpicked by 'Umar, the puritanical second Caliph of Islam, to be the military leader in Syria. Mu'awiya was a brilliant commander but was otherwise a peculiar choice, for he was the son of Abu Sufyan, the leader of pre-Islamic pagan Mecca, and attracted to his court many of the officials of the old Byzantine empire as well as members of the traditional aristocracy of Arabia. When his cousin 'Uthman was chosen as the third Caliph of Islam in 644, Mu'awiya's authority grew ever greater – so much so that he was later able to foment civil war against Ali, the principled fourth Caliph of Islam. After Ali's assassination in 661, Mu'awiya was confirmed as the ruler of the rapidly expanding Islamic empire. In less than 30 years Damascus had been propelled from a Syrian provincial city to the capital of the great Umayyad empire, which stretched all the way from Tunisia in the west to Afghanistan in the east.

In the cosmopolitan court of Umayyad Damascus, scholar officials from the old ruling classes of Byzantium and Sasanid Persia, from the Yemen and from Egypt, mingled with singing girls, poets and nomad huntsmen belonging to the old tribal courts of Arabia. The polyglot scholarship of St John of Damascus, whose father was a Christian treasury official to the Umayyads, is one of the monuments to this era. The other is the Great Umayyad Mosque of Damascus, built by Caliph al-Walid (705–15) over the site of the Christian basilica, which until that time had been used by both Christians and Muslims as a house of prayer.

The caliph poured seven whole years of imperial revenue into the building, reusing the ancient sacred enclosure, and fusing Byzantine craftsmanship and architectural forms with the traditions of the first house-mosque of the Prophet. The gorgeous golden mosaics seem to play with the image of an idyllic landscape inspired both by Damascus's Barada riverbank and above all by the Koranic promise from Sura 13, 'Such is the paradise promised to the righteous; streams run through it; its fruits never fail; it never lacks shade.'

In 750, the supporters of Ali at last had their revenge on Mu'awiya's Umayyad dynasty. Every Umayyad was hunted down, their bodies burned, their palaces obliterated, their tombs flattened and their bones ground into dust. Only the Umayyad mosque was permitted to survive – one of the great wonders of the early medieval world. Overnight imperial Damascus decayed back into a Syrian trading city and Baghdad (p. 103) rose up to be the new Islamic capital. The fortunes of Damascus would be revived in the 11th century when the brutality of the Crusades, especially the sack of Jerusalem, drove thousands of refugees to take shelter behind its walls and a brand new Citadel fortress. Damascus would resist three Crusader sieges, and rally behind its emir Saladin in the reconquest of the Holy Land.

# CHANG'AN

## Capital of Tang China

VICTOR C. XIONG

*Hundreds of houses, thousands of houses – like a go board.*
*The twelve streets like a field planted with rows of cabbage. In the*
*distance perceptible, dim, dim – the fire of a torchlight procession;*
*and a single row of stellar lodges lying to the west of the Five Gates.*
BAI JUYI (772–846)

Located in Guanzhong ('within the passes') in the central Wei river valley in present-day south Shaanxi, Chang'an was the capital of China during one of its most illustrious epochs, the Tang dynasty (618–907). With an enclosed area of 84 sq. km (over 32 sq. miles) and a population estimated at over 1 million in the early 8th century, it was at that time the largest city in the world, and the dominant power centre of China, with a vibrant cultural and commercial life.

Before the rise of the Tang dynasty, Guanzhong had already played host to three national capitals: those of the Western Zhou (11th century–771 BC), the Qin (221–206 BC) and the Western Han (206 BC–ad 9). The strategic importance of Guanzhong was clear in Han times: protected by natural barriers such as mountain passes, it could fend off enemy attacks from the east with relative ease; supported by the fertile Wei valley and with access to the riches of the Sichuan basin to the southwest, it could serve as an effective launching pad for military campaigns to conquer the Central Plain and the rest of the Chinese world.

The Chang'an of Han had lost its capital status after the fall of the interregnum dynasty of Xin (AD 9–23) and the founding of the Eastern

Han (AD 25–220) in Luoyang (in present-day Henan). In the subsequent centuries, the city served intermittently as capital of dynastic entities that controlled only part of China proper.

In 582–83, the emperor Wen of the newly founded Sui dynasty (581–618) built another capital city southeast of Han Chang'an, named Daxingcheng after the emperor's predynastic noble title. After the Sui dynasty gave way to the Tang, Daxingcheng was renamed 'Chang'an', later known as 'Tang Chang'an' or 'Sui-Tang Chang'an', to distinguish it from its Han namesake.

The builders of Chang'an were indebted to two traditions. First, they followed an age-old practice of positioning the palace quarter (the Palace City) in the northernmost part of the city. Second, as they apportioned various functional quarters, they attempted to follow the interpretations in the *Book of Changes* on the six solid lines of the hexagram *qian*, which were matched with the six horizontal lines that dominated the city site. However, a conflict arose from the area south of the marketplaces, which is indicated in the *Changes* as the place fit for a sovereign. The solution was to place two monasteries, one Buddhist and one Daoist, in the area against the possible rise of a sovereign.

Rectangular in shape, the city was built on a gridiron plan that was typical of medieval Chinese metropolises. The imperial residence was in the centre of the Palace City; immediately to its south was the government quarter (the Imperial City). Two rectangular marketplaces were embedded in the centre of the city, south of the palace-government area. Most of the space, however, was taken up by more than 100 residential wards, each of which was a mini-city in itself, complete with criss-crossing avenues, walls and ward gates. The residential wards fitted perfectly into the city grid defined by the streets. Accentuating the axiality of the city layout, the central north–south thoroughfare originated in the Palace City in the north as an imaginary line on which the main palace structures were centred. As it re-emerged south of the Palace City to enter the Imperial City it became a physical street. Its extension to the south, Vermilion Bird Street, served as the central dividing line between the two halves of the city. From Sui to Tang, the general layout of the city remained essentially the same. One major change, however, was the addition of two palace complexes: the Daming Palace, as an accretion north of the city proper; and the Xinqing Palace, converted from one and a half wards in the northeast.

The city's population is estimated at slightly under half a million in 609 under the Sui, but in the turmoil at the end of the dynasty and in the early years of the Tang, it no doubt dropped, along with that of the rest of the country. In 742, Chang'an's inhabitants reached the 1 million mark before another serious decline during and after the cataclysmic An Lushan rebellion (755–63). It probably regained pre-rebellion levels in the early 9th century.

When the Arab traveller Ibn Wahab visited the city, probably in the late 870s, he took special notice of the water-filled ditches, with banks lined with trees and tall houses adjacent to one another. He was also impressed by the city's enormous size, wide central street and large population. As attested by textual records and archaeology, the most salient feature of Chang'an is perhaps its spaciousness. Two of its widest streets – Heng Street south of the Palace City and Vermilion Bird Street – were 441 m and 150–55 m wide (1,445 and 492–508 ft) respectively; and more space was enclosed at its founding than could be utilized by the city. Urban congestion was never a problem, except perhaps in certain parts of the two marketplaces, where shops were squeezed closely together.

Houses varied in size and quality. The largest, the Hanyuan Basilica in the Daming Palace, measuring 76 by 41 m (250 by 135 ft), was only one of dozens of palatial structures scattered throughout the three urban palace complexes. In the residential quarters, the rich and powerful often had spacious homes. Under the Sui, two imperial princes each had a mansion as large as a residential ward. Under the Tang, the largest non-royal mansion belonged to the most powerful general, Guo Ziyi (697–781), covering a total area of 137,970 sq. m or 34 acres. Guo lived there together with 3,000 of his entourage and relatives. At the other end of the spectrum, commoners lived in simple houses in the west and south parts of the city, where land was less valuable. An ordinary home usually comprised a main hall and two wings, often surrounded by a garden for trees and vegetables.

Tang Chang'an played host to such cultural celebrities as Du Fu (arguably the greatest poet in Chinese history), Li Bai (a romantic poet born in Central Asia) and Bai Juyi (the most popular Tang poet), as well as the painters Yan Liben, Li Sixun (the foremost landscape painter) and Wu Daozi. A quintessential cosmopolitan centre, Chang'an was the city of choice for many foreigners who became its long-term residents: Nestorians, Manichaeans, Zoroastrians, Indian Tantrists, Korean and Japanese students, and Sogdian traders. Among the more illustrious foreigners were Prince Firuz (son of Yazdgerd III of Sasanian Persia), Abe no Nakamaro from Japan and Choe Chiwon from the Silla kingdom in Korea (both eminent men of letters who served in official posts in Tang China), and the Buddhist Subhakarasimha from India, who brought Tantrism to China.

The enlightened cultural atmosphere of Chang'an was poisoned by a series of persecutions perpetrated by the Daoist emperor Wuzong (r. 840–46) against foreign religions, especially Buddhism, in 843–45. The Japanese monk Ennin was amazed to witness the draconian measures taken against religious properties and clergies. The city then suffered a devastating blow in 881 during the invasion by the rebel Huang Chao and never fully recovered. Subsequent efforts to revive the city failed to prevent its fall in 904, when the warlord Zhu Wen decided to move the capital east and ordered a systematic destruction of palace structures, official buildings and civilian residences.

# BAGHDAD

## and the Abbasid Caliphs

DORIS BEHRENS-ABOUSEIF

*The city of Baghdad formed two vast semicircles on the right and left banks of the Tigris … The numerous suburbs, covered with parks, gardens, villas and beautiful promenades, and finely built mosques and baths, stretched for a considerable distance on both sides.*

YAQUT AL-HAMAWI, 1224

Baghdad was the capital of the Muslim world at the apogee of its brilliance and achievements between the 8th and 13th centuries and represents the epitome of Arab Islamic civilization in its classical age. It was also one of the major settings for the fabulous tales of the *Thousand and One Nights*, when the city was governed by the caliph Harun al-Rashid. Like all Islamic cities, its development mirrored the power and changing fortunes of its rulers. Its devastation in 1258 by the Mongols created a hiatus in the history both of Islam and, in particular, the Arab world.

The city was founded in 762 on the western bank of the Tigris by the second Abbasid caliph, al-Mansur. The Abbasids had overthrown the Umayyad caliphate of Damascus (p. 94) and sought to establish the centre of their caliphate further east, closer to their power base in Iran and Iraq. Al-Mansur carefully selected the site of his city, following strategic, climatic and economic considerations. He called his capital 'The City of Peace', associating it with Paradise. European travellers often confused it with Babylon, but it was a new Islamic foundation (though the name Baghdad is pre-Islamic and belonged to a previous minor settlement).

Arab medieval historians provide us with detailed descriptions of the city and information about its history. It was built around a fortified round city, a plan already known in the ancient Near East. In the centre of the round city was an esplanade that included the caliph's palace, topped by a monumental green dome 48 m (159 ft) high, itself surmounted by the effigy of a mounted lancer. Next to it was the great mosque and the administrative quarter.

Around this central complex a network of streets – linked to four equidistant gates in the outer brick fortification walls – was deliberately designed to accommodate dwellings in hierarchical order, as well as markets and open spaces. On the southern side of the round city extended the commercial hub, while the military quarters were to its north. Al-Mansur and his successors built palaces and military quarters on the eastern Tigris shore, which were connected by floating bridges to the west bank. Initially, only the round city was surrounded with walls; however, following military unrest the caliph al-Musta'in (r. 862–66) ordered the fortification of the eastern city also. A system of canals dug in antiquity to connect the Euphrates with the Tigris supplied the city with water. These canals, crossed by stone bridges, were a characteristic feature of Baghdad's cityscape and played an important part in its social life; other canals were subterranean.

Following the civil war in 814 sparked by the rivalry between Harun al-Rashid's two sons, al-Ma'mun and al-Amin, the round palatial city was ruined and abandoned, and was gradually absorbed by the surrounding urban agglomeration.

Baghdad's history as Abbasid capital was interrupted when the caliph al-Mu'tasim transferred the seat of power to the newly founded city of Samarra in 836, to avoid confrontations between the population and the new Turkish army recruits. Following the return of the court from Samarra in 892, the caliph resided in one of the palaces of the east bank, which eventually expanded to become a sort of palatial city within the capital, composed of several buildings and residences, with courtyards, ponds and gardens, and even a zoo. In 1095 the caliph al-Mustazhir surrounded the palatial complex with walls, which were maintained and restored in the following centuries.

Abbasid Baghdad rivalled Constantinople (p. 79) in extent. Modern historians estimate its area between 5,000 and 7,000 ha (12,355–17,297 acres), but are uncertain about the size of the population, with estimates ranging from 280,000 to 1.5 million. The higher figure is based on the reported number of 1,500 hammams, or baths, which would each serve 200 households of approximately five people. At a time when other great cities had only one congregational mosque, Baghdad had six.

Baghdad was a metropolis of superlatives. Its rich urban culture was shaped by its ruling aristocracy, together with the military establishment, bureaucrats, merchants, craftsmen and intellectuals and academics. All were members of an international and diverse population, reflecting the structure of an Arab caliphate that had come to power with the support of an Iranian clientele and relied on Turkish military recruits from Central Asia; it integrated local Christians, Jews and Zoroastrians, and enjoyed a prestige and wealth that attracted people from all over the Muslim world and beyond.

As a result of the cultural patronage of the caliphs and their officials, Baghdad was the centre of religious and secular scholarship that shaped Islamic civilization for centuries to come. Theology, law – notably the Hanafi and the Hanbali schools of Sunni Islam – historiography, grammar, natural sciences, belles-lettres, along with arts and crafts, all flourished, and were disseminated from the city throughout the entire Muslim world.

The House of Wisdom, an academic institution founded by al-Ma'mun (r. 814–833), played a seminal role in the translation of Greek sciences. Study and scholarship took place in mosques and houses, as well as in a number of public or semi-public libraries which were sponsored by notables and scholars to function as academies for religious and secular sciences.

Baghdad was also a centre of medical knowledge and possessed a number of hospitals founded in the 9th and 10th centuries.

As well as being the intellectual centre of the medieval Muslim world, Baghdad was also its commercial heart. The wealth of its markets and the luxury of their products inspired many of the tales of the *Thousand and One Nights*. The city's prosperity was based both on the rich agriculture of its hinterland and on a vast trade network within the Muslim empire and beyond, stretching to the Indian Ocean and China, Africa, the Atlantic and Europe. Its markets, which were laid out according to trades and supervised by inspectors, sold goods from all over the world and were at the same time centres of production and of financial transactions.

Baghdad's heyday came during the first half of the 10th century, when the caliphs cultivated a refined lifestyle in their glorious palaces along the Tigris. In 945 the Buyids, a Shi'ite dynasty who ruled in western Iran, occupied the city and deprived the caliphate of its authority. They were ousted in turn in 1055 by the Turkish Saljuks, also from Iran, who reinstated Sunni Islam, which they boosted through the institution of the madrasa, introduced in 1067 by Nizam al-Mulk the great vizier of the Malikshah, the third Saljuk sultan. The madrasa was an official establishment for teaching and boarding, which from this beginning spread throughout the Muslim world as the standard institution for religious studies.

Baghdad was already in decline when the Andalusian traveller Ibn Jubayr visited it in 1185. Floods, fires, popular revolts and sectarian turmoil had damaged the medieval city, but the fatal break that terminated its brilliant history was its sack by the Mongols in 1258 and the overthrow of the caliphate by Hulagu, who ordered the killing of the last caliph. Today no physical evidence of the round city is recognizable and only a few vestiges of the great Caliphate period remain, including a palace and two mausoleums attributed to the caliph al-Nasir (r. 1180–1225), two city gates restored by him in 1221, and the madrasa founded by the caliph al-Mustansir in 1232.

# CÓRDOBA

## Brilliant Capital of Moorish Spain

DORIS BEHRENS-ABOUSEIF

*In four things Córdoba surpasses the capitals of the world.*
*Among them are the bridge over the river and the mosque ...*
*but the greatest of all things is knowledge – and that is the fourth.*

AL-MAQQARI, EARLY 16TH CENTURY

Córdoba's age of splendour began after the fall of the Umayyad Caliphate in Damascus in 750 (p. 94), when prince 'Abd al-Rahman escaped the massacre of his family and fled to Spain, where he founded a new caliphate. The Arabs had conquered Córdoba earlier in the 8th century and declared it the capital of al-Andalus, the Arabic name for Muslim Spain. Córdoba's Umayyad Caliphate lasted until 1031, after which the city became a republic for 60 years before succumbing to a new dynasty, the Almoravids, followed in 1148 by the Almohads. In 1236 it fell to Ferdinand of Castile as part of the Reconquista, and its special status as one of the major cities of the Mediterranean world, Christian or Muslim, came to an end.

For nearly 500 years, and especially during the 10th century, Córdoba was a beacon of civilization, enjoying a greater degree of peaceful government and toleration than perhaps any other city of the period. The city was a cultural melting pot, with a mixed population of over 100,000, including Arabs, Berbers, Iberians (Vandals and Visigoths) and Jews. The caliph's court was the centre of a brilliant cultural flowering that surpassed all contemporary European capitals. Echoing the court of Baghdad (p. 103), it attracted foreign scholars and stimulated great achievements in science, medicine, philosophy, poetry and art. The late 10th-century ruler al-Hakam

II established one of the largest libraries of Islam in the city, estimated to have held over 400,000 volumes. The markets of Córdoba were renowned for their luxury goods, in particular textiles, jewelry, leather goods, weapons and carved ivory. The book market was one of the most prominent, acting also as a copying and publishing centre. Later, the highly influential Andalusian philosopher and polymath Ibn Rushd (1126–98), who was known to Christian Europe as Averroés, lived and worked here. On the ground today virtually the only substantial vestige of the Caliphate period – except for the city's walls – is the great mosque, the Mezquita, now a Christian cathedral.

The Mezquita was founded by 'Abd al-Rahman I (r. 756–88), 30 years after his accession, in the precincts of the existing Christian church of San Vincente, which he demolished (he authorized the Christians to build a substitute). It was completed a year before his death. Four successive enlargements by later caliphs testify to the dynastic significance of this great building, which came to epitomize Muslim rule in Spain. Like its only rival, the Great Mosque in Damascus, it follows the tradition going back to the Prophet's own time of a large courtyard with a prayer hall aligned on one side.

The mosque's architecture combines Syrian Umayyad and indigenous features. The superposed arches of the prayer hall recall Roman aqueducts in Spain and their horseshoe profile follows a Visigothic tradition. Many of the varied columns and capitals were spoils from earlier buildings from as far away as Constantinople, Alexandria and Nîmes. The 19 aisles of the ultimately completed prayer hall run perpendicular to the main wall, as do the naves of a church, with the wider central aisle leading to the prayer niche. Initially the courtyard was without arcades and there was no minaret. 'Abd al-Rahman II (r. 822–52) enlarged the mosque to the south, while in 956 'Abd al-Rahman III expanded the courtyard and added at its northern wall a rectangular minaret, which is part of the present church tower. Al-Hakam II's (r. 961–76) enlargement turned the mosque into a spectacular monument. The prayer hall grew to be 104 m (340 ft) deep, with a magnificent triple prayer niche roofed with three ribbed domes and decorated with glass mosaics executed by Byzantine craftsmen. In 978 the vizier al-Mansur widened the arcades by adding eight more aisles to the north, and he enlarged the courtyard accordingly.

The Mezquita not only fulfilled the religious functions of a mosque, but also acted as a political forum, seat of justice and teaching institution. Next to it lay the royal palace and centre of government, the Alcázar. The city was crossed by one major artery leading to the river on a north–south axis. The urban area extended beyond the city's walls, with their 132 towers and 13 gates, erected by 'Abd al-Rahman I, who also built another palace in the western suburb. Other extramural palaces and suburbs spread in all directions, except the river side. Between the river and the wall a quay called Arracife functioned as a public square for both popular entertainment and displays of political authority. The foundation by 'Abd al-Rahman III of a new palatial and administrative centre at Madinat al-Zahra, 6 km (4 miles) to the west of Córdoba, boosted urban expansion on that side of the city. Another courtly city, al-Madina al-Zahira, was founded by al-Mansur to the east.

When Córdoba was conquered by the Christians the Mezquita became a church and in 1523 it was irredeemably damaged by having a *coro*, with screens, altar and choir-stalls, built in its very centre. True, this occupies a relatively small space in comparison with the whole, and it is possible to ignore it and enjoy the original building, but one cannot help agreeing with the emperor Charles V who wrote to the authorities: 'You have built here what you or anyone could have built anywhere else, but you have destroyed what was unique in the world.'

The Moorish walls of Córdoba and their gates survive, and many of the churches and palaces built after the conquest are notable in their own right. Yet it remains true today, in the words of the 19th-century historian Rodrigo Amador de los Rios, that 'Cordoba, in the throes of the prostration that holds it in its grip, yearns for its past'.

# THE MEDIEVAL WORLD

By the time our story reaches the year AD 1000, great cities have appeared in four of the world's continents; and in the following 500 years, these cities developed prodigiously. In north Italy alone, the great city-states of the early Renaissance – represented here by Venice and Florence – made their own incalculable contribution to the civilization of the West; while in the south, the dazzling though tragically short-lived Norman kingdom of Sicily combined the three great cultures of the Mediterranean – Latin, Greek and Arab – as never before or since. North of the Alps, medieval Paris was a thriving metropolis; Lübeck and the other Hanseatic cities were opening up trade in Russia, Scandinavia and all over the Baltic; and Kraków – capital of the largest of European states – was the seat of a university which drew students from all over the continent.

Europe no longer held many secrets for geographers. Merchants and diplomats had travelled across it and maps drawn of it were reasonably accurate. Nobody, on the other hand, could begin to chart the other continents, which, even if their existence was known, remained virtually unexplored. In Africa, even Cairo – by now pre-eminent as a centre of Islamic scholarship and enriched by several of the most magnificent mosques to be found anywhere – was almost unvisited by western travellers. Our two other African cities, Benin and Timbuktu, were to Europeans little more than legends. But, as the following pages demonstrate, the fact of their being unknown to Europe in no way detracts from their greatness.

The same can be said of our two American cities, Tenochtitlan and Cuzco, of which nobody in Europe had heard at all – the entire continent of America being undiscovered by Europeans until the final decade of our medieval period. Of the Aztec capital, barely one stone now remains on another – apart from the great temple-pyramid, discovered next to Mexico City's cathedral some 40 years ago; but read the account of the Spanish conquest by Bernal

Díaz del Castillo, and you will be left in no doubt of the city's magnificence. Cuzco too has suffered, both at the hands of the conquistadors and also from disastrous earthquakes; but enough of the old Inca buildings have survived – with that astonishing technique of stonemasonry which can be seen to still greater advantage at nearby Sacsayhuaman – to convince us that here, too, was a city of surpassing splendour.

Of another of our cities a poet wrote:

*Sweet to ride forth at evening from the wells*
*When shadows pass gigantic on the sand,*
*And softly through the silence beat the bells*
*Along the Golden Road to Samarkand.*

But even without James Elroy Flecker's lines, there can be few more evocative place-names than that of Tamerlane's megalomaniac creation, capital and burial site. The Central Asian steppe is hardly a region in which one might expect a great city, let alone one of the most opulent and sumptuous cities of its time. Much of modern Samarkand is marred by Soviet brutalist architecture; but in the 15th century its beauty left visitors speechless, and of that beauty something lingers.

Finally we come to Angkor, which remained hidden in the jungle, for centuries unknown to European travellers, until its rediscovery only 150 years ago. Partly, perhaps, for this reason and partly owing to its immense size, it was never deliberately destroyed; its principal enemy has been the surrounding forests, which have undermined foundations, split buildings in two and occasionally, like monstrous boa constrictors, almost literally consumed them. Both Hindu and Buddhist, in its heyday it attracted pilgrims in their thousands. Now it has to contend, like so many other cities, with the infinitely more destructive mass tourism – and also with thieves in the night: more and more of the smaller decorative sculptures are sawn off, to reappear a week later in the antique shops of Bangkok.

# ANGKOR

## Khmer City of Glory

### MICHAEL D. COE

*These prodigious works … in the construction of which patience, strength and genius appear to have done their utmost in order to leave future generations proofs of their power and civilization.*

HENRI MOUHOT, 1864

The medieval city of Angkor in northwestern Cambodia has fascinated the western world since its 'discovery' by the French explorer Henri Mouhot in the 1860s. At that time largely buried in dense tropical forest, its magnificent ruined temples inspired Mouhot and other travellers to wonder who had built Angkor, and what had caused its downfall. The modern name of the city – Angkor – is a Khmer-language version of the Sanskrit noun *negara*, meaning 'capital city'. Its ancient name was Yashodarapura, 'City of Glory', a fitting designation for an enormous urban complex that during its apogee under Jayavarman VII (r. AD 1181–c. 1215) acted as the administrative centre of an empire covering most of mainland Southeast Asia.

Angkor occupies a flat, gently sloping plain between the Kulen hills to the north and northwest, and to the south the Great Lake or Tonle Sap, the largest body of fresh water in Southeast Asia. Fed both by streams originating in the Kulen range and by a branch of the Mekong river, the extremely shallow waters of the Tonle Sap reach their greatest extent during the monsoon (rainy) season of May to mid-November, and then shrink to one quarter of this depth in the winter dry season. This lake still provides the Khmer people with copious amounts of fish, and was a major source of protein for the inhabitants of Angkor. But rice was always the staple crop.

Angkor was founded after AD 802, when Jayavarman II declared himself the 'universal ruler' and established his capital in what is now the southeastern part of the city. There he and his successors built state temples both to the gods – principally Shiva, patron of the royal line – and to their ancestors on fairly orthodox Hindu plans, with central shrines of brick and/or sandstone representing the sacred Mount Meru (mythical home of the gods in the Himalayas), flanked by four smaller shrines in a quincunx pattern. Each of these temple complexes was surrounded by a rectilinear moat symbolizing the cosmic seas that ringed Meru.

Towards the end of the 9th century, Yashovarman I moved the administrative centre of the city about 20 km (12 miles) to the northwest and immodestly named the reconstituted city after himself (derived from Yashovarman. 'Protected by Glory').

In the early 12th century, Suryavarman II built what is surely the largest, and many think the most beautiful, religious structure in the world, Angkor Wat. Dedicated to Vishnu (the 'preserver god' of the Hindu Trinity), and maintained by Buddhist monks ever since the eclipse of Angkor as a city, it has always been the destination of pious pilgrims, both Hindu and Buddhist. In Angkorian times, as today, the devotee approached it on foot from the west, crossing the broad moat by a causeway, and entering the first of three quadrilateral galleries; in the outermost of these, the pilgrim would have made a clockwise circumambulation to view magnificent reliefs based on episodes in the Hindu epics of the *Ramayana* and *Mahabharata*, as well as the story of the creation of the cosmos. At the centre of a quincunx of increasingly elevated towers, at one time probably covered in gold, was the sanctuary and image of the god, presided over by Brahmin priests who were the intermediaries between the deity and the worshippers.

Our knowledge of what the city was like is in part based on the only eyewitness account known to have survived. This was written by Zhou Daguan, a commercial envoy from the Chinese capital, Beijing, who spent about a year in Angkor towards the end of the 13th century. The 'city' he describes in his spirited memoir is not 'Greater' Angkor but its inner core: Angkor Thom, the political and religious centre of Jayavarman's huge realm. Angkor Thom forms a square, 3 km (2 miles) on each side, surrounded by a moat and lofty walls. These were pierced by five great gates, tall enough to allow elephants with their passengers to pass through, and surmounted by towers with enigmatically smiling faces. The gate on the west (an unlucky direction) was, according to Zhou, a place of execution. At the very centre of the square lies the Bayon, Jayavarman's state temple, an enormously complex pile of four-faced stone towers and ritual chambers, largely dedicated to Mahayana Buddhism. Zhou tells us that the central tower was covered with gold, and that eight golden Buddhas were housed around the base of the complex.

In the quadrant to the northwest of the Bayon lay the Royal Palace. Unlike the stone structures of the great temples, built to house eternal gods, the royal dwelling was a huge complex of impermanent wood, covered with yellow glazed tiles; the principal chamber was roofed with lead. The size of the palace may be judged by the fact that quite apart from the king's five wives and their retinues, plus 3,000 to 5,000 'concubines and palace girls', bureaucrats, court dancers and musicians, over 2,000 women worked in it by day and returned to their homes at night. Within the palace compound were five royal bathing pools, and a family temple to which the king was said to retire each night to sleep with a 'snake princess'. The ruler gave audience in standard Southeast Asian style at a gold-framed window flanked by mirrors. Magnificently attired with a golden diadem and wearing around his neck some three pounds of pearls, with bracelets and rings of gold, he must have appeared an awesome figure to the supplicants prostrated before him. Whenever he left the palace, he carried the Sacred Sword of gold, the palladium of the Cambodian nation.

Fronting the royal palace at its eastern end was an enormous reviewing stand, faced with bas-reliefs of war elephants and their mahouts. From this the king and royal family viewed national spectacles, such as great military and civil processions, and even firework displays, as well as parades of family heads during the annual census of the empire's population. At the northern end of this structure is the so-called Terrace of the Leper King, now believed to be the cremation platform for the royal house.

Jayavarman VII was Cambodia's most indefatigable builder, and a powerful patron of the Mahayana Buddhist religion; among his foundations are three moated and walled complexes within Greater Angkor that may be thought of as Buddhist 'universities'. Each housed several thousand temple officials, various temple retainers (including dancers), commoners and slaves, all supported by revenues from lands granted to them by the king. The enormously wealthy Ta Prohm, for example, was supported by no fewer than 3,000 villages, which may have been scattered all over the empire.

An absence of currency seems to have been no hindrance to trade. Zhou has much to say about the merchants who lived within the city, and who seem to have been mainly Chinese – there are even lively depictions of Chinese merchants' households on the reliefs of the Bayon. Foreign trade seems to have been brisk in spite of the difficulties of navigating the waterways of the lower Mekong. Local products such as prized kingfisher feathers, rhinoceros horns and elephant tusks were exported abroad, in exchange for Chinese manufactures including silk textiles and Chinese celadon.

What kind of a city was this? Where did its people live? What was the purpose of Angkor's six enormous reservoirs? A century of archaeological and art historical research has concentrated on temples and inscriptions, and has provided no answers to these questions. But very recent ground and radar survey, together with excavation, has shown that most of Angkor's residents dwelt in pile-supported thatched houses near small artificial ponds (as Zhou had told us), interspersed with rice paddies; that this was a vast, low-density urban zone; and that the reservoirs were part of a massive, state-run, canal-irrigation system that ensured rice harvests throughout the year. The mystery is why all this fell into ruin at the end of six centuries of glory, although environmental degradation along with military pressure by the encroaching Thai must have played major roles.

# PALERMO

## Norman Jewel of the Mediterranean

JOHN JULIUS NORWICH

*The King's palaces are strung around the hills that encircle*
*the city, like pearls around the throat of a woman.*
*And in their gardens and courts he takes his ease.*
*How many palaces and buildings, watch-towers and*
*belvederes he has ... how many monasteries he has*
*endowed with rich lands, how many churches*
*with crosses of gold and silver!*

IBN JUBAYR, 1184–85

Of all the cities that existed in Europe in the middle of the 12th century, Palermo was surely one of the most brilliant. At the time of the conquest of Sicily by the Normans it was already a busy commercial metropolis of perhaps a quarter of a million inhabitants, boasting some 300 mosques and almost as many churches, together with countless markets and streets of craftsmen and artisans. The whole was surrounded not just by Ibn Jubayr's hills, but by parks and pleasure-gardens, murmurous with fountains and running streams of the kind that the Muslim world understands so well.

There had been Normans in south Italy since around 1015, when a group of Norman pilgrims had been approached by a Lombard nationalist in the shrine of Monte Sant'Angelo in Apulia. He made them a proposal which they found difficult to refuse: if a couple of hundred of their compatriots would only join the Lombards in their struggle against the Byzantine occupiers of the land, they could easily carve out vast estates for themselves in the region. The temptation proved too great to resist: over the next half-century a steady flow of footloose younger adventurers rode south across the Alps. By 1050 they had mopped up virtually all Apulia and Calabria; in 1053 Pope Leo IX had led an army against them, but was defeated and captured; and six years later his third successor Nicholas II had invested the Norman leader Robert Guiscard with the Duchies of Apulia, Calabria – and Sicily.

At that time no Norman had set foot in Sicily, but the investiture was an open invitation. Robert and his younger brother Roger invaded the island in 1061 – just five years before their cousins fought the battle of Hastings. Sicily, which was populated partly by Greeks and partly by Arabs, proved a far tougher nut to crack – Robert and Roger did not reach Palermo till 1072, while William the Conqueror dealt with England in a matter of weeks – but the result of the Sicilian conquest was to be infinitely more dramatic. Clearly, it could be successful in the long term only if three very different peoples, with three different religions and speaking three different languages, could somehow be welded together into a single state; and this – after Robert had returned to his mainland duchies – was the almost superhuman achievement of two men: Roger I and his son Roger II.

They differed widely from each other. Roger I was a Norman through and through; Roger II, born in Sicily of an Italian mother, was a southerner and an oriental. Roger I had been content with the title of Great Count; for Roger II (after he had inherited his brother's mainland dominions in 1127), only a royal crown was good enough. And three years later, on Christmas Day 1130, thanks to a disputed papal election which enabled him to side with the weaker of the two candidates in return for a papal blessing for his coronation, he was crowned king in Palermo cathedral. It was on that day that Palermo's golden age began.

The kingdom was, first of all, superbly administered. The Greeks, being by far the best seamen, had responsibility for the all-important navy, based in Palermo's magnificent natural harbour. Its admiral – the word itself comes, through Norman Sicily, from the Arabic *emir al-bahr*, emir of the sea – was effectively the prime minister. The finances were inevitably entrusted to the Arabs, whose mathematics were much better than anyone else's. As a result, and owing also to the island's superb position in the dead centre of the Mediterranean – a crossroads and clearing-house between north and south, east and west – Sicily and Palermo soon became enormously rich. King Roger could afford the best and accepted nothing less, as can be seen from the monuments that he left behind him. The most astonishing of these is unquestionably the Palatine Chapel, or Cappella Palatina, in the royal palace of Palermo, which he built in the 1140s and which perfectly illustrates the Norman-Sicilian miracle.

The chapel is conceived on the western European model, with a central nave, two side aisles and steps leading up to the chancel; but the walls are covered with Byzantine mosaics, clearly the work of the most skilled Greek artists that could be found in Constantinople, while the stalactite wooden roof is purely Islamic work – a *tour de force* of oriental joinery that would be a credit to Córdoba or Damascus. Nor – though it should not properly belong here, being not in Palermo but some distance eastwards along the coast – is it possible to omit mention of the most inspired work of art that Sicily has to offer: the vast apse mosaic of Christ Pantocrator in Roger's Cathedral of Cefalù, for many of us the greatest portrait of the Redeemer in all Christian art.

But the king was not only a munificent patron; his court in Palermo was easily the most brilliant of 12th-century Europe. In the Middle Ages the two most important languages of science were Greek and Arabic, both of which were virtually impossible to acquire in northern Europe. A scholar wishing to learn Greek might go to Constantinople; one eager to tackle Arabic might settle in Andalusia; but for any intellectual determined to master both, there was only Palermo. By the 1140s Roger had given a permanent home there to many of the foremost scholars and scientists, physicians and philosophers, geographers and mathematicians of both Christendom and the Arab world; and as the years went by he would spend more and more of his time in their company.

Roger II died in 1154, and immediately the kingdom began to decline. His son William the Bad hardly merited his sobriquet but unfortunately possessed little of his father's energy or vision; and William's son, William the Good – his title equally undeserved – had inherited little from Roger but his passion for building: his great cathedral at Monreale just a few miles from Palermo, its walls covered with literally acres of mosaics, its cloister perhaps the loveliest in the world, stands almost – if not quite – on the level of the Palatine Chapel or of Cefalù. But William and his wife, Joanna of England (she was the daughter of the English king Henry II), were childless, and the throne then passed to his aunt, Roger's daughter Constance, who married the future Holy Roman Emperor Henry VI. As a result, the Norman Kingdom of Sicily was subsumed into the Empire. It was not properly defeated; it was thrown away. It had lasted just 64 years.

Palermo was never the same again. It moulded Henry and Constance's son Frederick, greatest of the Holy Roman Emperors and a Renaissance prince 200 years before such paragons existed; but later it fell on hard times. When Sicily became part of the Kingdom of Naples, Palermo lost its capital status. It was never to regain it. It is now essentially a baroque city, beautiful though sadly dilapidated. But the setting – the Conca d'Oro or Shell of Gold – is as lovely as ever, and the Sicilian parliament still meets in King Roger's old palace – so all, perhaps, is not lost.

# CAIRO

## Centre of Islamic Civilization

DORIS BEHRENS-ABOUSEIF

*We arrived in Cairo on Sunday 17 June, 1481. I had come to
see the Cairenes and their deeds. However, if I were to write
about its wealth and its people, all of this book would not be
sufficient. I swear that if it were possible to put Rome, Venice,
Milan, Padua, Florence and four more cities together, they
would not equal in wealth and population half that of Cairo.*

RABBI MESHULAM OF VOLTERRA, 1481

Cairo under Mamluk rule was at the heart of the Muslim world and 'a city
beyond imagination', according to the Arab philosopher Ibn Khaldun. It was
the capital of a sultanate that ruled not only Egypt, but also Syria, including large areas of southern Anatolia, and the Hejaz, with the holy cities
of Mecca and Medina. After the sack of Baghdad by the Mongols in 1258,
Cairo became the seat of the Abbasid Caliphate, and even if this was only
symbolic, given the caliph's merely ceremonial function, it earned the city
the spiritual and cultural leadership of all Muslims. Like ancient Memphis,
the much earlier capital of Egypt (p. 21), its location just south of the Delta
and at the junction of Upper and Lower Egypt, placed it on important trade
routes. Its wealth derived from the transit of lucrative spices between the
Indian Ocean and the Mediterranean, as well as agriculture, since it also
sits astride the fertile black lands, irrigated by the annual Nile inundation.

In fact, the city we know today as Cairo began as two separate sites:
Fustat, the initial capital founded when the Arabs conquered Egypt in
641, which expanded with subsequent satellite cities; and, to its north,

al-Qahira, founded in the 10th century as the palatial city of the Fatimids. Under the Mamluks the latter grew into a fully fledged city that gradually eclipsed Fustat. Unlike Fustat, founded along the Nile shore, Qahira was built further east along the Canal or Khalij, which branched from the Nile to the north of Fustat. The Citadel, founded by Salah al-Din (Saladin) in the 12th century, bridged the urban gap between the two centres, although they never fully merged. Fustat became an industrial suburb with a port on the Nile connecting Cairo to Upper Egypt, while Qahira enjoyed the major share of the royal monumental patronage. Cairo's evolution from the double capital Fustat–Qahira to the Mamluk metropolis was shaped by the intensive religious and urban patronage of the ruling establishment.

Having seized power in 1250, the Mamluks legitimized their rule with victories against the Crusaders and Mongols, leaving them free to concentrate their efforts on a pious patronage of unparalleled dimensions and grandeur. The magnitude of their endowment of mosques, colleges, monasteries and other charitable foundations led to a florescence of architecture, which reached new peaks of refinement, coupled with huge urban expansion. It has been estimated that by the end of the Mamluk period, Cairo had grown to almost five times its previous size, with a population of nearly half a million. It was always a cosmopolitan mix, even before the Mamluks, and continued to include, in addition to the Muslims, a Christian (Coptic) and a smaller Jewish minority, as well as Mamluks of Turkish and Circassian origin, Mongols, Syrians, Africans, Anatolians, Iranians and Central Asians.

Perhaps the most significant factor in the glory of Mamluk Cairo was the remarkable relationship between the aristocracy and their capital. In the second half of the 13th and the early 14th centuries sultans and emirs seemed to vie with each other to establish major religious foundations in the heart of the former Fatimid Qahira, in the street called Bayn al-Qasrayn. Among them was the complex of Sultan Qalawun, which consisted of a mausoleum, a college and the famous hospital, or maristan, which remained the major medical centre of pre-modern Egypt until the early 19th century.

The reign of Sultan al-Nasir Muhammad (1294–1341) was a golden age of Cairo's history, as a result of his exceptionally long and prosperous rule, coupled with his architectural and urban ambitions. Together with his emirs, he enlarged the urban area with numerous fine mosques that formed the nuclei of new quarters. Fresh land was available for building as the course of the Nile bed shifted westwards, coming to a halt by the early 14th century. Al-Nasir built additional bridges over the Canal to connect the western bank with the main city. The Canal and the ponds it supplied were flooded by the Nile in summer and filled with greenery during the rest of the year, making them magnets for residential quarters and pleasant venues for leisure and pastimes. The Canal also provided Cairo with drinking water. In the outskirts of the city al-Nasir built a number of squares or parade grounds. Surrounded by walls and residences, these included gardens and pavilions, and were the sites of ceremonies and festivities.

The building boom of al-Nasir's reign also included cemeteries to the east and south, where the emirs erected religious foundations to accompany their grand mausoleums. Al-Nasir also transformed the Citadel, founding new palaces and a new mosque. Perhaps the largest of its kind in the medieval world, the Citadel became a city in its own right, with palaces, offices, barracks, dwellings and shops. It now acted as an economic focus, attracting markets for horses and weapons to supply the the military aristocracy and the army, as well as princely palaces and mosques. It was during this period that the famous Muslim traveller and writer Ibn Battuta described Cairo as 'mother of cities ... mistress of broad provinces and fruitful lands, boundless in multitude of buildings, peerless in beauty and splendour'.

Following the invasion of Syria by Timur (Tamerlane) in 1400, which badly affected the Mamluk economy, as well as a series of natural catastrophes and political instability, many of Cairo's quarters and markets were abandoned or devastated. However, neither the building zeal of the ruling establishment nor the quality of the constructions declined. Throughout the 15th century, sultans and emirs continued to embellish the urban fabric. For instance,

Sultan Faraj Ibn Barquq's funerary complex in the desert was the first royal foundation outside the city and one of the most remarkable architectural achievements of this period. Al-Mu'ayyad Shaykh built a new pleasure complex in the northern suburb along the Canal (it did not survive his reign), and encouraged his courtiers to construct residences nearby, so as to be close to his court when he was there. He also built a religious complex near the Fatimid gate Bab Zuwayla, above which he erected a pair of towering minarets that are still a landmark of Cairo today.

Besides his own exquisite mosque and religious school in the cemetery, Qaytbay's (r. 1468–96) building programme was characterized by extensive restoration work on the city's religious and secular monuments. He upgraded previous foundations by restoring and reconstructing their estates, revitalizing the commercial infrastructure of the city. While the sultan concentrated his efforts on Cairo's monumental heritage, his great emirs pursued their own ambitious urban transformations. With spectacular feats of landscape design, Yashbak min Mahdi – the great secretary – and Azbak – the chief of the army – filled urban gaps in the northern and western suburbs respectively with mosques, palaces, apartment buildings and shops. At the very end of the Mamluk period, Sultan al-Ghawri founded a funerary complex of great originality in the urban centre, surrounded by markets and commercial structures. Cairo's major markets were concentrated in what was Fatimid Qahira, along the main avenue and its extension towards the Citadel. Shops and booths crowded beneath apartment buildings and mosques, while caravanserais housed markets or workshops on the ground floor, and dwellings or workshops on the upper floors.

The Mamluk sultanate came to an end in 1517 when it was conquered by the Ottomans, but its rulers had left Cairo one of the largest and richest cities of its day and endowed it with many jewels of Islamic architecture. In the narrow streets of Cairo today, monuments of all periods crowd together, and in the continuity of its history and the density of its urban fabric through many centuries, Cairo is surely unique.

# SAMARKAND

## Tamerlane's Chosen City

COLIN THUBRON

*Everything I have heard about the beauty of Samarkand is true.*
ALEXANDER THE GREAT, 329 BC

The name Samarkand – like Timbuktu or Xanadu – conjures a capital of fabled remoteness, where the maps in people's minds blur away. Long after Samarkand's decline, as it withdrew into the isolating deserts of Central Asia, it became the fantasy of Handel and Goethe, Marlowe and Keats, immortalized for its golden roads and exotic tyranny.

Of all great cities, Samarkand is the farthest from any ocean. It grew up instead on the human river of the Silk Road, and its earliest known inhabitants were the Sogdians, an Iranian people whose merchants came to dominate the trade of Central Asia. Samarkand was the richest of their cities. Alexander the Great, who captured it in 329 BC, declared it surpassingly beautiful. Literate and sophisticated, the Sogdians were said to have taught the Chinese the arts of glass-making and viniculture.

Even after its conquest by the Arabs in AD 712, Samarkand gained a new distinction: it became a centre of paper-making (taught by Chinese prisoners-of-war) and it was from here that the craft travelled on to the West. For centuries the city showed resilience under invasion. Some 50 years after its sack by Genghis Khan in 1220, Marco Polo reported it depleted but recovering, and soon afterwards the much-travelled Ibn Battuta still placed it among the finest cities in the world.

But this past glory pales before what was to come. In 1366 Samarkand fell to the cavalry of Timur, an obscure Turco-Mongol chieftain whose powerful but maimed physique inspired his name: Timur-i-leng (the Lame), the western Tamerlane. The city was his first and favourite conquest, and his chosen capital. Lodged where the Pamir mountains break down into the deserts of today's Uzbekistan, it stood – and still stands – on the gold-bearing Zerafshan river, thick with orchards famous for their apples, melons and pomegranates. The surrounding pastures and foothills supported vineyards, wild game and fat livestock, with ample crops of cotton and wheat.

From this elysium, for more than thirty years, Tamerlane marched across Asia in a series of campaigns that devastated every state and city in his path, sacking Damascus and Isfahan, Baghdad and Delhi, crushing the Golden Horde and the Ottoman Turks, and leaving behind him some 17 million dead. But always he returned to Samarkand, bringing back artisans and plunder from civilizations whose craftsmanship, refined over centuries, was now employed in the rebuilding and embellishment of a unique capital.

From its ancient plateau-citadel Samarkand expanded southwest, ringed by 8 km (5 miles) of moated walls. All through Tamerlane's 35-year reign the city was in an uproar of construction. Six highways passed through orchard villages – he named them contemptuously after the great capitals he had conquered – to monumental gates, and on through fountain squares among mosques and religious schools, gardens and caravanserais, to converge at last on the immense domed market of the Registan. Above the labouring brick-workers and ceramicists of conquered Persia rose a cloud of turquoise domes, ribbed or smooth, sheltering mosques and tombs. Architects, painters and calligraphers from Persia, Syrian glass-blowers and silk-weavers, Indian silversmiths and jewellers joined a stream of captive scientists and scholars, while in the imperial palace, alongside its treasury and archives, the vaults rang with the din of Anatolian gunsmiths and armourers, preparing for the next campaign.

In the administration of the city – and of the whole empire – the governors and military chiefs, typically, were Turco-Mongol, while finance and civic works were managed by a sophisticated Persian bureaucracy. For the populace of Samarkand was a mine of expertise: of diverse races and faiths, slave and free, of Arabs, Persians, Moors, Hindus, Armenians and a medley of Christian minorities. And all the produce of the known world, from Chinese jade to Indian spices and Russian furs, flowed to its bazaars along the Silk Road.

Within a few years Samarkand – 'Centre of the Universe,' 'Garden of the Soul,' 'Mirror of the World' – lived up to the epithets bestowed on it. Yet it was never, in fact, an immense city, as was Tang dynasty Chang'an (p. 99) or even contemporary Paris (p. 128). The visiting Castilian envoy Gonzales de Clavijo, mesmerized by its riches, reckoned it a little larger than Seville, with a populace of some 150,000. It was not its extent but its cosmopolitan splendour – the evocation of sheer power – that provoked wonder.

Perhaps never had a city been so purely the creation of one man. Genghis Khan had levelled civilizations to the earth, as if despising them. But Tamerlane, nearly two centuries later, coerced art and science to his own glory. In Samarkand, it seems, he aspired to concentrate and embalm the accomplishments of the entire world – a monument to himself, and perhaps to God.

Near the city centre he planned the most prodigious edifice of all: the royal mosque named Bibi Khanum, lanced with 49-m (160-ft) minarets. Thousands of master-craftsmen were poured into the site, while 95 Indian elephants lugged its marble into place. Tamerlane executed its superintendents for building its gates too low. Ageing and half-crippled, he flailed on its construction from a litter, tossing meat to favoured workers. So its architects raised the mosque too quickly, in terror, and it began to crack apart even before the emperor's death.

Yet the city depended on a ruler who was largely absent. Even after he returned from campaign, Tamerlane – a nomad still – would camp outside the walls. Here, in one of 16 garden-compounds, his palaces and pavilions were sheathed in Chinese porcelain, or frescoed impiously with his wars and loves, or surrounded by such huge parks that horses were lost there.

And here he might receive envoys in a gorgeous tent-city whose walls and ceilings were air-hung silks dripping with precious stones. The Spaniard Clavijo described tables of gold and flasks studded with astonishing jewels, and a barbarian banquet in which leather platters, mounded with sheep's heads and horse-haunches, were so heavy that they had to be dragged along the ground.

But the moment Tamerlane died, on his way to invade China in 1405, his empire fractured. Whereas the realm of Genghis Khan, divided among his descendants, was to hold together for over a century in the Pax Mongolica, the empire of Tamerlane was so dependent on its paranoid ruler that his death left behind chaos and bewilderment.

Yet the legacy of Samarkand rang down the centuries. For a while the city's eminence continued under Tamerlane's grandson, the astronomer-prince Ulug Beg, from whose observatory more than 200 new stars were discovered. Meanwhile at Herat, Tamerlane's son, Shah Rukh, and his successors maintained a hedonistic court, leaving behind rare miniatures and poetry and the ravaged remains of a brilliant architecture. Above all, after Samarkand had fallen to the Uzbeks in 1500, the emperor's great-great-great-grandson, Babur, fled the city to found the empire of Mughal India, where the Timurid domes would rise again to find their perfect fruit in the Taj Mahal.

Today, among the Soviet flat-blocks of Samarkand, the domes gleam in sudden fantasy. Ulug Beg's religious school shines over the Registan (which Lord Curzon called 'the noblest public square in the world') and the shattered hulk of Bibi Khanum is being restored. More gloriously, the faience gates to the tombs of Tamerlane's family and chosen emirs still glisten along their sacred stairway, and the tomb of Tamerlane himself survives in shocking beauty, where he lies buried under the largest block of jade in the world.

# PARIS

## Pinnacle of Gothic Architecture

CHRIS JONES

*By the five wounds of God, Paris is a very great city! There is
a chapel of which I am desirous; I will cause it to be carried
in a rolling cart Straight to ... London, just as it stands.*

SPEECH ATTRIBUTED TO THE ENGLISH KING HENRY III IN A
FRENCH SATIRICAL POEM, 1260S

By the early 14th century the inhabitants of Paris could, with some
justification, look upon their city as the greatest in the Christian world. Its
self-confident rulers had defied the Papacy, the supreme spiritual authority in
Christendom, with impunity. The city's Gothic taste in art and architecture
had imprinted itself on the western European landscape. The University of
Paris was, by comparison with other centres of learning in Europe, a sun
that had risen and outshone the stars. But it had not always been this way.
For much of the previous millennium Paris had played a less than significant
role in Europe's history.

The origins of the city lay some two centuries before the birth of Christ,
when a tribe known as the Parisii had established themselves on an island
in the river Seine, later to become the Ile de la Cité. Called Lutetia by its
Roman conquerors, the city, which spread from its original island to both
banks of the river, was certainly witness to some distinguished visitors,
including Julius Caesar himself in 53 BC. Some 400 years later the last
pagan ruler of the Roman empire, Julian the Apostate, was lifted up on
a shield and declared emperor by his army within the city's bounds. Yet
Paris, as it became known from the latter part of the 4th century AD, was

not even the provincial capital, and remained something of a backwater under Roman rule, a trading post and little more.

As the Romans withdrew from their western provinces the city shrank until it was little more than a fortified island in the Seine. Falling into the hands of the Franks, one of the tribes who had filled the vacuum left by the departing Romans, the city enjoyed a brief period of importance under the tribe's Merovingian rulers before being virtually abandoned to a combination of slow decay and Viking raiders. It was not until the 12th century that Paris was to emerge from its obscurity.

This change in Paris's fortunes was in large part due to the decision of the Capetian kings of France to make it their principal place of residence from the 12th century. The presence of the court and its officials helped fuel the Parisian economy and made the city the centre of the political life of the French kingdom. It was here, for example, that the final gruesome acts in the history of the Order of the Temple took place: in 1314 the last Grand Master, Jacques de Molay, was convicted of heresy and burnt, under the watchful eye of the man who had brought about the Templars' downfall, King Philip IV. A decade earlier the city had witnessed the holding of the first representative assemblies in the French kingdom, assemblies which Philip had used to recruit support in his dispute with the Papacy. The presence of the royal court did more, however, than bring the political issues of the day to the doors of Parisians; it transformed a trading post into a capital fit for a king.

Offended by the stench from the city's streets, one of the first actions of an earlier king, Philip II, had been to order their paving in 1186. Increasingly worried by the belligerence of the English rulers of Normandy, the same king, in conjunction with the merchants of the Right Bank, began the arduous task of enclosing the city of Paris within a set of defensive walls. Completed between 1190 and 1215, little today survives of these walls, although traces of them are still to be found in the basement level of a Parisian car park and inconspicuously bordering a community sports ground. The most striking feature of these defences was the Louvre, a massive castle constructed on the western edge of the city next to the river and buried today beneath the modern museum.

Philip II's efforts to transform Paris were continued by his successors. Philip IV's Grand'salle, only the lower levels of which survive, offers only one example. Within this vast enclosure, statues of all the kings of France – whose aspect, as Jean de Jandun remarked, was 'so expressive that at first sight one would believe them to be living' – gazed down on those conducting the business of government.

Of all the royal building projects undertaken in Paris none was more magnificent than the Sainte-Chapelle constructed in the midst of the palace complex on the Ile de la Cité. This royal chapel was built to house the relic of Christ's Crown of Thorns acquired by King Louis IX ('Saint Louis'). The chapel, completed by 1248, is remarkable for the soaring stained-glass windows that dominate its structure and which recount, in over 1,000 panels, stories from the Bible and the journey of the relic to Paris. Elements of the building's design were emulated across Europe and the spectacle of this chamber of light so bedazzled the English king Henry III that one witty contemporary suggested he wanted to carry the chapel off to London, as quoted above.

The royal palace occupied the western end of the Ile de la Cité, and royal authority was counter-balanced at the eastern end of the island by the cathedral of Notre Dame. Begun in the Gothic style in 1163, Notre Dame was, like the Sainte-Chapelle, remarkable for its spectacular stained glass, in this case in the form of rose windows.

While Paris owed its late-medieval reputation to a combination of factors, perhaps none of them cemented its international renown as much as its university. In the course of the 12th century the school attached to the city's cathedral developed an increasing reputation for learning, attracting scholars from across Europe. Among the earliest of these figures was Peter Abelard, who became famous as much for a calamitous love affair with his pupil Héloïse, as for his contribution to the study of logic. The story of the couple's love, enlivened by the drama of Abelard's castration – an act of reprisal inflicted on the unfortunate scholar by Héloïse's uncle – became one of the period's most celebrated tales.

As the 12th century turned into the 13th, the students and masters of the cathedral school gradually established their independence. With both royal and papal support the new university grew to dominate the Left Bank of the Seine, its increasing numbers leading to the foundation of colleges. The most famous of these, established in 1254, took its name from its founder, a royal chaplain, Robert de Sorbon. Once Paris had established a reputation as Europe's premiere seat of learning, the problems of Christendom were brought before its scholars. As Pope John XXII found to his cost, the theologians of Paris could rebuke even popes when their ideas were felt to be less than orthodox.

A concentration of students and scholars fuelled many of the city's trades, but none were more dependent on the presence of the university than those involved in the book trade. The parchment makers, scribes and binders, however, formed only a small proportion of the rapidly increasing Parisian populace. When Abelard had arrived at the beginning of the 12th century the city's population was perhaps as little as 3,000 souls; some 200 years later it had risen to 200,000, making Paris the largest city in the West at that time.

Alongside those artisans involved in the copying and decoration of books, contemporary Parisians were especially proud of their city's sculptors, painters, armourers and, in particular, its bakers. As one university master remarked in 1323, these last were 'gifted with an astonishing superiority in their art ... the bread that they make acquires an unbelievable degree of goodness and delicacy.' The same master, Jean de Jandun, was also astounded by the sheer number of houses in the city and by the richness of the goods on sale in its markets. Paris's vibrant economy, which had at its roots the activities of merchants who exploited fully the opportunities for trade offered by the Seine, was fostered, in particular, by the city's most important inhabitant: the king. It was King Philip II who, in 1182–83, and at the expense of Paris's Jewish community, was to clear land on the Right Bank and organize the construction of the covered market known as Les Halles.

Today, Notre Dame cathedral, at the heart of modern Paris, remains the most visible reminder of the city's medieval glory, a grandeur which, by the mid-14th century began to slip away as first the Black Death and then English armies arrived at the city gates.

# LÜBECK

## and the Cities of the Hanseatic League

WILLIAM L. URBAN

*Ihr seid Herren (You are lords)*
CHARLES IV TO THE LÜBECK CITY COUNCIL, 1375

The island in the Trave river was inhabited long before Count Adolf II of Holstein founded a castle and walled city there in 1143. Its location on a north–south crossroads, with a good harbour for fishermen and merchants sailing into the Baltic Sea, was ideal for commerce. It was these character-istics, however, that also ensured its repeated destruction over the years by jealous enemies.

Indeed, calamity almost befell Count Adolf's city of Lübeck, which within two years was partially burnt by the neighbouring Wends. Two years later the missionary Vicelin became bishop of nearby Oldenburg. His success in converting the Wends to Christianity allowed the Count to attract farmers and burghers from as far away as Flanders. Then in 1158 the city was seized by the powerful Saxon duke, Henry the Lion, who opened north Germany to Lübeck's merchants, assisted the bishop of Oldenburg in relocating to the city, and permitted its first government to be formed. Political struggles from 1180 onwards brought the citizens under the rule first of the emperor Frederick Barbarossa, and later of the king of Denmark. Only in 1226, after Danish power was broken, did Lübeck become a free imperial city; henceforth its citizens governed themselves, minted money and traded freely.

Lübeck's merchants sailed to the eastern Baltic, where crusaders were conquering Prussia and Livonia, and to Sweden, then on to Russia, carrying

Flemish cloth, and German iron and salt from nearby mines. They traded with Hamburg by land and Bremen by sea, selling fish from the Baltic Sea and Norway, Russian wax and furs, Polish grain and Prussian timber. From the trading port at Visby on Gotland they learnt the advantages of co-operation, and after 1356 the international merchant community often met at Lübeck to discuss mutual problems. Each member city promised the others honest weights, low taxes, reasonable market fees and access to housing, warehouses and banks, medical care and worship. New cities appearing on the Baltic coasts adopted Lübeck law and increased their collective power; this, coupled with the regional dominance of its coinage, increased Lübeck's prestige significantly. It became, after Cologne, the second largest city in Germany.

The members of this loosely defined organization of 70 to 170 cities proudly called themselves 'free and Hanseatic cities' – the name the Hanseatic League first appeared in the mid-13th century, but did not become common until later. They met only when the need for collective action was obvious, but they managed to defeat pirates, to frustrate efforts to tax their vessels and to deal vigorously with potential competitors. The cities believed strongly in monopolies, both in guild life and trade, as long as the monopolies were their own. Lines of credit were essential to commerce, joint ventures reduced individual risk, and intermarriage with trading partners was common. Hanseatic merchants established 'factories' (*Kontore*) in foreign lands, along with hostels, churches and warehouses; in segregated districts in Novgorod, London, Bergen, Cologne, Bruges and other cities, they were protected against harassment and judicial misconduct.

In the 14th century Lübeck was filled with multi-storeyed brick homes, sturdy warehouses, and richly ornamented churches and welfare centres. Large restaurant-bars and inns were available for burghers and visitors. The city hall, the focus of public life, was a masterpiece of northern Renaissance architecture, with rich decorations and furnishings. Lübeck's marketplace was crowded with stalls, and the names of some of its streets reflected the trades that were carried on there – fishmongers, coppersmiths, butchers, bell-makers and others. Each occupation formed a guild, and these guilds chose the 24 members of the city council – from whom four mayors were selected.

There was occasional labour unrest, with the workers complaining that merchants were taking an unfair share of the earnings from trade and holding excessive political power. This was both true and probably unavoidable if each city was to remain independent and prosperous.

The 11-day visit of Charles IV to Lübeck in the autumn of 1375 became the stuff of pride and legend. Experienced, powerful and forceful beyond any other Holy Roman Emperor of living memory, Charles needed money. He brought such a large retinue that the citizens worried whether it was safe to let them through the gates; he was also a collector of relics, and what should the city council do if he asked for some? Charles tried to flatter the councilmen, but after listening to his request for money, they gave him mostly honeyed words in return. They housed him in the city hall and built a covered bridge to the building opposite, where the empress was staying. Legend has it that the citizens watched to see if they could observe him coming out of his window and crossing to hers. One night the empress locked him out, until the crowd of spectators grew so large that she had to open the window. He left richer than he had come, but not by as much as he had hoped.

Nothing lasts forever, and the Hanseatic League was no exception. It was not able to shield every member from regional lords, and each loss made it more difficult to protect the remaining cities. Those cities could impose embargoes on trade and they could raise navies, but they could not provide land armies; they also found it impossible always to block competitors from their markets or to compete with the larger vessels of England and Holland. These were fatal weaknesses. The Reformation brought further stresses, including a decreased demand for fish during fast days; and many cities were sacked during the Thirty Years War. The last formal meeting of the League took place in 1669, and only Lübeck, Hamburg and Bremen remained independent into the 19th century.

Lübeck's last decades of independence were described in Thomas Mann's *Buddenbrooks*, a novel of 19th-century life subtitled, 'the decline of a family'. But pride in the citizens' achievements and those of the Hanseatic League is still evident today; the name Lufthansa, for instance, is a reminder of the days when the Hanseatic League ruled the waves. Lübeck itself is today a World Heritage site and a centre for tourism.

OPPOSITE Detail of an anonymous painting depicting the flight of the Brilliant Emperor (Xuanzong), with his concubine and his imperial entourage, from Chang'an to Shu. The rebel An Lushan, a military leader who rose to prominence in the northeast of China, had declared himself emperor and marched on the capital, forcing Xuanzong to abandon the city.

ABOVE Aerial view of Angkor Wat, looking east. Built in the first half of the 12th century, the temple complex was dedicated to the god Vishnu, patron deity of Suryavarman II. It stands on an artificial island surrounded by a huge rectangular moat.

BELOW The monastery of Monreale was founded by William II of Sicily (r. 1166–89) on a hill overlooking Palermo. Its cathedral, with its astonishing mosaics, is among the treasures of Sicilian art. Notable in this cloister are the sculptured capitals and mosaic-decorated columns.

ABOVE The skyline of Cairo displays many sublime monuments built by the Mamluks. In the foreground is the carved masonry dome of the funerary mosque of Qanibay Qara from the early 16th century, with its double-headed minaret to the right.

LEFT Many of the older areas and streets of modern Cairo retain their medieval form and feel. Khan el-Khalili market, a warren of alleys and stalls, still holds workshops making many of the objects on sale, just as in Mamluk Cairo.

OPPOSITE The Bibi Khanum mosque of Samerkand. This architectural prodigy was raised by Tamerlane in 1399–1404 as he strove to create the greatest mosque in the world. Its entrance gate soared over 35 m (115 ft) high, but it began to crack apart even before Tamerlane's death, and was later abandoned. Now restored, it again dominates the Old City.

S. anto   S. sanct   S. dyon   S. r̄ S. el.

partūt

Istos prelatos ad se pater iste uocatos
admonet ut presto sint hij certamine gesto.
ppe gestor seriem deferre suorum

OPPOSITE The 3rd-century bishop and martyr St Denis (seated) brought Christianity to Paris. The lower register depicts scenes of 14th-century Paris: a covered wagon on its paved streets and wine merchants on the Seine. From a manuscript of Ives de Saint-Denis's *Life of Saint Denis*.

ABOVE Street scene in old Timbuktu. The Sankore mosque has the typical 'perch' silhouette of a Saharan mosque, and its adobe minaret is reinforced by embedded wooden scaffolding.

BELOW The 13th-century Palazzo da Mosto (left of centre) is among the oldest palaces on Venice's Grand Canal. The famous explorer Alonso da Mosto was born here in 1432 and it was later a well-known inn where Emperor Joseph II stayed.

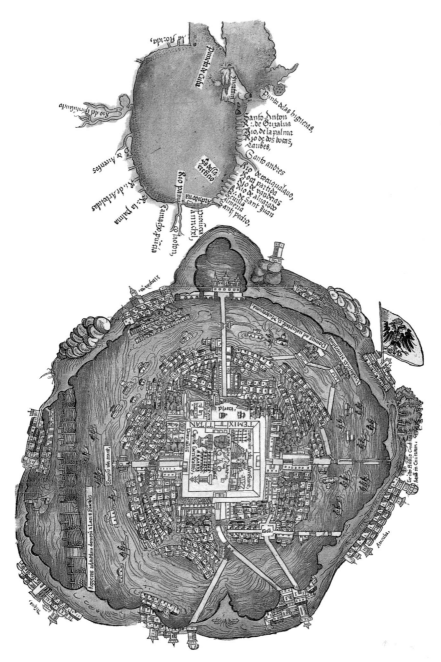

A map of the island city of Tenochtitlan from an early European account of the Aztecs in 1524. It shows the island city's many causeways and the wickerwork dyke separating the freshwater lake from more brackish water. The Templo Mayor ritual precinct dominates the central island.

ABOVE The sack of Baghdad by the Mongols under Hulagu in 1258, and the murder of the last caliph, marked a turning point in the history of Islam. Miniature from Rashid ad-din's *Universal History* (late 14th century).

BELOW The forest-like interior of the Mezquita mosque in Córdoba reused classical columns from as far away as Constantinople and Alexandria. Its superimposed arches in alternating coloured stone echo Roman aqueducts, but their horseshoe shape is a Visigothic form.

# KRAKÓW

## Renaissance City of the North

ADAM ZAMOYSKI

*Toruń gave birth to me, Kraków polished me with the arts.*
COPERNICUS

In the late Middle Ages, Kraków was the capital of the largest state in Europe and the centre of gravity of a dynastic imperium that stretched from the Baltic in the north to the Black Sea in the south, from the shores of the Adriatic in the west to a couple of hundred miles short of Moscow in the east. This was reflected in the size of its main square, the largest market-place in Europe, which contained a 12th-century Burgundian Romanesque chapel, a 14th-century German Gothic church and a hybrid High Gothic town hall, surrounded by houses of the city's merchant princes redolent in style of the palazzi of Italian cities. While the church of the Virgin Mary was dominated by one of the masterpieces of northern medieval art, Veit Stoss's carved triptych, the frescoes in the Franciscan church showed the unmistakable influence of Giotto. The streets teemed with people whose dress betrayed French, Flemish, German, Italian and Ottoman influences, and rang with the sound of languages as varied as German, Italian, Armenian, Yiddish, Ruthene and Magyar.

The city's origins are bound up with the rocky outcrop of Wawel Hill dominating the river Vistula and its legend of a ravening dragon slain, according to taste, either by the chivalrous Prince Krakus or by a cunning cobbler. The hill bears the remains of a 10th-century castle and basilica, and the city was recorded as an important trading centre in the year 965. It became the nominal capital of the Kingdom of Poland in 1040, but its golden age did not begin until King Kazimierz III, known as 'the Great', ascended the throne in 1333. It was a good age for Poland as a whole. A warming of the climate favoured advances in agriculture, while the Black Death, which ravaged Europe in 1348–49, halving the population of some areas, largely bypassed Poland, which additionally profited from an influx of Jewish refugees from witch-hunts connected with the plague.

King Kazimierz provided all the conditions for a boom, codifying the laws, regulating the coinage and investing in infrastructure. Kraków acquired a number of new buildings, new city walls and, in 1364, a university. Coming 14 years after the foundation of the Charles University in Prague, it was the second in Central Europe, pre-dating most of the German universities.

Kazimierz was succeeded by his nephew Louis of Anjou, king of Hungary, and then by his daughter Hedwig (Jadwiga), who married the Grand Duke of Lithuania, thereby opening up relations with a vast swathe of territory to the east and turning Poland into a major power. Her husband, who reigned in Poland as Władysław II, would defeat the Teutonic Knights at the battle of Grunwald (Tannenberg) in 1410, and his envoys would play a major role at the important Catholic ecumenical Council of Constance five years later. He was courted by Henry V of England, and his son, Kazimierz IV, would wear the Garter as he received embassies from the Ottoman Sultan Murad II. In the next century, their descendant Zygmunt Augustus, whose mother, of the Sforza family of Milan, was a first cousin of François I of France and a close relative of the emperor Charles V, would consider a match with Mary Tudor before marrying a Habsburg princess.

By the mid-1400s Kraków had become a cultural crucible. With no more than 15,000 inhabitants, it was not a particularly large city, but it made up for that in vitality. The next hundred years would witness an extraordinary explosion of intellectual, cultural and political activity, which placed it firmly within the mainstream of European life. While many Poles travelled abroad to study – in 1480 one became rector of the Sorbonne, and by 1500 they made up a quarter of the student body at the university of Padua – the University of Kraków attracted scholars from as far afield as England and Spain. The Italian humanist Filippo Buonaccorsi of San Gimignano, better known as Callimachus, who took up a teaching post in 1472, was delighted to discover that, thanks to the excellent postal service, he could keep up a regular correspondence with Lorenzo de' Medici and Pico della Mirandola, while the establishment of a printing press in 1473, four years after Venice and three before London, meant that he would not want for books. In 1488 he was joined by the German humanist Conrad Celtis, who founded a literary association which, unusually, included lady poets.

Celtis had been drawn to Kraków by the renown of the university's chair of mathematics and astronomy. These disciplines fascinated many, who believed that they held the key to ultimate knowledge, and one who supposedly studied there was Dr Faustus. A less sulphurous scholar, admitted to the university in 1491, was a young student from Toruń, Mikołaj Kopernik, who would publish his astronomical findings under the name of Copernicus.

The university's cloistered Collegium Maius, which dates from 1494, resembles a northern European version of an Oxford college. Flemish and north German influences are also visible elsewhere in Kraków, particularly in some of its brick Gothic churches and city walls and gates. But by the late 1400s the strongest influences were coming from the south – from Hungary and above all Italy.

As the realms of Poland's ruling dynasty, the Jagiellons, bordered with the Republic of Venice (p. 149), it is not surprising that there was much traffic between Italy and Poland, and not only the new humanism but also the art of the Renaissance flooded in. In 1502 the heir to the throne, Prince Zygmunt, returned from a trip to Italy, bringing with him a Florentine architect, Francesco Fiorentino. Four years later, as King Zygmunt I, he commissioned Fiorentino to rebuild the Gothic royal castle on Wawel Hill. The project was carried on after Fiorentino's death by another Florentine, Bartolomeo Berecci, whose funerary chapel for Zygmunt I, completed in 1531, was one of the first, and remains one of the finest, Renaissance buildings north of the Alps. These two Florentines were followed by other Tuscan architects, who transformed the cityscape and dotted the surrounding countryside with Renaissance villas.

The court on Wawel Hill was by now one of the most glittering in Europe, famous for its lavish displays and musical life. But Kraków was also at the centre of some of the most profound changes taking place in Central Europe. Poland's parliamentary system had developed by leaps and bounds in the second half of the 15th century, and in 1505 the act *Nihil Novi* turned the Polish parliament, the Sejm, into the sole legislative. The Sejm was the mouthpiece of the Polish political nation, the noble *szlachta*, and since they were not only obsessed with the issue of individual rights, but also included Muslims and Jews, it is not surprising that the Reformation in Poland was not the bloody affair it was elsewhere. Kraków became the refuge for religious and political dissidents from other countries, a centre of debate and the printing-house of much religious and political literature which was disseminated throughout Europe.

But it was the development of Poland's democracy as much as anything else which brought about Kraków's decline. From 1569 the Sejm began to meet at Warsaw, and a couple of decades later the court moved there too. But the buildings, the university, the libraries and works of art remain.

# VENICE

## Mistress of the Mediterranean

JOHN JULIUS NORWICH

*For here treachery has no place ... here reigns neither*
*the cruelty of harlots nor the insolence of the effeminate,*
*here there is no theft, or violence, or murder*

PIETRO ARETINO TO DOGE ANDREA GRITTI, 1530

At the beginning of the 15th century Venice was at the height of her power. A thousand years before, she had been a simple place of refuge for the peoples of the great mainland cities from the barbarian invasions; now she was mistress of the Mediterranean, the world's greatest trading nation, with commercial colonies extending to the Middle and even to the Far East. Both her navy and her mercantile fleet were in superb condition; the 15,000 workers in her Arsenal could turn out a fully rigged ship every few days. And she grew steadily richer. In the rest of Europe, where the feudal system still prevailed and where nobility was based on the ownership of land, trade was despised; in Venice, where there was no land, it was the highest calling that could be followed. The merchant prince, everywhere else a contradiction in terms, was an accurate description of the aristocratic Venetian.

To what did Venice owe such success? There were three principal causes. The first was security. Throughout the Middle Ages, mainland Italy was a constant battleground. After the collapse of the Roman empire in the West and the continuing barbarian incursions, the peninsula was hopelessly divided, with the Papacy, the Byzantines, the new empire of Charlemagne and his successors, the great northern cities such as Milan, Verona and Padua, the maritime city-republics such as Genoa and Pisa in the north and

Naples, Amalfi and Gaeta in the south – the list is far from exhaustive – all at loggerheads. But Venice remained apart. Those 3 km (2 miles) of shallow water – a far more effective defence than deep – served as a gigantic moat, giving her total protection from her envious and unruly neighbours and enabling her to turn her back on Italy and look to the East: to Constantinople, to the Black Sea, to the Indies and Cathay. There, in the silks and spices, the gold and the furs and the slaves of the Orient, lay her wealth.

The second cause was her stability, which was in turn due to her extraordinary system of government. From the time that she declared herself independent of Byzantium in AD 727, Venice had chosen to be a republic. So indeed had most of the other great cities of north Italy; but over the years virtually all of them were to be taken over by one leading family or another – the Medici in Florence, the Sforza and Visconti in Milan, the Gonzaga in Mantua, the Este in Ferrara. Not so in Venice, where the fear of such an eventuality was almost pathological. This was not a democracy, however; in 1298 membership of the Maggior Consiglio – the Great Council of the Republic – had been restricted to the noble families, whose names were listed in the *Libro d'oro*, the Golden Book. Still, Venice was determined that no one man should assume too much power, and would go to almost any lengths to ensure it. Thus the system for the election of the Doge (head of state) was quite grotesquely complicated, the more so in that once elected he enjoyed virtually no effective power – less, probably, than the Queen of England has today. The actual business of government was entrusted to innumerable faceless committees, many of them serving only a few months, whose decisions were all taken by a majority vote. Consequently Venetian political history contains the names of practically no great men; but for around 700 years until her final defeat by Napoleon in 1797 the government of the Most Serene Republic remained rock solid.

The third cause of its success was of a rather different kind, and little to Venice's credit. It was the Fourth Crusade. In 1201 those planning it appealed to Venice to provide transport for their fleet. Venice agreed – for a price – also offering to provide a military contingent of her own; but the Crusaders were deflected from their objective and turned instead against Christian Constantinople, which in 1204 they sacked and largely destroyed, expelling the Greek emperors and replacing them with a line of Frankish thugs, who allowed what was left of the city to go to ruin. Half a century later the Greeks returned, but found only a pale shadow of their former capital.

Byzantium's loss was Venice's gain. By the terms of the treaty with the Crusaders, Venice gained three-eighths of the city and its empire, plus free trade throughout the imperial dominions, from which her principal rivals, Genoa and Pisa, were rigorously excluded. In Constantinople, she appropriated the whole central district surrounding St Sophia; beyond, she helped herself to an unbroken chain of ports from the Venetian lagoon to the Black Sea – including the western coast of the Greek mainland, all the Peloponnese, the Ionian Islands and several of the Cyclades, the Thracian seaboard and the all-important island of Crete. Henceforth the Doge would assume the resounding title of Lord of a Quarter and Half a Quarter of the Roman Empire; it would be no more than the truth.

The 14th century had been a good deal harder for Venice than the 13th. There had been two attempts at revolution – though both pathetically inept – and a Doge, for the only time in the city's history, had been disgraced and executed. In the second half of the century the Black Death returned with remorseless frequency every few years to cut another great swathe through the population. Worst of all, the Ottoman Turks had invaded Europe and were rapidly occupying the Balkan peninsula. On the other hand, Venice's commercial success had brought huge gains in international prestige and in the influence that she would be able to wield in the whole of western Europe, where her trading position was immeasurably strengthened.

Meanwhile, much of Venice's hugely increased income was spent on the development of the city itself. In 1400 there were even more canals than there are today – many have since been filled in – navigated by boats very like modern gondolas. The Basilica of St Mark, now just three centuries old, already boasted its four bronze horses – loot from the Fourth Crusade – and an early Romanesque campanile, though the other three sides of the Piazza were as yet unbuilt. The finishing touches were being put to the Doge's Palace. For the rest, most of the lovely Gothic churches and palaces were already in place, though it would be another half-century before Gothic was reluctantly to give way to the classicizing architecture of the Renaissance.

As to the future, Venice's confidence was buttressed by the one huge advantage that she alone possessed over all her rivals: that, in so far as any city could ever be, she was impregnable. Despite her new terrestrial image, she still belonged to the sea, being both protected and enriched by it – and by the 3,300 ships and 36,000 seamen that she possessed in 1400. No other major Italian city could claim to have remained inviolate for close on a thousand years. And no other could boast such wealth. Not only was she nearer than any of her competitors to the eastern markets – the source of all those luxuries which Europe, having once acquired a taste for, was demanding more and more insistently; but the fact that the sea was, almost literally, her home had obliged her to achieve a mastery over it that her rivals might occasionally challenge but could never match for long. Furthermore, she was trusted. She had built up a network of trading contacts halfway across the world, together with a reputation for fair dealing – which did not exclude hard bargaining; and then there was the Venetian character: tough, hardworking, determined, with an ingrained respect for wealth and a boundless ambition to acquire it. Finally came the firm discipline, born of long experience, imposed by the state.

Was it therefore any wonder that the citizens of Venice accounted themselves privileged? They might have little say in their government, but there was no indication that the populations on the mainland were any better off. Besides, it was surely better to be well governed, even without political influence, than subject to the whim of an ambitious and tyrannical despot. If that was the price of living in the richest, safest, best ordered and most beautiful city in the civilized world, they were prepared to pay it.

# FLORENCE

## The Magnificence of the Medici

CHARLES FITZROY

*Florence altogether gave herself up to the arts and pleasures of peace,
seeking to attract thither men of letters, to accumulate books, to
adorn the city, to make the countryside fruitful.*

SCIPIO AMMIRATO, 1647

Florence occupies a unique position in history. It was in this small Italian city-state that the Renaissance began, a movement that has changed our perception of the world. Situated on the river Arno in central Tuscany, Florence grew in power during the Middle Ages, expanding beyond the limits of the original Roman settlement. Having formed an independent commune in the 12th century, by 1300 Florence was one of the five largest cities in Europe, its wealth based mainly on banking and the woollen-cloth industry. The florin, named after the city, became the standard gold coin throughout Europe.

The Middle Ages in Italy was, however, a time of political unrest, with a prolonged civil war between the papal Guelphs and the imperial Ghibellines; Florence was a champion of the former. Unlike its neighbours, who were ruled by tyrants or a small clique of nobles, at this time the Florentine middle-class played a significant part in civic life, with the guilds, representing the most important trading bodies, administering the evolving Florentine Republic. Every two months an election was held for the governing body, the Signoria – six members represented the major guilds, two members represented the minor guilds, and a ninth took office as Gonfaloniere.

Medieval Florence was also an outstanding cultural centre. During the 13th and 14th centuries it produced artists of the calibre of Cimabue and Giotto, as well as the writers Dante, Petrarch and Boccaccio, the greatest names in medieval Italian literature, all three deeply versed in classical civilization. By the late 14th century Florence had become the intellectual and artistic centre of Europe. There was growing interest in the concept of humanism – that 'Man is the measure of all things'. These humanists drew inspiration from the study of the world of antiquity, with the art and literature of the ancient Romans and Greeks viewed as the pinnacle of human achievement. And they saw Florence as both the heir to Rome and a bastion of liberty.

Florence's growing political and economic power coincided with the development of a new artistic style in the years around 1400. The Florentines, having defied a threatened invasion by the powerful Duke of Milan in 1402, celebrated their success by commissioning major works of art. Initially in the field of sculpture, a new naturalistic style was created, based on the study of classical prototypes. Three figures of genius dominated Florentine art in the early 1400s. The architect Brunelleschi, who had spent 12 years studying the ruins of ancient Rome, invented the science of perspective, built the great dome of the Duomo, Florence's cathedral, and was the first to use the classical forms of architecture. The sculptor Donatello and the painter Masaccio created figures which possessed a realism and psychological intensity inspired by a close observation of nature and classical art. The new ideas dominated politics as well as art. Humanist scholars such as Coluccio Salutati and Leonardo Bruni, author of an important history of Florence, served as chancellors of the Florentine Republic.

From 1434, when he returned from exile, the astute merchant Cosimo de' Medici became the unofficial ruler of the city, a position he retained until his death in 1464. Cosimo was banker to the Papacy and used his influence to persuade his friend Eugenius IV to hold the Council of Florence in his native city in 1439 – a meeting between the Pope and the Byzantine emperor John Palaeologus. Although the Council failed to unite the Greek and Latin churches, it encouraged Florentine humanists, already busy collecting classical manuscripts, to pursue their study of ancient Greek civilization. Leon Battista Alberti, the brilliant humanist, described the change in attitude in Florence from the medieval view of art as a symbolic expression of theological truths, to the new humanistic outlook based on scientific naturalism.

As well as being a skilled politician and businessman, Cosimo de' Medici was also a judicious patron of the arts. Brunelleschi and Donatello, the architect Michelozzo, and the painters Fra Angelico, Filippo Lippi and Paolo Uccello all created masterpieces for him in the new classical style. Cosimo was, however, a modest man, living in a typical Florentine palace with a fortified exterior and an internal courtyard to let in light. It served as the family headquarters, with the ground floor devoted to business and the servants' quarters; the main reception rooms were on the *piano nobile*, their walls decorated with frescoes and tapestries, and with just a few windows filled with glass – still a precious commodity. The upper floors housed the kitchen and rooms for lesser members of the family.

The Florentine Renaissance reached its apogee under the benevolent rule of Cosimo's grandson, Lorenzo the Magnificent, an immensely talented and versatile man. Although Lorenzo was not a successful banker, and barely survived an assassination attempt by the rival Pazzi family in 1478, in which his brother Giuliano was stabbed to death, he was a popular ruler and used his great personal charm and gifts as a diplomat to dominate Florentine politics and resolve disputes all over Italy.

An accomplished poet, Lorenzo was a close friend of the neo-Platonic philosophers Marsilio Ficino and Pico della Mirandola, who attempted to produce a synthesis between the classical world – represented by the writings of the Greek philosopher Plato – and Christianity. During Lorenzo's period in power the visual arts continued to flourish, with Botticelli, who was strongly influenced by neo-Platonism, Verrocchio, Leonardo da Vinci and the young Michelangelo creating masterpieces that astounded their contemporaries all over Europe.

Florence's golden age came to an abrupt end with Lorenzo's death. The next 40 years were to witness great political upheaval. In 1494 the Medici were expelled following the French invasion of Italy. For the next four years Florence was ruled by a theocracy under the fanatical Dominican friar Girolamo Savonarola, before the Florentine citizens, tiring of his puritanical regime, burnt him publicly in the Piazza della Signoria. Between 1498 and 1512 Florence was a republic again, but in reality merely a pawn between the invading powers of France and Spain.

In 1512 the Medici, under Lorenzo's son, Giuliano, soon to become Pope Leo X, were invited back, but not for long. In 1527, after the Sack of Rome, they were expelled once more. They returned in 1530 following a disastrous siege by the army of the emperor Charles V, an ally of the Medici pope Clement VII. Although Alessandro de' Medici was soon assassinated, his crafty and calculating cousin Cosimo, who succeeded in 1537, proved an able ruler and was created Grand Duke of Tuscany in 1568. In the 16th century the family, now the dominant force in central Italy, cemented its European reputation by producing three popes and two queens of France.

Despite political uncertainty, the arts were still thriving. During the first decade of the 16th century, Leonardo, Raphael and Michelangelo were all working in Florence. Michelangelo's heroic and gigantic naked statue of *David*, unveiled in 1505, was immediately adopted as the symbol of the city. Vasari, in his influential *Lives of the Artists* (1550), placed these three men at the summit of artistic achievement, the first to surpass the greatest artists of antiquity. Their successors, Pontormo, Bronzino, Cellini and Giambologna, all working in Florence and masters of the late Renaissance style known as Mannerism, influenced art throughout Europe.

The Florentine genius was not restricted to the visual arts. Francesco Guicciardini produced his magisterial *History of Florence* in 1530, and Niccolò Macchiavelli's *The Prince* was an influential work that championed the cynical use of power. Florence was already a renowned centre of map-making, and it was the Florentine, Amerigo Vespucci, who was the first to realize that Christopher Columbus had discovered a wholly new continent and who gave his name to America.

It is thanks to the generosity of the last Medici, Grand Duchess Anna Maria, who died in 1743 and bequeathed her family's fabulous collections to the city in perpetuity, that it is still possible to see the great works of art, particularly those of the Quattrocento, the golden age of Florence, in the city for which they were commissioned. This allows us to assess the enormous impact that this small city-state, the cradle of humanism, has made on the world. Later European civilization owes an incalculable debt to the Florentine Renaissance – the rebirth of the arts, based on an intense study of the classical world, with man taking his place at the centre of the universe.

# BENIN

## West African City of the Ancestors

PATRICK DARLING

*Benin has an extraordinary fascination for me which I cannot explain
... No one who went there came away without being impressed.*

CYRIL PUNCH, 1892

Benin, in southern Nigeria, has been described as the City of Love, the
Land of Vexation, Land of the Powerful Oba and Great Benin. Its incredible
bronze and ivory artwork astounded a late 19th-century western world still
in denial of black African civilization.

Linguists calculate that Edo-speakers ancestral to Benin began shifting
south to the rainforest some 8,000 years ago. About 2,000 years ago,
iron technology and plantain cultivation helped the population grow
sufficiently to sustain permanent communities, which dug vertical-sided
ditches around their farmlands as protection against nocturnal devastation
by forest elephants. So began a vast 16,000-km (10,000-mile) long earthen
record of settlement growth over time. This record shows that, around
1,000 years ago, land shortages triggered a migration westwards; and by
the 13th century AD, the new settlements encompassed the territory which
was to become Benin.

The migrants brought with them their ancient beliefs linked to the rural
cultural landscape, where new villages planted 'everlasting' *ikhimwin* tree
shrines before any house-building, farming or sexual congress could begin.
Their linear earthworks separated the real world from the spirit world and
were crossed only by women. Regional cults based around hero-deities (*ihen*)
characterized the petty chiefdoms. One of these, Benin, initially accepted

the *ihen* of its incoming migrants, contributing to its cosmopolitan success. The leaders of Benin also created a strong spiritual power-base of its own, centred on shrines featuring so-called potsherd pavements and deep *iha* pits to hold those sacrificed to the earth.

Benin's potsherd pavements may link it to the widespread state-formation myth based on the holy city of Ife, and heralded the late-13th century *Oba* dynasty. This dynasty, ruled by kings who were regarded as divine, had its own palace snake-cult and other practices which enhanced the dynastic power mystique. Radiocarbon dates for the city ramparts at Benin and its rival, Udo, indicate that power was consolidated at both centres around the early 14th century, coinciding with Ife's 'classical period' of spiritual suzerainty in the 13th/mid-14th century, which saw the creation of superb naturalistic bronzes and terracottas.

In the mid-15th century, *Oba* Ewuare stormed and burnt Benin, ejected the city's *ihen*, deepened the rampart, buried charms under its nine gateways and established the *Eghaevbo n'Ore* Executive Council and the *Iwebo* Senior Palace Society to endorse his divine-kingship and attend to its ritual requirements. His military strategy of dividing his armies into nine sections to surround enemies extended Benin's sphere of influence, capturing thousands of slaves and resettling them under provincial chiefs to produce an annual tribute of yam and palm-oil. This new organization fundamentally realigned Benin.

Sixteenth-century Europeans compared Benin favourably with their own cities: they noted its impressive 20-m (66-ft) deep rampart, its great extent, broad streets thronged with people, bustling markets full of food and medicinal products, and house walls of mud polished with snail-shells to shine like red marble. In addition to recording around 40 busy trade guilds involved with woodcarving, dyeing, weaving, pottery-making, blacksmithing, brass-casting and mat-work, mid-17th-century visitors also noted that the women did all the work; men strolled around, drank palm wine and smoked tobacco.

The *Oba*'s palace, surrounded by a 6-m (20-ft) wall, occupied much of the city: it was a labyrinth of open courtyards, storerooms and closely guarded women's quarters, with accommodation for hundreds of palace attendants, polished floors of imported pink weathered granite, and 12-m (40-ft) high turrets, each carrying a large bronze-headed python or surmounted by a spectacular bronze ibis with outstretched wings. Long galleries were hung with beautifully executed bronze plaques depicting past exploits and ceremonial activities.

After *Oba* Ehengbuda drowned in a canoe accident in the early 17th century, *Obas* ceased to be warrior-kings and became tied to an annual round of over 200 state ritual ceremonies. Spiritual introspection followed; the dead were exposed along the broad Akpapava Street; skulls lined the palace environs; and the numerous extra sacrifices made in an attempt to halt the 1897 British conquest unfairly earnt Benin the epithet City of Blood.

The conquest exposed the inner palace sanctum of ancestral altars: amid iron hand bells and ancient stone axes were striking bronze heads depicting each past *Oba* wearing ceremonial red coral necklaces and headgear. On top of each head were placed enormous ivory tusks, skilfully carved with a timeless iconography, to receive annual offerings. The western world hailed this magnificent 'art', but many missed the real significance of Benin: it was the last great African city-kingdom fully practising ancient beliefs in a magical universe – beliefs deriving from the original roots of all mankind's quest for immortality.

# TIMBUKTU

## City in the Sands

BARNABY ROGERSON

*Salt comes from the north, gold from the south,*
*but the word of god and the treasures of*
*wisdom come from Timbuktu.*

TRADITIONAL SAHELIAN SAYING

Timbuktu is a city on the southern edge of the Sahara constructed of one part history and two parts myth. It stands just 15 km (9 miles) north of the Niger river, surrounded by the Sahara desert. It first sprang into the consciousness of the wider world in the 14th century, when the ruler of the Muslim Mandingo empire, Mansa Musa, went on pilgrimage to Mecca and proved himself to be so well supplied, and prodigiously generous, with West African gold that a legend was born. Ever afterwards, travellers, writers and diplomats set out to find the source of this gold and returned disappointed. For the reality of Timbuktu, a typical Sahelian trading town built of mud bricks that was swept by sand and dry desert winds, could never live up to the expectations of a mysterious city of gold hidden among the vast wastes of the sand dunes of the Sahara.

Among the medieval historians and travel writers of the Maghreb, the Tangier-born Ibn Battuta, the Tunis-born Ibn Khaldun and the Granada-born Leo Africanus (Hassan al-Fasi) make mention of historical Timbuktu, the latter two having been specifically sent there by instruction of the sultans of Morocco. Leo reported that the 'rich king has many plates and sceptres of gold, some weighing 1,300 pounds, 3,000 horsemen and a great store of doctors, judges, priests and other learned men.'

In the late 18th century the colonial rivalry between France and Britain extended even to the mapping of Central Africa, driven in part by a desire to discover the mysterious source of this gold, and rival societies fostered missions of exploration. Mungo Park brought back a description of the river Niger but did not reach Timbuktu itself, which was first visited by Major Gordon Laing (coming south across the Sahara from Tripoli), although he was to be murdered outside the city walls in 1826. A year later, the Frenchman René Caillié journeyed to there from Senegal disguised as an Egyptian Muslim and returned with the first European account of the city, though in scholarship this would be superseded by the German explorer Heinrich Barth's methodical study in 1854. Barth identified the different ethnic communities within the city (the Songhai, Tuareg, Fulani and Mande), the three historic mosques – the Djinguereber founded in the 14th century, the Sidi Yahya founded in 1440, and the 15th-century Sankore, though its origins are older – and the Kasbah fortress that the Moroccans established here in the 16th century. A generation later, in 1894, the French general Joffre occupied the town.

It was only after the colonial presence of the French had ended that the true history and wealth of Timbuktu were revealed in the form of the great private libraries that their scholar citizens had patiently copied, preserved and transcribed. The manuscripts tell of the foundation of the city in the 11th century from an old camping ground of the Tuareg nomads based around 'Tim-Buktu', the well in the dunes. Over the 11th century this grew into a trading centre that attracted Muslim merchants from all over North Africa. It was important to them that Timbuktu stood just north of the river Niger in the desert sand dunes, because this allowed them to feel that they were part of Dar-Islam, where the normal contractual processes concerning trade, marriage and proper worship followed Islamic law. The Koran, the hadith, the histories, grammars and commentaries were taught in the shadow of the mosque courtyards. The much larger trading cities and political capitals further south were heavily influenced by the traditional practices that surrounded kingship – the drinking of beer and the wearing of gold, not to mention blood sacrifices.

So Timbuktu stood a little apart, a self-consciously Muslim town set on the periphery of the teeming millions of West Africa. It was well placed to benefit from the trade in rock salt, carved by slaves in the mid-Saharan quarries at Taoudeni, which could then be traded for gold dust, black slaves, ebony, ivory and ostrich feathers. The actual source of the gold may not even have been known by the traders of Timbuktu themselves – they acquired alluvial gold dust that had been panned from small clearings among the equatorial forests near the headwaters of the rivers Niger and Senegal.

Timbuktu passed under the influence of the Kingdom of Mali (also known as Mandingo), which was established by Sun Diata Keita by 1235. It was his grandson, Mansa Musa (literally 'great King'), who so impressed the world with his wealth, causing a collapse in the Egyptian gold price. Mansa Musa also brought back scholars, architects and manuscripts to enrich his kingdom – at his bidding Timbuktu's Sankore mosque and the adjacent palace of Madugu were built by the Andalusian architect and scholar Abu Ishaq al-Sahili in 1327. But even in these high days of wealth and scholarship, Timbuktu was only one among 300 Sahelian cities, such as Walata, Tadmekka, Kabara and Dia that might be visited by the royal court and itinerant scholars. Scholarship in the 14th century, was highly mobile, with entire libraries transported on camels in red kid-skin book bags. Teachers and their students also moved within the framework of nomadic migrations, while markets and annual festivals meant that towns mushroomed into cities of tents for a few weeks, before returning to half-empty compounds for the rest of the year.

In the 15th century the expansionist Sultan of Songhai, Sunni Ali, used the excuse of leading a jihad to overwhelm Mandingo, and he conquered Timbuktu in 1468. Over a century later, a Moroccan army sent south by Sultan Ahmed el Mansour under the command of Judar Pasha defeated the Songhai army and established their principal base at Timbuktu.

The descendants of this army dominated the region as the Ruma until the mid-18th century, after which the town passed under the control of various feuding sultans, whose power was based on either Tuareg or Fulani cavalry, until the French came.

The commercial lifeblood of towns such as Timbuktu had been sucked away centuries before, however, for the inland trans-Saharan caravan routes were already being replaced by seaborne traffic in the 15th century, and the first Portuguese traders were soon followed by their French, Dutch and English rivals. What has kept Timbuktu in existence for the last 400 years was neither gold dust nor slaves, but pride in a thousand years of Muslim scholarship and a carefully guarded inheritance of thousands of manuscripts.

# CUZCO

## Imperial City of the Inca

BRIAN S. BAUER

*The city of Cuzco was the home and dwelling place of gods,*
*and thus there is not in all of it, a fountain, or road,*
*or wall that they did not say contained a mystery.*

JUAN POLO DE ONDEGARDO, 1571

The Inca empire was the largest state to develop in the New World. Last in a series of complex Andean societies, it emerged in the south-central mountains of Peru and expanded across the western highlands and coast of South America, ultimately encompassing a territory that stretched from modern-day Colombia to Chile. By the time of European contact in AD 1532, the Inca ruled over a population of at least 8 million from the city of Cuzco, their capital and the ancestral home of the 11 dynastic rulers who are said to have reigned before the arrival of the Spaniards.

Cuzco lies at the northern end of a large and agriculturally rich valley. The city developed between two small rivers, the banks of which were walled and canalized within the city and for some distance outside, with the water flowing over flat paving stones. Numerous bridges crossed the rivers and offerings were made each year at their confluence. At its height the city of Cuzco held more than 20,000 people, with many thousands more living in numerous large villages scattered across the valley. But Cuzco was more than simply the royal seat for the ruling dynasty and the political hub of the Inca polity – it also represented the geographical and spiritual centre of the empire.

Located on a slight rise in the heart of Cuzco, near the confluence of the two small, canalized rivers, was the most famous sanctuary in the Inca empire, the Coricancha, called Templo del Sol (Temple of the Sun) by the Spaniards. The name Coricancha translates as 'Golden Enclosure', deriving from the gold sheets that were attached to its walls. Built with the exquisitely cut stone blocks for which the Inca are justifiably famous, it was the focal point for the major imperial rites that were staged in the city.

The Coricancha actually consisted of a series of temples to different deities, as well as various rooms to house the support personnel and materials offered to the gods, all surrounded by a large exterior wall. Together, these buildings and courtyards formed an impressive architectural complex that dominated the centre of the city and was visible from a great distance. Accounts of its gold-covered walls were included in the Spaniards' initial reports of the Inca empire and helped to fire public imagination about the great riches of the New World.

The importance of the Coricancha for the Inca cannot be underestimated. They visualized their empire as composed of four great geopolitical quarters that radiated out from it, and it thus marked the central and most sacred spot in the universe. Soon after the Spaniards seized control of Cuzco, the sanctuary was taken over by the Dominican order and construction began on a church and monastery. Today, nearly five centuries later, the sanctuary is still run by the Dominicans.

Cuzco's central plaza was also an important ceremonial area. Thousands of people gathered there several times a year to attend the city's elaborate festivals and to see the ruling Inca. These festivals included, among others, the June and December solstices, as well celebrations for maize in both August (planting) and May (harvest). At these times the mummified remains of the previous Cuzco rulers were taken from their palaces and set, in order of their rule, in the plaza.

Many important compounds surrounded the central plaza, including the palaces of these ancient kings. The city centre also held temples for various gods, numerous royal storehouses and a wide range of other state institutions and facilities. Among these was the large complex of the Allcahuasi (House of Chosen [Women]), which housed hundreds of women who dedicated their lives to serving the state.

Cuzco and its environs were endowed with a host of smaller sacred locations. Indeed, the entire city was considered sacred, and travellers offered prayers and sacrifices on the mountain passes when Cuzco first came into view. There were three to four hundred shrines in the vicinity of the city, many of them organized into 42 lines that radiated out of Cuzco, like the spokes of a wheel, from the Coricancha. This complex of shrines, now known as the 'Cuzco ceque system', has been the subject of recent investigations.

The most important site outside the city, but still within the Cuzco valley, is the massive structure of Sacsayhuaman. It is located on a steep hill that overlooks the city and provides an impressive view of the valley. Excavations and surface collections of ceramics indicate that the site dates back to pre-Inca times, but the complex was greatly expanded during the period of Inca imperial rule (c. 1400–1532). Thousands of workers toiled for decades to construct what is now one of the most impressive archaeological sites in the New World. The stones of its walls are often multi-angled and are among the largest used in any pre-industrial building, displaying a precision of fitting that is unmatched in any other ancient culture. Because of its location high above Cuzco and its immense terrace walls, Sacsayhuaman is frequently referred to as a fortress. However, early accounts of Cuzco indicate that it also included a sun temple, as well as numerous storage buildings.

At its height, the city of Cuzco was built on a loose grid system of large compounds divided by narrow streets. The compound walls were substantial constructions of superbly crafted stones, with some walls reaching 4–5 m (13–16 ft) in height. A few of these exterior walls have survived and can still be seen. Within the compounds, however, were once hundreds of smaller buildings, many of them also built of stone.

Almost all of these smaller buildings were destroyed after the Spaniards divided the compounds between themselves and began to transform the city according to European conventions. Much of Cuzco was rebuilt after a massive earthquake in 1650 and new Spanish structures were built on top of many of the important Inca buildings and plazas. Nevertheless, enough of the original Inca architecture has survived to justify the listing of the city centre as a UNESCO cultural heritage site in 1983. Today, more than a million people visit the city each year to admire its impressive ancient remains.

# TENOCHTITLAN

## Aztec City in the Lake

SUSAN TOBY EVANS

*When we saw so many cities and villages built in the water ...*
*and that ... causeway going towards Mexico [Tenochtitlan],*
*we were amazed and said that it was like the enchantments*
*they tell of in the legend of Amadis, ... great towers ...*
*rising from the water, and all built of masonry.*
*And some of our soldiers even asked whether*
*the things that we saw were not a dream.*

BERNAL DÍAZ DEL CASTILLO, 1560S

Set in a sparkling blue lake, its islands landscaped with jade-green willows, the Aztec capital Tenochtitlan was a lush paradise that bore little resemblance to the dusty home towns of the Spanish conquistadors – or to modern Mexico City (p. 222), the megalopolis that now overlies it. Like Mexico City, Tenochtitlan was the largest metropolis in the Americas in its day, with over 100,000 inhabitants living in the city proper – measuring about 13 sq. km (5 sq. miles) – and in its suburbs. In 1521, two years after Díaz entered the city with Hernán Cortés, leader of the Spanish forces, Tenochtitlan was destroyed in a three-month siege; Cortés sorely regretted being unable to deliver this urban jewel intact to his king.

Tenochtitlan's beauty was bought with the wealth of its empire, which extended from the Pacific to the Atlantic and drew tribute from at least 5 million people. Maintaining and expanding this wealth machine required military officers, administrative bureaucrats and priestly orders, most of whom worked in the city in its palaces, warehouses and religious buildings.

At its very centre was the ceremonial complex now called the Templo Mayor (Great Temple) precinct after its dominant structure. The causeways that linked the island on which Tenochtitlan was built to the mainland became wide roads leading to this precinct from the cardinal directions. Thus the Templo Mayor stands at an *axis mundi*, marking the intersection of the earth's horizontal plane with a vertical axis formed of the many layers of the heavens and the underworld.

Around the Templo Mayor precinct were ranged the city's other important monuments: the great plaza (now known as the Zócalo) just to the south served as a kind of public antechamber to the huge palace of Emperor Motecuzoma II (popularly known as Montezuma) on its east side. Each day, 600 courtiers came to wait upon the emperor in the palace courtyard, sharing gossip and enjoying the palace's entertainments and culinary largesse. Across the Zócalo were schools for young nobles and administrative offices. Just west of the ceremonial precinct stood an older royal palace, where Cortés and his men were housed during the months in which they shared courtly life with Motecuzoma and his nobles, before the Spanish diplomatic mission turned violent in 1520.

A little further to the west were the storehouses for the tributes that flowed in, set in a park-like property that also housed animals collected from all over the empire in habitats that were designed to recreate their natural environments. Just east of the Templo Mayor was another kind of zoo, where the fiercest of beasts were kept.

Tenochtitlan was an essential prestigious address for wealthy and powerful Aztecs and for foreign powers – allies who maintained diplomatic missions in the city. Díaz noted that 'These houses stood in the fresh water lake and one could reach them by a causeway' and that the houses were 'full of mantles and cloth … gold and featherwork'. Many of these goods were imported as tributes or luxuries, but the city itself was also an important centre for the production of such prestige items. The city's fine textiles were produced in palaces and mansions by noblewomen and their servants; the privilege of having a household with many wives was limited to the wealthy, and was itself a license to produce money, because woven mantles were an exchange medium. Other elite goods such as jewelry and featherwork were also produced in house compounds by high-ranking specialists.

To the north of Tenochtitlan proper was a smaller island city, Tlatelolco, founded at the same time by a group closely related to Tenochtitlan's Aztecs. Tlatelolco was eventually absorbed into the main city because it became so wealthy from long-distance trade that it was an irresistible prize. Tlatelolco's merchant guild consisted of related commoner families who served both commercial and diplomatic functions. Occasionally on trading missions their encounters escalated into military aggressiveness as the 'vanguard merchants' established an Aztec presence in previously unallied areas; they might even provoke hostility in order to give the emperor grounds for invasion. In their home city, the merchants were famous for their wealth and their exclusivity. They seldom displayed any of their riches in public, however, and their large dwellings, which also served as warehouses, had plain exteriors, again to deflect envy of their wealth. After Tlatelolco had been absorbed by Tenochtitlan, the merchants remained wealthy and active, but of necessity changed allegiance to their new masters.

'Tenochtitlan' is in fact a compound word combining elements describing a scene so iconic that it became the central motif on the modern Mexican flag: an eagle with a snake in its beak sitting atop a cactus growing out of a rock. The Tenochca Aztecs claimed that it was when they saw this scene that they knew they had reached their promised land on the boggy lake islands. Historically, it is more likely that they were permitted to settle on this spot because the entire mainland was already occupied, and their overlords wanted to both placate them and channel their violent vitality towards mercenary military sorties. The accepted date of the establishment of Tenochtitlan is 1325, and the first construction may have been a packed-earth platform with a thatch shelter for the sacred bundle of their patron deity, Huitzilopochtli. Six rebuilding episodes and 196 years later, this

Templo Mayor would impress the Spaniards, and today its ruins are the centrepiece of an archaeological park.

The Templo Mayor's successive rebuildings tell a story of repeated urban renewals precipitated by disasters. Flooding destroyed the city several times. In 1449, it prompted the construction of a dyke 14.5 km (9 miles) long to protect the city from the lake. A string of famine years in the 1450s forced the Tenochca ruler to open the granaries, but the price was service on public works, particularly what is now labelled Stage IV of the Templo Mayor, and an expansion of the royal palace. The palace was rebuilt again in 1475, after an earthquake. In 1487, the fifth rebuilding of the Templo Mayor was cause for the greatest celebration ever staged in ancient Mexico, with tens of thousands of participants – many of them sacrificed at the high altars of the temples. In addition, the event called for programmes of urban beautification.

The city was heavily damaged yet again by the floods of 1499, and its reconstruction created the city that dazzled the Spaniards. The building of the palace of Motecuzoma II may have been part of this effort; it underlies the present National Palace of Mexico, making archaeological exploration unlikely. During this period adjacent islands were developed as pleasure gardens for the emperor. A map published in Europe in 1524 to accompany one of Cortés's letters shows them southwest of the city, with the label 'Domus ad Voluptase, D. Muteczuma'. Beauty and luxury were combined to great effect in these settings; we can imagine evening parties for the court, with torches casting flickering light across the water, the air scented by tuberoses, wood smoke and tobacco, while the revellers laughed and sang.

The Spaniards shared the pleasures of courtly life with the Aztecs for many months in 1519–20, and it is clear from their speed in claiming various properties after the conquest of Mexico that their enjoyment was heightened by the prospect of territorial acquisition. And, in a larger sense, the very reasons that made Tenochtitlan such a brilliantly located capital led Cortés to rebuild it as the capital of New Spain (p. 222). Yes, it was subject to flooding, and fresh water had to be brought by aqueduct from the mainland. But it was defensible, and its location in the lake and the extensive canal system throughout the city greatly facilitated transportation. Drainage projects had transformed the swamps surrounding the city into productive farm plots (the misnamed 'floating' gardens). The constraint on available land actually pushed the island community towards urbanization and thus sophistication. Tenochtitlan sustained higher densities of population and buildings than did surrounding communities, and its people became expert in artisanal activities and specialist roles as merchants and bureaucrats. From its Aztec origins to the present, this unique city has been home to ambitious achievers who relish their role as citizens of the capital of their world.

# THE EARLY
# MODERN WORLD

The break between the third and fourth sections of this book marks almost precisely the moment, in the very last years of the 15th century, of the two near-simultaneous events that changed the political and economic history of the world: the discovery by Europeans of the American continent and of the Cape Route to the Indies. This brought a certain change of emphasis: the vastly increased importance of Lisbon, for example – the key city to the Age of Discovery – and the corresponding downgrading of the Mediterranean, which lost much of its status as an international waterway, to regain it only four centuries later with the opening of the Suez Canal.

Those two discoveries would have been impossible without the impressive advances which had been made during the late Middle Ages in the arts of navigation and shipbuilding, advances which continued apace during the centuries that followed. In 1500 sailors were still brave men indeed, who with every voyage took their lives in their hands; by 1800 they were sailing the world's oceans with confidence, and more of the blank areas of the map were being filled in with every year that passed. The world was no longer a mystery; men did not now believe legends like those of El Dorado or Prester John. Every great city on earth was known to every other.

And what were those cities? Let us take the imperial capitals first. Europe in the Middle Ages had known two empires only, the Holy Roman in the west and the Byzantine in the east. The former, originally Frankish (with its founder Charlemagne) and then German, was now in the hands of the Austrian House of Habsburg. Its true capital was Vienna; but in the later 16th century, under the alchemist-emperor Rudolph II, it moved temporarily to Prague. The Byzantine empire had been conquered by the Turks in 1453; but its old capital, Constantinople, survived under the additional name of

Istanbul, fulfilling the same function under its new masters, the Sultans of the Ottoman empire. It remains the only city in the world to have been an imperial capital for over fifteen hundred years.

By now, however, a third empire had taken shape, the Russian, and in 1703 Peter the Great inaugurated his new capital of St Petersburg. Meanwhile, away in the East, four new imperial capitals had revealed themselves: of Safavid Persia at Isfahan, of Mughal India at Agra, of Ming dynasty China at Beijing and of Japan at Kyoto – a city which had always been the residence of the emperors but which in the 17th century enjoyed a dramatic new flowering of art and culture. In the West, Mexico City was not yet an imperial capital; during the 17th and 18th centuries, Mexico was still a colony of Spain. But its eponymous capital city – built on the bed of the great lake, now long dried up, which had surrounded Aztec Tenochtitlan – was of a size and splendour that rivalled many capitals in the Old World.

Returning to Europe, we cast an astonished glance at Renaissance Rome, where a cynical and ambitious Papacy continued to set a somewhat ambiguous example to the faithful. The spotlight then swings northwards: first to Amsterdam, where we look at that almost unparalleled explosion of artistic and commercial genius which was the 17th-century Netherlands, then to Stockholm and Copenhagen, and finally – for the first time – to the British Isles. Here is the 17th-century London of Shakespeare, of Samuel Pepys, of the Great Plague and the Great Fire and of Sir Christopher Wren; here too is 18th-century Edinburgh, home of such luminaries as Adam Smith, David Hume, Robert and John Adam and Robert Burns, all of them products of another extraordinary phenomenon – the Scottish Enlightenment, given architectural expression by the neoclassical elegance of the New Town. In Ireland, Dublin, though not perhaps at first of comparable importance in the political field, had acquired a cultural and literary distinction of its own, long before its more recent prosperity in the European Union.

# LISBON

## in the Age of Discovery

MALYN NEWITT

*Mas temo me de Lisboa*
*Que ó cheiro d'esta canela*
*O reino nos despovoa.*

*I fear for Lisbon, which is depopulating the*
*land with the scent of its cinnamon.*

SÁ DE MIRANDA, C. 1533

Lisbon was built by the Romans on a hill on the north bank of the river Tagus, overlooking the greatest natural harbour on the coast of Atlantic Europe. For some five hundred years a Moorish city, with a large Christian (Mozarabe) and Jewish population, it was captured by English Crusaders in 1147, after which it became the capital of the new kingdom of Portugal. By the 14th century it had become an important commercial centre and was used by Venetians and Genoese for their trade with northern Europe.

A new wall (the Cerca Fernandina) with 77 towers and 34 gates, built in only two years to surround the city, was complete when in 1383 a national rising against Castile, in which the guilds of the city took a prominent part, placing João of Avís on the throne. In the following year the city had to withstand a siege by Castilian forces. Thereafter Lisbon became the centre of a successful and expanding state. Dom João built a fortified palace in the central square of the Rossio, and his Constable, Nun'Alvares Pereira, founded the imposing Gothic Carmo monastery. The city also contained the archives housed in the Torre do Tombo, the high court (Desembargo do

Paço) and, after 1460, the Casa da Guine (later the Casa da India), which administered the country's overseas expansion. There was also a thriving shipbuilding industry and gun foundry, and it was from Lisbon that most of the exploratory voyages of the 15th century departed.

Lisbon had always contained large communities of artisan Moors and Jews, with their mosques and synagogues, and the city's Jewish population had grown as refugees fled the attacks on Jews in Castile in 1391. Although the Jews had traditionally been protected by the Portuguese kings, in 1495 their expulsion was made the condition for a royal marriage with Castile. Instead of being expelled, the large numbers assembled in Lisbon, were forcibly baptized and, as New Christians, were allowed to remain in Portugal, with the promise that they would not be further molested for 20 years. In 1506, however, a week of rioting led to large numbers being killed. King Manuel, blaming the city authorities for the troubles, then drastically curtailed the privileges under which Lisbon had been governed.

In 1497 Vasco da Gama set out from Lisbon on his epic voyage to India, and by 1505 Lisbon was replacing Venice as the principal European emporium for eastern spices. Damião de Góis, the city's first historian, called Lisbon and Seville the 'Queens of the Seas', deliberately displacing Venice from its maritime primacy. Dom Manuel, contemptuously called *le roi épicier* by the French king, François I, spent lavishly to embellish his capital. A new royal palace was built on the waterfront between 1500 and 1505 and Góis described seven other monumental buildings that made Lisbon one of the most magnificent cities of Europe – the Misericórdia, the Hospital, the Estaus Palace, where visiting ambassadors were housed, the Public Granary, the Customs House, the Casa da India and the Armoury, where 40,000 suits of armour and artillery for the 200 ships that maintained the Portuguese empire were stored. The king processed through the streets with elephants brought from India and attempted to stage a public fight between a rhinoceros and an elephant, before sending the former as a gift to the pope.

A vast new Jeronimite monastic complex and a fortress to guard the entrance to the river were begun at Belem, 8 km (5 miles) down the river. These were built in the exotic late Gothic Manueline style, unique to Portugal. Lisbon now became a centre for map-making, through which knowledge about Africa and the East entered the intellectual bloodstream of Europe. Writers such as Gil Vicente, Sá de Miranda, Garcia de Rezende and Bernardim Ribeiro, as well as Damião de Góis, the friend of Erasmus, flocked to the court, making it a focus for literary and cultural activity and one of the most brilliant Renaissance courts of Europe. In 1536 the Inquisition was established, with its Lisbon tribunal having jurisdiction over West Africa, Brazil and the Atlantic islands. From that time regular *autos-da-fé* were held in the capital and executions were carried out in the great square outside the royal palace. By 1550 Lisbon's days as a centre of humanistic culture were over.

The slave trade brought large numbers of Africans to Lisbon, where they were baptized and increasingly took over the menial jobs in the city. They had their own confraternities and were employed by their owners in street trading and prostitution. By the middle of the 16th century they may have constituted a tenth of the city's population. Large colonies of foreign merchants, especially Italians, were concerned with freighting the carracks that set out for the East and marketing the spices, silks, cottons, lacquer ware and porcelain that formed the return cargoes.

Although an administrative and ecclesiastical centre of importance (in the early 17th century there were 3,500 clerics in the city, more than the manpower employed in the shipyards), Lisbon owed its special character to its harbour. In 1578 Dom Sebastião assembled a vast armada of 800 ships in the port of Lisbon to take his army to Morocco, where he was killed at the battle of Alcazarquebir. When his successor Cardinal Henry died childless in January 1580, Philip of Spain claimed the throne. On his behalf, an army led by the Duke of Alba and a fleet under the Marquis of Santa Cruz converged on Lisbon, and the forces of the pretender, Dom António, were dispersed at Alcântara outside the city. Philip took up residence in the royal palace until 1583, apparently contemplating making Lisbon the capital of his vast empire. He was, however, put off by two outbreaks of plague, which killed thousands of the city's population towards the end of the century.

Lisbon was central to Philip's plan to establish naval supremacy in the Atlantic. It was there that the 150 ships of the Armada were equipped and from where they sailed towards England under the Duke of Medina Sidonia in May 1588. The following year an English fleet under Francis Drake attacked Lisbon, but did not venture into the Tagus, while the land army led by John Norris, having burnt the suburbs, was unable to assault the city's defences. English losses in this campaign equalled those of Spain in the great Armada of the previous year.

Lisbon remained the second city of Philip's monarchy and the base for his naval operations as well as for the dispatch of the trading ships to the East. In spite of the frequent outbreaks of plague, the city's population grew from 65,000 in 1521 to 165,000 in the early 17th century. Its wealth and importance were reflected in the great churches built during Philip's reign. São Vicente da Fora constructed on the hill above the Alfama and the Jesuit church of São Roque on the Bairro Alto brought the latest mannerist architecture to the city. The approach to the port was further strengthened with the building of Fort Bugio, which made Lisbon virtually impregnable to attack from the sea. Only in the 17th century, with the increasing exodus of New Christian merchant families, was it overtaken by Amsterdam and London as the centre of Europe's trade with the East.

# ROME

## and the Renaissance Papacy

CHARLES FITZROY

*God has granted us the papacy. Let us enjoy it.*
POPE LEO X ON HIS ELECTION, 1513

Following the fall of the Roman empire in the 5th century AD, the importance of Rome had lain in the power of the Papacy. With the exile of the
popes to Avignon during the 14th century, followed by the papal schism
(1378–1417), Rome was reduced to a shadow of its former glory, wracked
by feuds between the Orsini and Colonna families. It was not until 1420,
when Pope Martin V Colonna returned to his native city, that Rome began
to emerge from one of the darkest periods in its history.

Through the 15th century the city's fortunes slowly revived. Martin V
and his successors Eugenius IV and the humanist Nicholas V restored
Rome's churches, repaired her fountains and aqueducts, and tried to clear
the mounds of rubbish filling every street. Gradually, the dirty, crumbling
medieval city was transformed into one full of beautiful Renaissance palaces.
At the same time, the popes attempted to restore Rome as the undisputed
centre of Catholicism and heal the damage caused by the papal schism,
although Pius II, a passionate antiquarian, was unsuccessful in launching
a crusade against the Turks, who had captured Constantinople in 1453.

It was not so easy for these popes, whatever their personal qualities, to
re-establish their spiritual authority. As rulers of the Papal States, they were
drawn into Italian secular politics and were widely seen as corrupt. Unlike
a hereditary monarch, the pope, often an old man when elected, needed to
reward his family and followers swiftly before his power base disappeared on

his death. As a result, simony (the selling of ecclesiastical offices for cash) and nepotism were rife. Many Renaissance popes had illegitimate children, whom they rewarded lavishly. The reign of Alexander VI Borgia (1492–1503), an intelligent, unscrupulous and sensuous Spaniard, became a byword for depravity: his son Cesare was believed to have ordered the murder of both his own brother and brother-in-law, and Alexander's daughter, Lucrezia was, with less justification, reputed to have poisoned her many lovers.

Whatever their personal morality, these popes proved enlightened patrons of the arts and transformed Rome into one of the great cities of Europe. Their main residence was the palace of the Vatican. Sixtus IV founded the Vatican Library in the late 1470s and commissioned Perugino, Botticelli, Ghirlandaio and other leading Tuscan artists to decorate the walls of the newly constructed Sistine Chapel. Twenty years later in the Borgia apartments, Pinturicchio painted a delightful fresco cycle for Alexander VI. In the city itself, leading nobles and prelates erected a series of splendid Renaissance palaces, such as the Palazzo della Cancelleria, begun in 1486 and built on the proceeds of one night's gambling between two cardinals, favourite nephews of successive popes.

Julius II, who succeeded Alexander VI, proved one of the greatest patrons in the history of art. In 1506, with astonishing boldness, he instructed his favourite architect, Bramante, to tear down the basilica of St Peter's, founded by the emperor Constantine, and erect an enormous new church. It was the grandest of the entire Renaissance, and his own tomb, designed by Michelangelo, was to stand at its centre, beneath a vast dome. In 1508 the young Raphael was commissioned to paint Julius's private apartments in the Vatican, known as the Stanze, with a series of splendid frescoes, while in the nearby Sistine Chapel Michelangelo began to paint the ceiling with an array of heroic figures depicting scenes from the Old Testament. These masterpieces were to inspire future generations of artists throughout Europe and beyond.

The artistic supremacy of Rome was not matched, however, in the field of politics. The economic wealth and political disunity of the Italian states had encouraged France and Spain to invade the peninsula in the 1490s. The Papacy struggled, with increasing desperation, to retain its independence. Cesare Borgia had some success and Julius II, a tough and resilient character, made a determined effort to drive foreign armies out of Italy.

Julius II was followed by the pleasure-loving Leo X de' Medici, who preferred diplomacy to warfare. During his pontificate (1513–21) his favourite artist, Raphael, together with his followers, created a series of artistic masterpieces. But the necessity of raising money by simony to fund his extravagant habits, and the mounting costs of rebuilding St Peter's, caused widespread protests and encouraged the activities of Martin Luther in Germany. During the pontificate of Leo's cousin, Clement VII, disputes with the Protestants threatened to destroy the Papacy. Rome itself was brutally sacked by the troops of the emperor Charles V in 1527, and the pope barely escaped with his life. Many of the most talented artists fled the city, thus bringing to an end the glorious era known as the High Renaissance.

Although peace returned to Rome, the fear engendered by the sack of the city endured. The Papacy was unable to challenge the military might of Spain, and the temporal power of Rome was much diminished. But, in this dark moment, as so often in its history, the Eternal City showed once again its astonishing power of renewal – not only artistic, particularly through the works of Michelangelo, who settled in Rome for the last 30 years of his life, but also through the spiritual leadership of the Counter-Reformation.

The career of Paul III Farnese is indicative of this new direction. In his youth he had fathered illegitimate children and built the enormous Palazzo Farnese on the proceeds of the money his beautiful sister Giulia had gained as the mistress of Alexander VI. As pope, however, Paul instigated the fight back against Protestantism by convening the Council of Trent in 1545 (it lasted until 1563), and inaugurating the Jesuit order to spearhead the Counter-Reformation. The order's main church of the Gesù, built by Giacomo Barozzi da Vignola, designed specifically for preaching and lavishly decorated, was copied all over the Catholic world.

The pope had always admired Michelangelo and he persuaded the ageing artist to become the architect of St Peter's and redesign the Capitoline hill. Michelangelo also painted the powerful *Last Judgment* for the altar wall of the Sistine Chapel, a work that reflects the prevailing dark and sombre mood following the sack of Rome, with Christ portrayed as a wrathful judge. In another manifestation of this mood, Paul IV Carafa (1555–59) championed the Inquisition and confined the Jewish community to a ghetto.

The Counter-Reformation did not, however, completely crush the spirit of the Renaissance. The Villa Giulia, built for Julius III, and the beautiful gardens of the Villa Medici and the Villa d'Este at Tivoli, designed for eminent cardinals, all dating from the second half of the 16th century, are imbued with the classical spirit. The order of the Oratorians, founded by St Philip Neri, stressed beauty in worship, both visual and musical (hence the word oratorio), and had a strong influence on artistic life in Rome.

The most important pope of the later 16th century was Sixtus V, who transformed Rome during his brief pontificate from 1585 to 1590. A town-planner of genius, Sixtus lost no time in restoring the city's water supply and repairing her bridges before laying out a series of long, straight avenues and star-shaped squares, with fountains and obelisks sited at focal points. Additions were made to papal palaces and Michelangelo's great dome over St Peter's was finally completed, over two decades after the artist's death. By the time of his own death Sixtus had made Rome one of the most modern and beautiful cities in Christendom.

Rome's artistic dominance continued into the 17th century, when the painters Caravaggio and Annibale Carracci and the sculptor Bernini were inspired to create the new baroque style, which was to spread throughout Europe. In the middle of the 18th century, Rome once again provided the inspiration for a new movement, neoclassicism. Young noblemen on the Grand Tour flocked to the city to study and collect the great works of antiquity and of the High Renaissance, when Rome had reclaimed her position at the summit of European art.

# ISTANBUL

## City of the Sultans

JASON GOODWIN

*I know of no state which is happier than this one; it is furnished with all God's gifts. It controls peace and war with all, it is rich in gold, in people, in ships and in obedience: no state can be compared to it.*

REPORT OF THE VENETIAN AMBASSADOR, 1523

On Tuesday, 29 May 1453, the Ottoman Sultan Mehmet II rode into Constantinople, the Red Apple of Islamic myth. Famously, he went first to Hagia (Saint) Sophia, the Church of Holy Wisdom, where, in a sign of humility, he dismounted and sprinkled a handful of dust over his head, before ordering the church to be converted into a mosque. Tradition allowed a conquering army three days to pillage a fallen city that had shown resistance, but the Conqueror may have halted the destruction at the end of the first day. That night he wandered the imperial palace murmuring the lines of a Persian poem: 'An owl hoots in the towers of Afrasiab, / The spider spins his web in the palace of the Caesars.' He was 21 years old.

The Ottoman conquest was a renaissance for Istanbul (as it later came to be called). It became once more the capital of a vigorous and expansive empire, and the population soared. Greeks who had fled the city were invited to return, and Mehmed's share of prisoners from his conquests in Europe were resettled along the Golden Horn. Thousands of Jews found refuge there after their expulsion from Spain in 1492, followed by Arabs from Granada. Land was given to the Conqueror's followers; they were encouraged to build mosques – or convert churches – around which Muslim Constantinople would coalesce. The so-called *millet* system was applied: every faith group became, in effect, self-governing under its own ecclesiastical authority, submitting to the Ottoman courts only in criminal cases.

The Orthodox monk George Scholarius was made Patriarch by Mehmed himself on 1 January 1454. An imperial firman (decree) ordered that 'no-one should vex or disturb him'; he was given the Church of the Holy Apostles, although the Patriarchate eventually settled in the Church of St George, where it is today. Similar agreements were made with Bishop Hovakim, the Armenian Patriarch, and Moshe Capsali, the Chief Rabbi. The semi-autonomous Genoese district of Galata lost much of its defensive wall, and several yards were shaved from its celebrated watchtower; but it retained a measure of self-government, as well as the right to trade, travel and to own property. Ottoman policy towards non-Muslim subjects did not much alter in subsequent centuries.

In 1463 the Church of the Holy Apostles was torn down to make way for the Conqueror's own mosque, the Fatih Camii, the first of the great mosques whose domes and minarets were to shape the city's unforgettable skyline. A mosque, with its ancillary buildings, was more than a house of prayer: it was a nucleus of Islamic life in the city. Fatih Camii provided eight madrasas (religious schools), a hospice, hospital, public kitchen, caravanserai, primary school, library, hammam (bath), market and graveyard. The market was considerable, and indicated how the currents of trade had flowed back to the Bosphorus. It had 280 shops, 32 workrooms and 4 storehouses, and the income from these went towards the maintenance of the other institutions. Lesser but similar endowments were made by prominent men and women in other parts of the city, each complex defining a district.

Mehmed established the Covered Bazaar, that huge emporium on the Third Hill (the city, like Rome, is built on seven hills), created on the site of the old Byzantine market, and a mosque complex at Eyüp, at the head of the Golden Horn, where the body of the Prophet's standard-bearer, killed during the Arab siege of Constantinople of 674–78, had been miraculously rediscovered. Eyüp became one of the holiest places in the Muslim world, second only to Mecca and Jerusalem in Turkish eyes, and henceforward it was beside this tomb that each new sultan was girded with the sword of Osman, in a ceremony akin to a coronation.

Reunited with its hinterland, restored as the turnstile between Ottoman Asia and Ottoman Europe, as between the Black Sea and the Mediterranean, and protected from attack by the Pax Ottomanica, Istanbul sprang alive, and grew. Each month a great caravan of 2,000 mules and camels arrived from Persia and Syria. Western merchants were encouraged to do business in the city, and luxuries poured in, particularly to the palace, from all over the known world: silks and spices from the east, furs and amber from the north.

Between the great mosques, palaces and bazaars ran narrow, twisting streets of wooden houses, prone to disastrous fires from cooking pots. But at least the pots were always full: while domestic building was haphazard, Istanbul was fed and watered with astounding care. Market prices were rigorously controlled, both by market judges and by the ubiquitous guilds that regulated all trade and manufacture. Across an empire stretching from the Danube to the Nile, from the Crimea to the plains of Hungary, a complex system of requisitions, tribute-gathering and advance orders ensured that food in the city was plentiful and cheap. In 1577, for instance, no sheep were slaughtered in the Balkans – they were all driven to Istanbul instead, where, in the mid-17th century, 7 million sheep were eaten in a year, 18,000 oxen each month, 250 tons of bread in a single day. One-tenth of it all was consumed in the palace. Every year 2,000 ships unloaded grain and other foodstuffs into the warehouses along the Golden Horn.

The city was as splendid as it was rich. Here was the Arsenal, whose ships controlled the Black Sea and the eastern Mediterranean; here were the barracks of the fabled janissaries, the only standing army in Europe; here was Topkapı Palace, which by the end of Mehmet's reign in 1481 had achieved something like its final form. With its kiosks, courtyards and tree-lined gardens overlooking the Bosphorus, Topkapı resembled an encampment in stone, sheltering an army of cooks, gardeners, janissaries and viziers, as well as the Palace School, in which the Ottoman ruling elite were trained and raised. An elaborate protocol surrounded the Sultan, the grandest monarch of his age, whose servants communicated in sign language, the better to maintain a dignified and awful silence. Rather than attend the daily divan, in which his viziers dealt with imperial business, he might listen to their deliberations through a screen; foreign ambassadors were led to audience between two chamberlains gripping their elbows.

Within a century, Istanbul had half a million inhabitants. Muslims were a scant majority, but it was very much an Islamic city as Suleyman the Magnificent (r. 1521–66) began to reshape his capital. The sultans were open-handed with their wealth, and their followers were encouraged to emulate. Fountains, bridges, mosques and schools were set up as endowments, or *vakif*.

Suleyman was fortunate to command one of the greatest architects in Ottoman history. Probably from a Christian family in Anatolia, Sinan had already enjoyed a career as a military engineer when, in 1538, Suleyman appointed him head of the imperial architects. One of his first commissions was the *külliye*, or mosque complex, which the Sultan presented to his wife, Roxelana, as a birthday surprise. Sinan went on to erect dozens of buildings across the empire; some 85 of them are still standing in Istanbul, 22 of them mosques, including the Suleymaniye on the Third Hill, completed in 1557. While work on the sultan's mosque was going on, Sinan built a delightful public bath for Roxelana. He also renovated the city's water-supply system.

Suleyman's reign marked the apogee of empire. Ahmed I's Blue Mosque of 1610, named for the beautiful tilework of its interior, spelt the end of building on a grandiose scale, until the 19th-century sultans began to erect European palaces along the Bosphorus. Yet Istanbul survived, in all its grace; and on the walls of old mosques and mansions throughout the Balkans and the Middle East, you find it represented still: a city of hills and kiosks, cypresses, minarets and shady planes rising gracefully above the slim caiques – the Ottoman gondolas – which skim the water, like a glimpse of an earthly paradise.

# AGRA

## City of the Taj Mahal

EBBA KOCH

*What a city! A perfumed garden, newly blossomed,*
*Its buildings have grown tall like cypress trees.*
ABU TALIB KALIM, IN PRAISE OF AGRA, 1630S

The court historian 'Abd al-Hamid Lahauri reported in the official history of
the emperor Shah Jahan (r. 1628–58) that on 6 February 1643, corresponding
to the Muslim year 1052, the illumined tomb – the Taj Mahal – had been
completed. This, the most magnificent of all Mughal mausoleums and the
tomb of the emperor's favourite wife, Mumtaz Mahal, was not built in a
special or prominent site, but was integrated into the urban landscape of
the main capital of the Mughal empire, the city of Agra.

Agra was founded long before the Lodi Sultans made it their seat
of government in 1505. Twenty years later, in 1526, when the Mughals
established themselves in Hindustan, Agra became their first capital and
acquired its distinctive character as a riverfront garden city. The Mughals,
coming from Central Asia via Kabul, were accustomed to residing in
formally planned gardens. Babur, the founder of the Mughal dynasty, and
his followers, therefore began to lay out gardens along both banks of the
available water source at Agra – the large, slow-flowing river Yamuna,
Jamna, or Jaun, as the Mughals called it. The Timurid concept of a formally
planned garden was here creatively adapted to a riverfront situation. In
this scheme, the main building was placed on a terrace overlooking the
river, with the garden on the landward side. The buildings were flanked
by towers and, to those viewing it from a boat or from across the river, the

whole riverfront presented a splendid panorama of a band of pavilions, towers, trees and flowers.

The gardens constituted the residences of the imperial family and the highest-ranked nobles, and the city as a whole reflected the concept of the garden as the primordial residence of the Mughal dynasty; in a wider ideological sense it also served as a symbol of the blooming of Hindustan under the just rule of Shah Jahan. After his accession, Shah Jahan renamed Agra, calling it Akbarabad, 'the city of Akbar', in honour of his grandfather, but the new name did not gain permanent acceptance. By his time, Mughal Agra had become one of the great cities of Asia – as much a focus of the arteries of trade both by land and water as a meeting-place of saints, sages and scholars. In 1638 the German traveller Mandelslo judged Agra 'at least twice as big as Isfahan'; other travellers felt that it was one of the largest cities in the world. The impression that Agra made on contemporaries is put in flowery words by Shah Jahan's historian Muhammad Salih Kanbo:

> On either side of that sea [Yamuna] full of pleasantness, buildings and gardens of paradisiacal space are placed together in such a handsome close way that ... it appears that garden is linked to garden and ... the desire to stroll in the garden of Paradise is completely erased from the page of memory ... In particular, the spacious buildings and wonderful pavilions of the princes of exalted origin and other famous amirs ... give a display of ... the palaces of the garden of Paradise.

The garden character of Agra also impressed the French physician François Bernier, one of the best observers of the Mughal court, who was in the city in 1659. He found that although it did not have the uniform and wide streets of Shah Jahan's new city Shahjahanabad (Delhi, completed 1648) – it made up for that lack with its 'luxuriant and green foliage ... Such a landscape yields peculiar pleasure in a hot and parched country, where the eye seeks verdure for refreshment and repose.'

Comparable waterfront schemes were developed in the capitals of the other two great Muslim empires: in Ottoman Istanbul (p. 184) royal and non-royal suburban garden villas lined the Bosphorus, and in 17th-century Safavid Isfahan (p. 193) garden residences were built on the banks of the Zayanda river. However, in its tight, systematic and uniform planning – in which a particular Mughal logic is manifest – Agra differs from these more informal arangements.

Mughal Agra is also different because here the suburban riverfront scheme formed the nucleus of the city, with the majority of the urban fabric situated to its west. Shah Jahan did, however, make some efforts to develop the rest of Agra. In 1637 he ordered the construction of an octagonal bazaar (now lost) which formed a link between the palace-fortress – the Agra fort – and the new Jami' Masjid, or congregational mosque, to its west, sponsored by his favourite daughter Jahanara. But still, even after the project was completed, the emphasis of the city remained the riverfront. Mughal writers and European observers found nothing of note to report beyond it.

The river Yamuna – one of the great holy rivers of India – formed the artery of the city, binding all the gardens together. It was a broad, water avenue on which one could travel by boat from one garden residence or tomb to another. When Shah Jahan visited the Taj Mahal, or the house of a member of the imperial family or of a noble, he would take the boat from his palace in the fort of Agra. The most famous garden at Agra was that of his daughter, Jahanara, which she had inherited from her mother, Mumtaz Mahal. The court poets were full of its praise and foreign dignitaries were taken on visits there. In May 1638 Shah Jahan entertained the Iranian ambassador Yadgar Beg with illuminations and fireworks in the garden of Jahanara.

Only the imperial family and the highest dignitaries of the empire resided close to the waterfront. The princes, imperial women and Mughal nobles held the garden residences only during their lifetime, however, and after their death the property reverted to the crown. The emperor either then kept it for himself or he might grant it to someone else. The indigenous Rajputs, who were integrated into the Mughal government, were in a better position than Mughal nobles, and were allowed to own heritable land. Shah Jahan acquired the land on which he built the Taj Mahal from Raja Jai Singh, of the ruling family of Amber near Jaipur, by giving him in exchange four houses at Agra.

Property could remain in the possession of a family if a tomb had been constructed on the garden site. In consequence, to avoid losing their property to the crown, more and more nobles started to build tombs along the river, thus introducing a funerary aspect. Today, the tombs are the main remnants of the riverfront scheme. One outstanding example belongs to I'timad ud-Daula (completed 1628), which Nur Jahan, the powerful Iranian wife of Jahangir and thus Shah Jahan's stepmother, had built in white marble inlaid with stone, forming a close forerunner to the Taj Mahal. Then there are also the tomb of Sultan Parwiz, a brother of Shah Jahan, as well as the tomb of Afzal Khan Shirazi, a noble from Iran, which was faced with tile mosaic in the style of Lahore, where he had been governor, and the tomb of Ja'far Khan, the brother-in-law of Mumtaz Mahal.

The best-known and most magnificent tomb of all is, of course, the Taj Mahal. More than simply a mausoleum set in a garden which represents the culmination of the sepulchral architecture of the Mughals, it was also a large complex consisting of numerous buildings serving a great variety of purposes. In the Islamic context it can be compared only to the *külliyes*, the great mosque complexes of the Ottomans, which also included the tombs of the builders. These were, however, smaller and laid out in a more informal way.

The oblong site of the Taj Mahal is divided into two main zones: the funerary and the 'wordly', reflecting the dialectics of the Islamic concept of '*din wa dunya*', the domains of the spiritual and of the material life. The architectural complex representing the funerary aspect – the mausoleum with its flanking mosque and assembly hall, garden and monumental gateway – is preceded by two complexes of ancillary buildings, consisting first of the transitional zone of the forecourt, flanked by quarters for the tomb attendants, subsidiary tombs and bazaar streets, and then the entirely mundane bazaar and caravanserai complex. These buildings served the funerary complex in a way that was both functional and formal, with the service area echoing the plan of the funerary unit. Adding urban quarters for foreign travellers and merchants to the mausoleum complex ensured that, as the French jeweller and traveller Jean-Baptiste Tavernier said, 'the whole world should see and admire its magnificence'.

Agra began to decline when Shah Jahan moved his court to his newly built residence Shahjahanabad (Delhi) in 1648. With the riverfront city abandoned by the ruling elite, the inhabitants of Agra took it over. The river and its banks became the centre of civic life and an outstanding swimming culture emerged, in which people from all walks of life and of all religious communities participated, young and old, rich and poor.

After the British takeover in 1803 the riverfront gardens continued to decline. In the 20th and 21st centuries the urban landscape of Mughal Agra was largely forgotten and absorbed by the ever-expanding city. The water level of the Yamuna was reduced by dams built upstream to draw water for irrigation, and what remains is heavily polluted. The river's edge, once the most privileged site, is used as a latrine, for garbage and for illicit gambling. It is still possible, however, to take a boat on the river in order to see the Taj Mahal in its original context and appreciate the garden city of the Mughals.

# ISFAHAN

## Shah 'Abbas and the Safavid Empire

STEPHEN P. BLAKE

*They say Isfahan is 'Half the World'. By saying this,*
*they only describe half of Isfahan.*

ISKANDAR MUNSHI, C. 1615

The Persian poets were not the only ones to be captivated by the new capital of the Safavid empire in Iran. To European travellers such as Jean Chardin, Isfahan was 'one of the great cities of the world' – a rival of Paris and London. Founded by Shah 'Abbas I (r. 1587–1629) in 1590, the city quickly grew in size and architectural splendour.

The Safavid empire (1501–1722) was one of three states to dominate the early modern Middle East and South Asia – the Mughal empire in India and the Ottoman empire in Anatolia, the Balkans, the Levant and North Africa being the other two. Shah Ismail (r. 1501–24), the founder of the dynasty, had been the leader of the Safaviyya Sufi brotherhood, a mystic order composed primarily of Turkish tribesmen. Ismail claimed to be divinely anointed – a reincarnation of Ali, the Prophet Muhammad's son-in-law, and a manifestation of God himself. His followers, convinced of his mission, overran the Turkish Aq Quyunlu forces at Tabriz and soon acquired control of the Iranian plateau.

While Ismail was the charismatic founder, it was his great-grandson, Shah 'Abbas I, who laid the institutional foundations of the mature state. To counter military challenges from the Turkish tribal chieftains, 'Abbas increased the number of cavalrymen in his household militia. Dependants or slaves, these men developed a deep personal attachment to the ruler. To fund his expanded bodyguard the emperor instituted a series of economic reforms. He redistributed agricultural land from the domain of the tribal leaders to the domain of the imperial household, he recruited a group of Armenian merchants to market the silk from his private lands and he established lucrative trade agreements with the Dutch and English East India companies. Finally, lacking the supernatural aura of his grandfather, he promoted the spread of Imami Shi'ism, building mosques and colleges, appointing Shi'ite clerics to important posts, and underwriting the rituals and ceremonies of Shi'ite Islam.

His institutional reforms underway, 'Abbas decided to found a new capital. Ismail had established his centre of rule at Tabriz, and Tahmasp, his son, had moved his headquarters to Qazvin. 'Abbas, however, chose Isfahan – closer to the Iranian heartland and to the ancient city of Persepolis, capital of the Achaemenid empire (559–330 BC). In 1590 Isfahan was organized around the old piazza, the Maidan-i Harun Vilayat, and 'Abbas's initial projects were limited primarily to renovation. But in 1602, after defeating the Uzbeks and recapturing Herat, 'Abbas shifted his headquarters to an undeveloped garden in the southwestern corner of the Isfahan oasis. The centre of the new city, the Map of the World Piazza (Maidan-i Naqsh-i Jahan), featured four monumental gateways which dominated the four sides of the square and gave access to four magnificent structures, each symbolic of a recently initiated reform.

The Ali Qapu (High Gateway) dominated the western side of the piazza. A five-storey structure, it served several functions: entrance to the imperial palace, audience hall for the reception of ambassadors and officials, and elevated balcony for viewing the spectacles below. The imperial palace itself, behind the Ali Qapu, comprised a vast complex of mansions, audience halls, gardens, stables and apartments. Two structures stood out: the Chihil Sutun (Forty Pillars) Audience Hall and the Hasht Bihisht (Eight Paradises) Mansion. The size and splendour of 'Abbas's residence – the beautiful mansions and apartments and the great retinue they housed – reflected the strengthening of the imperial household and its hard-won victory over the forces of the Turkish tribal leaders.

The northern end of the piazza was commanded by the Qaisariya (Imperial) Gateway to the imperial bazaar. A long arcade that connected the new piazza with the old, this bazaar was the central economic artery of the city, reaching its final form in the 1660s. Like the Ali Qapu, the Qaisariya Gateway was more than its name implied. A five-sided, two-storeyed semicircular structure, it enclosed a courtyard with a fountain. Its lower face was tiled with multicoloured porcelain squares, and its upper half was decorated with large colourful paintings: 'Abbas returning from a hunt; 'Abbas defeating the Uzbeks; a group of feasting Europeans; and a likeness of Sagittarius (the Archer), the astrological sign under which the city was founded. On the ledges that jutted from the lower storey jewellers, goldsmiths and cloth merchants displayed their goods, while on the balconies above imperial musicians played loud, martial music at sunset and midnight. The gateway proclaimed the indispensable role of the imperial household in the budding economy of the new capital. With the increased resources from his economic restructuring, 'Abbas was now able to provide a major stimulus – building roads, shops and caravanserais and offering a ready market to the merchants, artisans and artists of the city.

The last two gateways on 'Abbas's new piazza led to mosques. To the east was the entrance to the Sheikh Lutfallah Mosque. The first of the four defining structures to be completed, it was begun just after groundbreaking on the new square. Sheikh Lutfallah, an Arabic-speaking Shi'ite from Lebanon, was the chief cleric of the mosque – both prayer leader and teacher. A personal favourite of the emperor, he received a stipend from the household exchequer and spearheaded 'Abbas's efforts to spread Imami Shi'ism.

To the south was the magnificent gateway that led to the Masjid-i Shah (Imperial Mosque), the chief religious structure of 'Abbas's new capital. Flanked by two minarets and recessed to match the Qaisariya Gateway opposite, this entrance enclosed a small pool; a chain to keep out horses and other animals stretched across the threshold. The Masjid-i Shah was the congregational mosque for the new city and was, after the imperial palace, the largest complex on the piazza. It was said to contain 18 million bricks and 475,000 brightly coloured tiles, and included two colleges, four minarets and an underground chamber for escaping from the searing heat of midsummer. Symbolizing 'Abbas's campaign to convert the populace, the mosque was dedicated to the Mahdi, the apocalyptic Twelfth Imam of Shiite Islam. Above the niche which indicated the direction of prayer was a cupboard containing two relics: a Koran in the hand of Ali Riza (the Eighth Imam) and the bloodstained robe of Husayn (the Third Imam). The tiled dome covering the central sanctuary could be seen for miles around.

The Map of the World Piazza, with its four surrounding monuments, was the centre of a rapidly expanding urban area. By 1670 the population had reached nearly 500,000. The symbolic capstone to 'Abbas's new state, Isfahan's magnificence almost matched the poet's hyperbole. The end came some 50 years later. In the late 17th century a fiscal crisis erupted – silk exports dropped while imports from India and imperial household expenses continued to rise. The last emperor of the dynasty, Shah Sultan Husain (r. 1694–1722), had neither the energy nor the ability to confront the problems, and so when the Ghilzai Afghans surrounded the capital in 1722, the Safavids were totally unprepared. After a six-month siege that took a terrible toll on the inhabitants and the urban fabric, the invaders entered the city and beheaded the emperor. Amid the devastation and destruction that followed, the Safavid empire came to an end.

# BEIJING

## and the Forbidden City

FRANCES WOOD

*This city of Peking ... is so prodigious and the things*
*therein so remarkable ... I know not where to begin.*
FERNÃO MENDES PINTO, 1614


No traveller approaching the Beijing during the 16th and 17th centuries could fail to be struck by the vast grey mass of the city wall that rose high above the flat North China Plain. Fernão Mendes Pinto, a Portuguese explorer and adventurer who claimed to have spent a couple of months in the city in the mid-16th century, described 'the double fortified wall which surrounds the city, built of dressed stone ... inside this vast walled enclosure, there are, the Chinese assure us, 3,800 pagodas and temples.' The Persian historian Hafiz-i-Abru, who accompanied the Timurid embassy to China in 1420 to attend the opening ceremonies of the imperial palace, saw the walls as they were being built:

> *It was a very magnificent city ... All around the city wall ... still under*
> *construction there were set up one hundred thousand bamboo poles,*
> *each one of which being fifty cubits long, in the form of scaffoldings.*
> *Since it was still early dawn, the gates had not yet been opened, the*
> *envoys were admitted through the tower which was being constructed.*

Though there had been towns on this site for over 2,000 years, the city was created by the formal announcement in 1409 by the third emperor of the Ming, Zhu Di (r. 1403–24), known by his reign title of Yongle, or

'Everlasting Joy', that the capital would move north from Nanjing. Parts of it can still be seen today.

The first Ming emperor had founded a new capital in his personal power base, Nanjing, and had sent his sons to hold fiefs in distant parts of China. His fourth son, the future Yongle, established himself in Beijing, once the capital of the vanquished Mongol Yuan dynasty. After leading an insurrection, which ended in 1403 with Nanjing ablaze and the second emperor (his nephew) dead, the usurping Yongle Emperor decided to move the capital to Beijing, his military stronghold. It was also a strategic improvement upon Nanjing, which was too far from the still-contentious border with Mongolia, just to the north of Beijing. Even before this, work had begun on the outer walls of the city, which were still vulnerable to Mongol attacks; the old Yuan walls were newly faced with brick and the northern wall was moved southwards. The southern part of the city was not walled until 1553, by which time it had filled with people, temples, restaurants and places of entertainment. Ming Beijing, once enclosed, would cover 62 sq. km (24 sq. miles).

Having dismissed arguments that the good fortune of the site had been exhausted with the destruction of the Yuan dynasty, from 1406 the Yongle Emperor ordered the building materials for his palace. This was made easier by improvements to the Grand Canal, which brought materials as well as rice northwards. Some 10,000 households were moved east to Beijing from Shanxi province in 1404 to increase the population of the city, and a huge labour force including 7,000 artisans captured in Southeast Asia was assembled. Building work did not start until 1416, by which time timbers of catalpa, elm, oak, camphor and *Phoebe nanmu* had been assembled from all over China, along with floor tiles from Shandong and Suzhou, and red clay, yellow clay and gold leaf brought from all corners of the country.

The Forbidden City – the imperial palace complex – stood at the very centre of Ming Beijing, stretching nearly 1,000 m (3,280 ft) from north to south and standing on the main axis of the city, which ran from the Temple of Heaven complex through to the north wall. It consisted of nearly 9,000 'rooms', its outer walls washed dark red and its halls raised on carved white marble terraces and covered with yellow tiled roofs. One of the earliest westerners to see it, the Jesuit Nicholas Trigault, described it in the early 17th century: 'The royal colour, forbidden to all others, is yellow, and regal vestments are decorated with various designs of dragons ... The roof and tilings of the palace are also done in yellow and with various paintings of dragons.' Emperors conducted official business in three main halls inside the Gate of Heavenly Peace, while the private apartments clustered behind housed hundreds of palace women with their attendant eunuchs.

In the south of the city, the Temple of Heaven, first constructed in 1420, is the most significant building associated with imperial ritual. There were also altars to agriculture, the sun, the moon and the earth (constructed in the early 16th century) which the emperors visited for annual sacrifices. As the emperor was regarded as the 'son of heaven', the Temple of Heaven was the most important altar, traditionally visited on the eve of the winter solstice and in the first month of the lunar new year, when, seated in an elephant-drawn chariot, he proceeded south from the Forbidden City.

The growth of the Yongle Emperor's new capital can be seen in the increase in the number of temples, from perhaps 40 in the northern part of the city in 1401 to nearly 250 in 1550. These were mostly Buddhist and Daoist establishments but there were other cults, such as that of the city-god and Guandi, the god of war. Temples were not only places of worship: temple fairs were held on the birthday of the local god, when entertainers performed acrobatics and knife-throwing, magicians arrived with trained mice and monkeys, and itinerant traders set up shop. The temple courtyards were also thrown open to periodic markets. Mendes Pinto noted 'a hundred and twenty public spaces in Beijing where a fair was held every month and someone calculated that there were four fairs a day ... Then there were the specialist shops in separate streets where there was an abundance of silk, brocade, fabrics of gold, linen and cotton, skins of sable, ermine and musk-deer, aloes, porcelain, gold and silver, pearls, powdered gold and gold in ingots ... coral, cornelian, crystal ... ginger, tamarind, cinnamon, pepper, cardamom, borax, indigo, honey, wax.' Many of these goods were shipped, usually along the Grand Canal, from other parts of China – imperial silks came from Suzhou, porcelains from Jingdezhen and paper from Xishan.

Emperors aside, there were over a million inhabitants in Beijing by 1550. The rich built substantial houses beside the lakes in the northern city and villas in the Western Hills that surrounded the North China Plain to the north and west; the poor were crammed into small grey courtyard houses lining the chequerboard of tiny lanes that ran between the broad main streets, packed 'as close as the hairs on an ox', as the saying went. Annually, the city's population was swelled by the thousands of candidates who came to take the imperial civil service examinations and by merchants who travelled from all over China and stayed in the guild halls of their native provinces.

The extent of the influence of Ming China was seen in the exotica that the eunuch admiral Zheng He brought back to the capital from his sea voyages to Southeast Asia, India and Africa. From his fourth voyage, he returned in 1419 with lions, leopards, dromedaries, ostriches, zebras, rhinos, antelopes and giraffes for the imperial zoo, the giraffes particularly delighting the Yongle Emperor. Foreign envoys also flocked to Beijing. In 1420, Hafiz noted Japanese, Kalmucks and Tibetans, all come to join in the opening ceremonies of the Forbidden City. Within a few months, in May 1421, as Hafiz recounted, the three great halls 'supported on columns of ... lapis lazuli' were struck by lightning and burned as 'if a hundred thousand torches' had been lit. They were soon rebuilt and given new auspicious names, and throughout the Ming dynasty the Forbidden City continued to see processions of foreign envoys bearing tribute for the emperor. These included the first Portuguese embassy in 1520, and in 1601, the first Jesuit missionary to enter the Forbidden City, Matteo Ricci. It was to remain the imperial palace until the end of the Qing dynasty in 1912.

# KYOTO

## Pleasure Gardens and Vermilion Palaces

LESLEY DOWNER

*When you look out over the present Kyoto from the west gate
of Kiyomizu Temple, you see such long crowded rows of
white-walled storehouses that in summer, in the early sunlight,
the city sparkles as if on a snowy morning. The opulence of the
era is manifested by silent pines and by cranes diverting
themselves among the clouds ... Smoke rises, morning and night,
from the kitchen fires of all sorts of tradesmen.*

IHARA SAIKAKU, 1686

For most of its thousand-year history, the city we now know as Kyoto was
called simply Miyako – the Capital. For all but a few of those centuries,
however, power lay elsewhere. But Kyoto was the seat of the emperor, who
was of divine descent, and it was therefore a sacred city, revered as the capital.

Kyoto was founded in 794 by Emperor Kammu, who chose for his new
capital a location which fitted the rules of geomancy: a broad bowl-shaped
valley surrounded by tree-clad hills, bordered by sparkling rivers to east
and west. He named it Heian-kyo – the Capital of Peace and Tranquillity.
Poets called it the City of Purple Hills and Crystal Streams. Modelled on
Chang'an, the fabled capital of China's great Tang dynasty (p. 99), the
streets were laid out in a grid pattern, with the imperial palace, the home
of the emperor, to the north and the Rashomon gate guarding the south.

Heian-kyo was a city of vermilion-painted palaces where noblemen
and princes rumbled along the boulevards in lavishly decorated ox carts and
spent their days writing poems, mixing incense and conducting elaborate

courtships. This jewel-like civilization left one remarkable monument – the world's first novel, *The Tale of Genji*, written by a court lady in the 11th century, which depicts the lives and loves of those pampered courtiers.

Then in 1194 the first of a succession of warlords snatched power. Heian-kyo went up in flames. By the 16th century the city was known simply as Miyako, and the emperors had been reduced to penury. In 1600, after four centuries of war, Tokugawa Ieyasu defeated his rival warlords at the battle of Sekigahara. The emperor conferred on him the title of shogun, recognizing him as ruler of all Japan.

With peace came prosperity. Ieyasu ruled from his headquarters in the small fishing village of Edo, which quickly grew into a vast city; it would later be known as Tokyo (p. 334). But Kyoto, the sacred city, remained the capital, and there – among its aristocrats and nobles, its merchants and entertainers – began an extraordinary flowering of culture such as had not been seen since the golden days of the Heian period. The Dutch doctor Engelbert Kaempfer, who visited in 1691, found a city of some 3 million people which, he wrote, 'serves as the storehouse of all Japanese workmanship and trade'.

To consolidate his power, Ieyasu initiated a vast building programme. In Kyoto he ordered his defeated rivals to build him a spectacular castle. Lavishly decorated with coffered ceilings, carved transoms and gilded walls, Nijo Castle was designed to awe the nobility with its showy extravagance and magnificent gardens. But while the parvenu shogun flaunted his wealth, the aristocrats were developing a very different style. Tea ceremony was the art form that characterized the age. It underpinned an aesthetic of poverty and simplicity, often achieved – ironically – at great expense. The taking of tea was an experience which began with walking across cobblestones to a small, bare teahouse and creeping through a tiny entrance. Every item in the ceremony was a work of art, from the cherry-wood scoop to the tea bowl.

The epitome of tea taste was the Katsura Imperial Villa, whose garden was said to be the most perfect ever designed. Paths led around a large lake, past woods and groves, stone lanterns and moss-covered bridges. The whole world – mountains, hills and seas – was there in miniature. Every detail was precise, every tree and stone cunningly placed to enhance or conceal a view. There Prince Toshihito, the builder of the villa, sat on his Moon-Viewing Porch, sipping bitter green tea.

Meanwhile the ordinary folk too were enjoying a renaissance. Far from being refined, this one was lively, vulgar and rambunctious and produced some of Japan's most enduring and well-loved art. With peace established, merchants became extremely wealthy. But they were considered the lowest of the low because they dirtied their hands with money. A succession of edicts prohibited any display of wealth. Forbidden to spend money on houses or clothes, they turned to the ephemeral pleasures of the 'floating world' – the pleasure quarters, the kabuki theatre and the other 'bad places'. These quickly became the epitome of glamour. At the Shimabara pleasure quarters, merchants bankrupted themselves wooing courtesans who often refused them until the last silver coin was spent.

On the wrong side of the river Kamo, the carnival never stopped. There tea-selling women entertained with singing, dancing or more, depending on the depth of one's purse. Paintings show people in festive robes dancing through the streets and crowding to see puppets, wrestlers, jugglers and sword swallowers.

It was here that kabuki theatre developed. The first performers were courtesans, performing dances and comic skits to attract customers. When they became too disorderly the government banned women from public performance and thereafter kabuki was the preserve of men. Entertainers were even lower than merchants in the hierarchy, but nevertheless they were lionized. This wonderfully lively and vivid culture was immortalized in woodblock prints and the novels of comic writers such as Saikaku and Kiseki, themselves denizens of the floating world, who partook of its values.

By the beginning of the 18th century Edo was the most populous city on earth. Nevertheless Kyoto retained its grip on everything to do with culture, style and spiritual matters. The wealthy men of Edo went to Kyoto to enjoy the company of its charming geishas, who entertained in the new pleasure quarters of Gion. And it remained sacred. When westerners forcibly ended Japan's isolation in the mid-19th century, Kyoto was the city that was most firmly off limits. Then in 1868, after years of civil war, the Tokugawas were defeated. The new rulers of the country declared the restoration of the emperor, who moved to Edo, which – renamed Tokyo, the Eastern Capital – became the official capital.

Kyoto remained the cultural heart of the country, however, and was spared American bombs in the Second World War. Today the city is fighting a new war against encroaching concrete; it recently acquired a vast new station. But behind high walls its palaces, temples and gardens remain intact. It still sits amid purple hills and crystal streams; and geishas still patter through its shadowy streets lined with dark wooden houses.

# PRAGUE

## Rudolph II's City of Magic

COLIN AMERY

*Prague doesn't let go. Either of us. This old crone has claws.*
*One has to yield or else.*
FRANZ KAFKA TO OSKAR POLLAK, 12 JANUARY 1902

Prague has recently relaxed into its complex history, as a city always at the political crossroads of Europe. It wears its great beauty with a sense of calm acceptance that the worst is now over and a steady future has been won by its citizens. Its treasury of Gothic and Baroque architectural masterpieces is gradually being sympathetically restored and rescued from the slow neglect of the recent past. The architectural panorama of the city on the river Vltava is one of the most beautiful in Europe, but it cannot be admired on appearances alone. It is also important to remember how the city has survived and now flourishes. Anyone who witnessed the Velvet Revolution in November 1989 will never forget the powerful effect of three-quarters of a million people filling Wenceslas Square and the surrounding streets and surging across the Charles Bridge chanting *Havel Na Hrad* ('Havel to the Castle'). They refused to go home until the liberal and enlightened playwright turned politician Vaclav Havel was sworn in as President – they, and Prague, had won their freedom.

Not for nothing is the city known as 'Golden Prague' – the ochre stuccoed walls of so much of the city do glow in the sunlight, and the vision of a hundred spires seen through the mist rising from the river is one of the most beautiful sights in Europe. Prague demonstrates before your eyes the transformation of a medieval Gothic city into an almost encyclopaedic display of the baroque triumphalism of the Counter-Reformation. Under Emperor Charles IV (r. 1346–78) Prague had a great moment of glory as the capital of the Holy Roman Empire, which gave the city the famous Charles Bridge, the strong perpetual presence of Prague castle (the Hrad) and the Gothic spires of the Old Town.

The two jagged spires of the Church of Our Lady of Tyn contrast with the smooth dome of St Nicholas Church and encapsulate in their architectural styles the historical and theological contests that have shaped the city. The long struggle between Catholics and Protestants in Central Europe crystallized in Prague, and its martyrs are recalled in monuments and in many references to a peculiarly Czech way of dealing with differences of opinion – not by firing squad but by defenestration from high windows around the city. In 1421 followers of the Protestant reformer Jan Huss hurled some Catholic opponents from the windows of the Town Hall. In 1618 Protestant nobles feeling angry at imperial restrictions on their rights threw reactionary royal officials from the castle windows. Shortly before the communist takeover in 1948 Jan Masaryk, foreign minister to the fledgling republic, 'fell' from his office window in the Czernin Palace near the castle. All three defenestrations precipitated long periods of conflict and upheaval in Prague and Central Europe.

Central Prague today falls neatly into four historic districts. Two of them are on the left, or west, side of the Vltava river. The Hradcany ('castle complex'), which dates back to the 9th century, occupies the higher ground and surveys the entire city from its rocky bluffs. The lower sloping ground that runs down to the river from the castle is now the part of the city known as the Mala Strana ('Little Quarter'). Remarkably there are still terraced gardens and orchards here in the heart of the city. On the east bank, in the bend of the river, there were originally two towns, which have now been absorbed as districts into the larger city. Closest to the river is the Staré Mesto ('Old Town'), which goes back to the 11th century, and encircling it in an outer crescent is the Nové Mesto ('New Town'), which began its life in the 14th century. Adversity and poverty have left these older parts of Prague in a remarkably well-preserved state. The 19th century added a substantial area of unmemorable architecture, with the exception of some intriguing Art Nouveau and Secessionist experiments. Communism luckily built its dreams of a regulated paradise on the distant outskirts of the city.

Prague's political flowering in the late 20th century is as remarkable as its intellectual renaissance in the 16th century during the extraordinary reign of Rudolph II (1576–1612). In 1575 the Bohemian Estates approved the election of the young Archduke Rudolph as King of Bohemia, while asking the emperor, Maximilian II, to ensure that his son and successor would remain in Prague and learn Czech. By 1583 Rudolph had decided that Prague should become the seat of the imperial residence, at a distance from Vienna and the ever-present threat of the encircling Ottoman empire. Few would have expected Rudolph to become so captivated by Prague castle that he seldom left it or that his highly individual court would become a magnet for so many artists and intellectuals from throughout Europe. Rudolph may have brought political and cultural importance to Prague but his court was a puzzle to his fellow rulers. In 1606 the Archdukes of Vienna declared:

> *His majesty is interested only in wizards, alchemists, Kabbalists and the like, sparing no expense to find all kinds of treasures, learn secrets and use scandalous ways of harming his enemies … He also has a whole library of magic books. He strives all the time to eliminate God completely so that he may in future serve a different master.*

In fact, Rudolph filled Prague with the wonders of the age – he was a fanatical collector and ordered great paintings from Italy to be carried over the Alps. He was fascinated by intricate automata and ordered maps and models of the heavens to be specially made. Rudolph's greatest possessions were people – the astronomers Johannes Keller and Tycho Brahe, the almost mythical magus John Dee and the philosopher Giordano Bruno were all welcomed to Prague. One of his artists in residence was Giuseppe Arcimboldo – his bizarre heads composed of fruit, flowers and vegetables appealed to Rudolph's almost surreal tastes. The paintings reflected the acquisitive character that lay behind Rudolph's *kunstkammer* – where among the curiosities and treasures were a dodo, a unicorn's horn and some of the nails of Noah's Ark. Rudolph may have had a strange character and a wilful temper, but he brought Prague to the forefront of Renaissance ideas and moved it out of the medieval age.

Rudolph II is still very present in Prague, giving the city the sense of the esoteric and the occult which it has never quite shaken off. To visit Golden Lane – a street of tiny buildings along the walls of the castle near the White Tower – you experience the places where Rudolph's alchemists and goldsmiths worked to enrich his collection and struggled to find the elixirs of life. Magic is the word for the heart of Prague and it is one of the few places in Europe where intellectual struggle can be sensed through the survival of so many untouched quarters and buildings. You can walk from the medieval castle to the surviving baroque palaces and theatres where Mozart's *Don Giovanni* was first performed. The dark history of more recent times is being banished by the delight the new Czech Republic takes in its renewal as a centre for the exploration of European urban ideas.

ABOVE The Torre de Belem in Lisbon is a structure of great elegance and strength: both a defensive tower for the port and a ceremonial gateway to the city. It was built in the Portuguese late Gothic, or 'Manueline' style between 1514 and 1519 by Francisco and Diogo de Arruda.

BELOW Michaelangelo's mighty dome overlooks Bernini's greatest work of architecture, the Piazza San Pietro (1656–67) in the Vatican City, Rome. The curved colonnades leading up to the basilica's façade act as an immense pair of arms, enfolding the faithful.

OPPOSITE The buildings and gardens of Topkapı in Istanbul, 1584. It was both the home of the sultan and his extended 'family', and the administrative centre of the sprawling empire. Some 1,000 cooks worked in the kitchens alone.

ABOVE The Taj Mahal complex at Agra, seen from the river. The Mihman Khana, or assembly hall (left), mausoleum and mosque are set on the riverfront terrace, framed by towers.

BELOW At Isfahan, Shah 'Abbas set out to create a capital worthy of his empire. The vast, tiled Map of the World Piazza at its heart served as a market and a stage for great events, its four monumental gateways leading to magnificent structures such as the Imperial Mosque (right).

OPPOSITE The domes, cupolas and spires of Prague's breathtakingly well-preserved skyline: an architectural journey from the medieval to the baroque, with detours into art deco and art nouveau. The dome to the left crowns the Church of the Knights of the Cross.

ABOVE A plan of Amsterdam published in Braun and Hogenberg's atlas of 1572, with the small city set on and surrounded by water, but not yet girdled by its semi-circular system of canals.

BELOW Market stalls inside one of the barbican gates in Beijing's wall sell antique vessels, fans, ink stones and books. At the rear, a reader sits cross-legged beside a white sheet on which books in their blue cotton covers are displayed; to his right is a pedlar with a red sack and a small hand drum. Officials in their black flap-eared caps stroll through the market.

OPPOSITE The original settlement of Stockholm, Gamla Stan (Old Town), is the most picturesque part of the city. The iron fretwork spire marks the church of Riddarholmskyrkan, where the great Swedish warrior kings are buried.

ABOVE The central square of Mexico City painted in 1695 by Cristóbal de Villalpando. Richly dressed Europeans in carriages parade in the foreground, while native traders sit at their stalls. Behind looms Popocatépetl.

RIGHT Detail from a view of the Thames by Jan Visscher, 1616. The old St Paul's Cathedral towers above the north bank; to the south we see the Globe Theatre.

ABOVE Dublin in 1800: James Malton's painting looks south from Capel Street across Essex Bridge and the river Liffey to the dome of the old Royal Exchange (now City Hall) at Cork Hill.

BELOW The Winter Palace in St Petersburg, was completed in 1762 by the architect Franco Bartolomeo Rastrelli. Once the principal imperial residence in the city, the palace is now home to the State Hermitage, one of the greatest museums of the world. Its splendours are haunted by the violence and misery of the revolutionary masses who gathered outside in 1917.

# AMSTERDAM

## and the Dutch Republic

SIMON SCHAMA

*Hence Amsterdam, Turk-Christian-Pagan-Jew /
Staple of sects and mint of schism grew: / That bank
of conscience, where not one so strange / Opinion but
finds credit, and exchange.*

ANDREW MARVELL, 1653

Amsterdam is a miracle. A place from another century – from 1640 to be more exact – caught in a time-net like a thrashing codfish only much, much prettier. Nowhere else in the world – except of course the Other Canal empire on the Adriatic lagoon – grants this uncanny sense of graceful admission to its built memory. And the waters, history, have been kinder (or its magistrates wiser) to Amsterdam than to Venice. The impoldering, draining large tracts of the Zuider Zee, creating cultivable, habitable East Flevoland, took away the threat of deluge (only to bring a whole new set of problems, social and ecological, for although the city is not dying or descending into the sea, the balance of marine life has been badly damaged). The city tugs you up alleys of time, because the thing about Amstelredam is that, of all cities in the world, it rose to fortune so quickly and, once arrived, decided not to push its luck and stayed put. There were 30,000 Amsterdammers around 1600; 200,000 a century later, but also 200,000 or even slightly fewer in 1900.

Amsterdam has an undeserved reputation for modest understatement. It is no Las Vegas, but it has always blown its own trumpet whenever it could, as if not quite believing its luck. The first full-on eulogy to its glories of untold wealth, fame, freedom, was Johannes Pontanus's *Rerum et Urbis Amsteldodamensium*, published in 1614 when Amsterdam was still relatively small beer. Twenty-four years later, in 1638, the city officially received Marie de' Medici, the Queen Mother of France, estranged from her son Louis XIII and his government, dominated by Cardinal Richelieu. She had been the subject of the most spectacular cycle of allegorical paintings ever made by a Netherlandish artist, albeit a Catholic Fleming, Peter Paul Rubens, in which she features as an omnipotent, omniscient, all-benevolent quasi-deity, and was greeted with triumphal arches, firework displays, masques staged on floating islands, processions and banquets.

Soon, like most of those who came to Amsterdam in the golden 17th century, she was busy shopping, haggling like an old hand with the merchants. And because Amsterdam had indeed become the *emporium mundi*, there was nowhere else she needed to go to buy anything her queenly heart desired: spices and ceramics from the Orient; perfumed tobacco from America; steel and leather from Iberia (for being at war with Spain was no bar to doing business with its traders); Turkey rugs; Persian silks; Russian sables; or perhaps even an exotic animal for a princely menagerie, one of the lions or elephants that Rembrandt had sketched.

But Amsterdam's spectacular fortunes were built on provisioning the bulky commonplace needs, not just the luxuries, of 17th-century Europe. Before it could become the place you went to buy Malacca cloves or Brazilian emeralds, it was the place that supplied wheat, rye, iron, cured fish, linens, salt, tar, hemp and timber for markets near and far. Why would you go there if you were, say, from Norwich or Augsburg, rather than just have the things shipped directly from source? Because you knew they would be available and cheaper. And why was that? Because Amsterdam's merchants had understood that the key to market domination was the transformation of shipping. So they had used their accumulation of capital (the Amsterdam Exchange Bank was established in 1609, the first year of a 12-year truce with Spain) to finance an extraordinary interlocking system of shipbuilding and bulk carrying. Whole Norwegian forests were bought in advance, harvests of Polish rye likewise, in return for making money immediately available to hard-pressed landowners. Timber, hemp – the wherewithal needed to build a fleet – were consigned to the satellite towns and villages in the countryside north of the city. Each specialized in a particular stage of shipbuilding – some, in the yards on the Zaan, in carpentry; others in casting anchors; others still in making canvas and sails. The components of ships, designed to be sailed with smaller crew and to maximize cargo space, were then brought by barges down to the shipyards on the Ij and the Amstel. Whether a venture was off to the Baltic, to the White Sea or to the Mediterranean, the voyage could be accomplished at a freight cost that made it impossible for merchant fleets to compete. And so the world came to Amsterdam to do its shopping and to take in the outrageousness of a city built to sate the appetites.

But it might also come for freedom. More than anywhere else in the world, Amsterdam and the Dutch saw that becoming a world city – providing living space for those who were confined to ghettos elsewhere, or who were allowed only a clandestine life – Jews, Mennonites, Muslims – was also good for business. Sephardi Jews in particular brought with them from their half-life as Marranos in the Spanish world a great chain of personal and commercial connections from the tobacco and sugar colonies of the Atlantic to the great bazaars of the Maghreb. In Amsterdam they became – as they could not in Venice – merchant princes, allowed to build spectacular synagogues and handsome dwellings in the heart of the Christian metropolis. Amsterdam became the hub of liberty in other ways too – the centre of a free printing press and international book trade.

By the time that Jacob van Campen's great Town Hall, with its Maid of Peace holding her olive branch over the Dam, was completed in the 1660s, and the rotunda topped off, did the 'regents' of the great families who dominated Amsterdam – the Huydecopers, de Graaffs, Backers and Corvers – believe that all this would last forever, that somehow a great mercantile empire would be immune from the laws of hubris that had laid low others of that ilk to whom they constantly compared themselves – Carthage, Tyre and, more recently, Venice? If endurance as the unrivalled world city were just a matter of business they could be confident of their staying power. But it was not. Immense riches generated envy, fear and hatred from neighbours. Even within the United Provinces and the state of Holland, there were plenty who despised Amsterdam's habit of throwing its weight around; who wanted the Republic to be as strong in land power as Amsterdam insisted it should be at sea; and who thought the great city's pragmatism a drag-weight on building a secure state. In 1650 the Stadholder William II had actually marched on the city to impose his will upon it. But providence had, at least temporarily, smiled on Amsterdam. The Prince of Orange's soldiers got lost in a fog; the siege was barely begun and the Stadholder died shortly thereafter, precipitating an anti-dynastic coup in which the decentralized nature of 'Holland's Freedom' was institutionalized.

There was no sudden Carthaginian destruction (although the invasion of Louis XIV's armies into the Republic in 1672, combined with an English naval attack, came close to it). If you went to Amsterdam in the middle of the 18th century, you might have noticed more beggars and street whores; the houses of correction full, and as the poor got poorer, the rich swaggered in a more international way, with stone facings, pedimented and pilastered Frenchified double-doored buildings on the canal houses; more in the way of perruques and Italian singing masters catering to the plutocrats. But in most essentials, the lives of Amsterdammers, the copiously fed, riotously entertained lives, went on much the same way. Voltaire may have been churlish to the place where he could get published, calling Holland the land of 'canaux, canailles et canards'. But there was still true grandeur, bravery and business in the printing of freedom.

It was only the long, grim wars of the French revolution and Napoleonic periods, that sent the city, for a while, into smoky obscurity and hardship. Amsterdam became something that the regents of the golden age could never have imagined: a poor city, a church mouse commonwealth; cheese and beggary. For a while, during the Batavian Republic from 1795 to 1805, there was an upsurge of patriotic euphoria, a sense of the city taken back from the regents by its citizens. But as the brutal reality of Amsterdam's subjection to French military needs became apparent, that optimism disappeared in the mundane desperation of survival. Amsterdam had bent history to its purposes, but in the age of mass mobilization and munitions, it was rolling over Holland. In the 19th century the city suffered the most humiliating of all fates: quaintness – a cosy nook of Europe, tulips, clogs, skaters, pot-bellied stoves, pancakes and street organs.

The sweetness did burst forth again after the Second World War, and how it exploded! A technological revolution happened and Amsterdam went from sleepy cuteness to explosive modernism in the wink of an eye. Quaintness disappeared and sharpness rushed in. Suddenly it was on the cutting edge of design, architecture, painting, writing. It once more revelled in a cosmopolitanism that looked out towards the world without ever forfeiting its intricate, domestic peculiarity.

# MEXICO CITY

## Utopia in the New World

FELIPE FERNANDEZ-ARMESTO

*The city seems inert but it was made by volcanoes.*
JOSÉ EMILIO PACHECO, 1976

Behind the main square of Mexico City, painted in 1695 by the most fashionable painter in the Americas, a volcano looms: a reminder that the splendour of the city remained at the mercy of God. The rest of the painting celebrates the greatest city in the hemisphere. The grid of market kiosks and shopping arcades stamps the surrounding wilderness with order and geometry. The grandeur of the buildings that line the square testifies to the era's notions of the solemnity of civilization and of the ennoblement of nature. In the foreground, the elite appear, with elegant carriages and elaborate manners, parading wealth, status and European taste. Around a fountain, where the water-carriers gather, the thatched stalls of native vendors spread neatly, while native women – many in European dress – sit under fashionable umbrellas.

Throughout New Spain's colonial era, artists and writers of Mexico City conspired to project images of urbanity and excellence to the outside world. At about the time of Cristóbal de Villalpando's painting, the chronicler Agustín de Vetancourt likened the churches to Rome's and the convents to Lisbon's. For him, Mexico City was 'the capital of the New World, an imperial city of great size, space, concourse and population.' Even more challengingly, Mexico was the 'New Jerusalem' – 'the most devout and charitable city in Christendom', not just the aesthetic equal of European cities, but their moral superior.

Villalpando's painting, on the other hand, was frank about the social problems that accompanied madcap growth. Unassimilated Native Americans, beggars, lepers and lowlifes throng his canvas – the human refuse of a city of 100,000 people. When Aztec hegemony in Mexico collapsed in 1521, the Spaniards who replaced them ruled from the same place – 2,285 m (7,500 ft) above sea level, in the midst of the remotest valley from the sea (p. 169). This was a surprising choice for the capital of a maritime empire, thousands of miles and, on average, over two months' sail from the conquerors' homeland.

By tearing down most of the preceding rulers' structures, and rebuilding from scratch, the Spaniards were able to emphasize a break with the Aztec past and erect new edifices of what – to the natives – was a new aesthetic, daringly lavish with frail arches in an environment periodically convulsed by earthquakes. Three circumstances made these defiant ambitions seem manageable: the apparently providential nature of the conquest, effected against overwhelming odds; the novelty of the setting, which inspired new departures; and the abundance of labour in a densely populated region that was only beginning to experience the demographically catastrophic effects of the arrival of the unfamiliar diseases that Europeans brought with them.

In 1554, barely a generation after the conquest, a professor newly arrived for the newly founded university wrote a guidebook that described the effects. He imagined himself showing a visitor around. 'How the approach to the city makes the senses and spirit exult!' the imaginary visitor exclaims. 'The houses are all superb and highly finished, such as the richest and noblest cities deserve.' The noise and traffic made a mere street seem like a marketplace, overlooked by the richly decorated balconies of the Viceroy and his courtiers. 'To my mind,' the visitor continues, 'nothing in either world can equal' the main square – the 'forum', as the author calls it.

Surprise underlies the hyperbole. The visitor can hardly believe that the cathedral maintains a full choir and original music (as indeed it did, including a repertoire of sacred settings in the native language in the best polyphonic style fashionable in Europe). As he passes the pox hospital, the 'Domicile of Minerva, Apollo and the Muses', and the schools respectively for boys and girls of mixed Spanish and native parentage, the author expects his visitor to go slack-jawed. Gradually, more and more of the strange, exotic elements in the city are revealed – first, the indigenous population, then the native foodstuffs in the market. 'Unheard-of names!' exclaims the visitor, 'and fruits never yet beheld!'

The writer even makes a virtue of the unfinished nature of the city: when the Augustinians' house is finished, he claims, 'it could join as the eighth those wonders of the world'. Indeed, a massive building campaign enhanced the city from the 1560s. The streets were paved at the end of the century and the cathedral was rebuilt in its present form in the 1620s.

It may seem that the city's encomiasts protested too much. But the idea that the New World presented an opportunity for a new start was profoundly inspiring. Churchmen dreamed of restoring apostolic purity. Citizens dreamed of reconstituting antique virtue. Both impulses led to classical models and ideals of Renaissance town planning, unrealizable in Europe. In the Americas, utopians could apply Vitruvian nostrums and erect cities with broad, straight streets, right-angled intersections, spacious plazas, hierarchically ordered spaces and perfect geometry. Thomas More located Utopia in the New World just before Mexico was revealed. Mexico City really was the most perfect city of its day, according to the prevailing aesthetic. It remained the model for other colonial foundations, including most of those in North America.

Subsequent development followed the original plan, which appealed to the enlightened successors of the early colonial elite. Architects became adept at designing for seismic instability, but one big, unresolved problem remained: the lake-bound location condemned the city to flooding and slow sinking. Repeated efforts to drain the lake failed. In 1789 engineers hailed 'one of the most gigantic hydraulic works ever executed', but it was still not enough.

Meanwhile, three circumstances ensured that the artistic and scientific life of Mexico City would be vibrant throughout the colonial period: the presence of the Viceroy's court; the large number of religious orders that provided artistic patronage; and an emulous aristocracy – which, in the Spanish tradition, lived in the capital rather than the country – descended from the conquistadors and native dynasties. Shortly before ruinous revolts ended in independence and inaugurated Mexico's era of relative stagnation, Alexander von Humboldt hailed the capital as 'one of the finest cities ever built by Europeans in either hemisphere'.

# LONDON

## Renaissance to Restoration

A. N. WILSON

*The exterior of the Cathedral was adjudged to be complete.*
*It stood with its perfect dome and encircling colonnades,*
*its galleries and ball, and surmounting cross ... If ever there*
*was an occasion on which the heart of man might swell with*
*pardonable pride, it was the heart of Wren at that hour.*

H. H. MILMAN, 1868

The 17th century may be seen as the pivot of London's history. By the accident of a Great Fire, and by the prodigious joint talents of Londoners at this stage of history, a medieval city became a modern one. Moreover, not merely was London architecturally transformed. It became the epicentre of the two forces which would shape the future world itself: capitalism, and the scientific outlook.

The London into which John Milton was born in 1608 and which saw the latter days of Shakespeare was a small medieval city whose population had swollen beyond any manageable size. (In 1500 there were some 75,000 Londoners, by 1600 there were 220,000 and by 1650 this had risen to 450,000.) You have to imagine a small medieval town such as Bruges or Salisbury trying to accommodate the population of modern Brussels or Birmingham – and to accommodate it without any modern sanitation. Shakespeare's Globe Theatre, built in 1599, had a capacity for a little less than 3,000 spectators, but there were no lavatory facilities of any kind. Samuel Pepys, in a pre-Fire diary entry (of October 1660) recorded, 'Going down to my Cellar ... I put my feet into a great heap of turds, by which I find that Mr Turner's house of office is full and comes into my cellar.' One recent economic historian has said that the preparedness of 17th century Londoners to live in filth was one of the reasons for their extraordinary success: they reaped the benefits of high population, in terms of trade, and entrepreneurial activity, without being disconcerted by the smell. The Japanese and Chinese at a comparable period had elaborate systems of waste-collection, whereby human faeces and even urine were collected for fertilizer and taken to out-of-town farms. Orientals also wasted much time, which could have been valuably spent making money, in washing. In 1710 in England, by contrast, the sale of soap suggests that the population used a mere 0.2 oz per day.

London, then, was a filthy and an overcrowded city in the first six decades of the 17th century. John Stow, in his *Survey* of the late 16th century describes the parish of St Katherine-by-the-Tower as 'enclosed or pestered with small tenements and homely cottages, having inhabitants, English and strangers, more in number than some cities in England'.

It was this City of London, overcrowded and prosperous, which, as the early years of the 17th century unfolded, developed its firmly Protestant colouring. The Puritans had a hold not only of the institutions of the City – for Protestantism and money-making have often gone hand in hand in history – but also of its churches, many of whose vicars and rectors were Calvinist 'lecturers' who insisted upon the parishioners coming to hear their predestinarian interpretations of Scripture not only on Sundays but on weekdays also.

Meanwhile, during the 1620s to 1640s over in Westminster, Inigo Jones was Surveyor-General of the King's Works, and King Charles I was bringing about an architectural renaissance – Palladian houses around Lincoln's Inn, Queen Street and Long Acre, with the superb Banqueting House being built in Whitehall, and Covent Garden being laid out like an Italian piazza. In January 1649, Charles I was to walk through an upstairs window of the Banqueting House in Whitehall, on to a scaffold erected for his execution at the behest of Oliver Cromwell and his supporters in the City of London.

Cromwell effected a revolution which was not reversed by the restoration of the monarchy in 1660. Though the king came back, it had been established beyond any question that Britain was to be an oligarchy, governed by a coalition of aristocrats and mercantile wealth, rather than by an absolutist monarch on the French pattern. One of Cromwell's most inspired acts of tolerance (and he was a tolerant despot, except where Roman Catholics were concerned) was to end the 365-year banishment of the Jews from England. In December 1655, he gave permission for the Jews to come and live, work and worship in England. Their first synagogue in London was in Creechurch Lane, built in 1657. (Milton, already blind, but with good Hebrew, attended worship there.) Another, for a Spanish and Portuguese Sephardic congregation, was built in Bevis Marks, and is there to this day.

The Jews brought not merely synagogue-worship but – for they came from Amsterdam (p. 217) where it was invented – also the idea of credit capital, the basis of Britain's vast expansion of wealth and power in the 18th century. The creation of the national debt, to cover the huge expenses of the Dutch War, established the power of the city merchants who supplied the money. At the beginning of the century, if you wanted money, you had to obtain it physically, either from a scrivener (the profession of John Milton's father) or goldsmiths, who kept bags of the stuff, at great personal risk, on their premises. (Pepys sent his wife and servants into the country, at the beginning of the Dutch War of 1667, with as much gold as they could carry.) By the end of the 17th century another innovation from Holland – banks – had been established, and the personal householder was no longer responsible for keeping all his gold at home. Sir Francis Child was one of the first bankers in the 1690s, having been a goldsmith and Lord Mayor of London.

But the great event which signalled the change from the medieval London of Milton's boyhood, to the modern city which we know, was the

Great Fire of 1666. It destroyed the old medieval St Paul's Cathedral, all the hovel-tenements described by Stow and most of the churches: 87 churches, 44 livery halls, the Royal Exchange and the Guildhall.

The Lord Mayor of London formed a committee of experts to meet weekly and to formulate, with three city surveyors, the shape of the new city. They decreed that the old narrow streets be widened. Standards of building were laid down. It is no accident that 18th-century London was one of the finest cities the world had ever seen – it was planned by a group of some of the cleverest men who have ever lived.

Robert Hooke, astronomer, inventor of scientific instruments and speculative physicist, was one of the key figures in the rebuilding of London, as of course was his friend and colleague Christopher Wren. Between them, they designed the Monument, that symbol of 17th-century London's survival of the Fire, topped with its blazing gold flame, and with Hooke's observatory and laboratory. Hooke and Wren, together with pioneer mathematician and physicist Isaac Newton as well as Robert Boyle, who had worked on the weight, elasticity and compressibility of air, were founder members of the Royal Society. They all helped to lay down the foundations of modern science, just as their colleague John Locke, gathering friends together at Exeter House for his speculative society, worked out the foundations of empirical philosophy and of the political ideas which would shape modern democracy in Europe and America.

So late 17th-century London was much more than its trades, or its swarming population. It was an emblem of what Britain had become, in the amazingly short time since the death of Charles I. What the great Sir Christopher Wren left was, until later destructions, a symbol of this prodigious renaissance in science, commerce and political science. When he died, and his son had to write him an epitaph in the new-built St Paul's Cathedral, he came up with the immortal words, '*Si monumentum requiris, circumspice*' ('If you require a monument, look around you'). They refer not merely to the gigantic domed Cathedral, but to the whole of the rebuilt London, the resurrected phoenix. Wren built 52 churches of astounding variety and brilliance, and two great hospitals for retired or injured servicemen – the Royal Chelsea Hospital for soldiers and the Greenwich Royal Hospital for retired and disabled seamen. He also built or helped to restore 36 livery companies. And, at the point where the traveller passes from Westminster to the City of London, at the end of the Strand, is his Temple Bar. It is no accident that the London built by Wren, Hooke and friends coincided with the period of Britain's greatness, as a political world power, as a commercial prodigy without parallel in economic history, and as a centre of scientific, musical and literary excellence. Nor perhaps is it an accident that when the buildings of late 17th-century London were partially damaged by German bombs and utterly vandalized by post-war speculators, that the greatness of Britain itself could be seen to have crumbled into the rubble.

# STOCKHOLM

## and Sweden's Baltic Empire

CHARLES FITZROY

*Birger Jarl, that wise man,*
*Let the City of Stockholm be builded, With bounteous sense*
*and plenteous deliberation, A fair House and goodly city.*

THE ERIK CHRONICLE, EARLY 14TH CENTURY

The city of Stockholm, spread over 14 islands in a wonderful position on the west side of the Baltic, was founded in 1252 by the regent of Sweden, Birger Jarl. For several centuries Stockholm was a relatively unimportant trading base for the German-dominated Hanseatic League (see p. 133). The town played a part in the endless wars between Sweden and Denmark, notably the Swedish regent Sten Sture's victory over the Danes at Brunkeberg in 1471, and the Stockholm Bloodbath in November 1520, when 80 Swedish nobles were beheaded by the Danish king Christian II. Three years later Gustav Eriksson Vasa, one of the few nobles to escape, returned to Stockholm on Midsummer's Day 1523 and was proclaimed king. During his long reign (1523–60) he introduced the Lutheran Reformation and centralized trade on Stockholm. The monarchy became hereditary, with power centred on the castle of Tre Kronor on Gamla Stan (the Old Town), which became the permanent seat of the national treasury. Stockholm continued to increase in importance as the administrative centre during the reigns of Gustav Vasa's three sons. Between 1500 and 1600 its population trebled.

Sweden's golden age begins with the accession in 1611 of Gustavus Adolphus, or Gustav II Adolph as he is known in Sweden. Having secured Sweden's position in the Baltic, he introduced much-needed reforms in finance and education, with the government's offices based in Stockholm. In 1630 Sweden entered the Thirty Years War by invading Germany. A brilliant military tactician, Gustavus Adolphus was enormously successful and was acclaimed as the Protestant champion, known as 'the Lion of the North'. Although the victorious king was killed at the battle of Lutzen in 1632, his army remained a powerful presence in Germany, even capturing Prague in 1645, and Sweden made considerable territorial gains at the treaties of Westphalia and Osnabrück in 1648, becoming the dominant power in the Baltic.

Swedish foreign policy was driven by two overriding concerns: to avoid encirclement by her enemies and to profit from trade in the Baltic, where the Netherlands now replaced the Hanseatic League as Sweden's most important trading partner. The majority of the export trade of the key industries of copper and iron passed through Stockholm. Sweden's expanding navy was housed on the island of Skeppsholmen, taking full advantage of Stockholm's superb natural harbour. The splendid *Vasa* warship, now housed in a fine museum in Stockholm, shows the full extent of Swedish naval ambition.

Following Gustavus Adolphus's early death, his daughter, Christina, succeeded at the age of six. She grew to become an intelligent and gifted woman, and corresponded with leading scientists and philosophers, including René Descartes, who came to the royal court in Stockholm in 1650. The queen's cultural aspirations coincided with the desire of her regent and chancellor Axel Oxenstierna to make Stockholm, created the capital in 1634, a city that reflected the power and strength of Sweden as the centre of a burgeoning empire.

The nobility, enriched by Sweden's wars, were encouraged to build splendid palaces such as Riddarhuset (House of the Nobility), erected in the Dutch Baroque style in 1641–47. In 1661 Nicodemus Tessin was created city architect for Stockholm. He erected a series of fine palaces, including the beautiful royal palace of Drottningholm, just outside the city. With a substantial growth in population, from under 10,000 in 1600 to over 50,000 in the 1670s, the city expanded well beyond Gamla Stan, with its cobbled streets and medieval alleyways. An English ambassador described Stockholm as having a 'general impression of a distinguished and beautiful city'.

Despite these changes, Christina found Sweden very constricting and, following her conversion to Roman Catholicism, abdicated in 1654. Her cousin, Charles X, inherited his uncle's martial qualities and was victorious over the Danes after boldly leading his army across the frozen waters of the Baltic to attack Copenhagen. The Treaty of Roskilde in 1658 made the Baltic effectively a Swedish inland sea. Charles, however, died just two years later.

Charles XI, who acceded to the throne in 1660 at the tender age of four, grew up to become an able general like his father. He led his army to victory over the Danes at the battle of Lund in 1676, consolidating Sweden's hold on the rich southern province of Skane. The king transformed Sweden into an absolute monarchy, reformed the country's administration, and built up a strong army and navy; however, the effort of retaining a Baltic empire virtually bankrupted the economy, and the complete destruction of Tre Kronor Castle by fire on Charles's death in 1697 was a harbinger of things to come.

On his accession, the 15-year-old Charles XII faced a formidable alliance of Denmark, Russia, Poland and Saxony, all envious of the Swedish empire. In 1700 his enemies attacked. Against overwhelming odds the young king won a series of startling victories. But Russia, with far greater resources, regrouped, and in 1709 Peter the Great inflicted a decisive defeat on the Swedes at the battle of Poltava. The continuing war bled Sweden dry, and in Stockholm alone, a series of plague epidemics and crop failures reduced the population by one-third. Charles himself was killed in 1718 and at the peace that followed, Sweden lost her overseas empire, retaining only Finland and the province of Skane.

Thus ended the greatest age in Sweden's history. Despite the loss of empire, however, Swedish culture, particularly science and industry, flourished in the 18th century, with Carl von Linné (Linnaeus) establishing a reputation as the leading botanist of his age. Stockholm enjoyed a vibrant cultural life, centred on Tre Kronor castle, which was rebuilt as a Roman-style palace by Tessin the Younger. By the mid-18th century Stockholm was enjoying modern amenities such as street lighting and traffic regulations. Gustav III, who reigned from 1771 to 1792, was a great lover of the arts and music, and gave his name to the Gustavian style, a pure form of neoclassicism strongly influenced by French culture.

# DUBLIN

## and Georgian Elegance

THOMAS PAKENHAM

*Dublin the beautie and eie of Ireland ... is superiour to
all other cities and townes in that realme.*

RICHARD STANYHURST, 1577

On 27 July 1662, the new viceroy of Ireland, the Duke of Ormonde, sailed
into Dublin Bay to take charge of the country for the recently restored king,
Charles II. On Dublin sands the Catholic peasantry came out to welcome
him, singing (in Irish): 'we have brought summer with us'. It was high
time. Dublin, first a Viking outpost, then an Early Christian centre, and
after 1172 the capital of England's earliest colony, had been battered by a
century of intermittent civil war. When Ormonde arrived at Dublin and
its medieval castle, he found it encircled by 17 towers and gatehouses, with
two cathedrals, all verging on collapse. The population had shrunk to about
9,000, most of whom lived in tumbledown cabins.

Ormonde, like his royal master, had spent part of the years of exile
in Paris, and was no stranger to continental ideas for re-planning cities.
Splendour was the guiding principle of the Renaissance city. But who would
pay for it? In the event Ormonde made three dramatic changes to Dublin
which laid the foundations for its role as a ceremonial capital. He bought
up 1,500 acres of the high ground on the north bank of the river Liffey,
west of the city. Here he created Phoenix Park for the public to enjoy – a
royal park more splendid than any open to Londoners. On the south bank,
he created a Royal Hospital for old soldiers, modelled on the Invalides in
Paris. The huge building was completed in 1684 and remains today the most

magnificent monument in the whole of Ireland. And Ormonde began the task of creating a series of French-style quays along the river to form the main east–west axis for the city.

Inspired by Ormonde, the city fathers enclosed their ancient commonage at Stephen's Green and created a vast new square, larger than any in London. North of the river, they built a large market (named after the viceroy) and a Bluecoat school, and constructed four elegant new bridges to span the Liffey.

Ormonde had made a start in giving the city confidence in itself. But it was only a start. For Protestants the next century was to be their golden age – as it was for Dublin also. No one would today attempt to defend their narrow ideals and the penal laws they imposed on the Catholics, yet they had a sense of style and a sense of pride – colonial nationalism of a sort – that set them apart from a mere English garrison taking its orders from London. The men who shaped Dublin were not content to imitate the metropolis. They would go several times better. The streets would be wider, the squares larger, the monumental buildings more splendid. It took less than a hundred years. And in the process the city became a masterpiece.

Of course, the private landlords who planned the elegant brick-and-stone houses of Georgian Dublin were primarily interested in making money. That explains the most striking feature of Dublin's domestic exteriors: their plainness. A minority of the people who bought leases in the new terraces and squares were the peers and upper gentry who controlled Parliament. Most of the new householders were lawyers, doctors, businessmen, clergymen. It suited their pocket to rely on neoclassical restraint, on sober grey brickwork and handsome cut-stone door-cases, reserving the rococo excitements (if they could afford a few hundred pounds extra for a stuccador) for the drawing room and staircase of the interior.

Two rival families of landlords – the Gardiners and the Fitzwilliams – made most of the running. Luke Gardiner was a *nouveau-riche* banker. From 1714 he began to buy up building land north of the river. His first great work was a row of palatial houses in Henrietta Street. Today it is a palatial slum, marooned on the commercial side of Dublin. But no Dublin street has richer plasterwork or finer panelling. Henrietta Street was followed by two large squares (now Parnell Square and Mountjoy Square) and a huge mall (now O'Connell Street). A few public buildings were included, notably the Rotunda, the first public maternity hospital in Europe.

Meanwhile, on the south bank of the Liffey, the Gardiners' supremacy was challenged by Lord Fitzwilliam, who launched an ambitious programme for laying out squares and terraces in the same sober idiom as Gardiner.

In parallel with the Protestant landlords who were making their families rich by building squares and terraces, the fixers and jobbers of the Dublin Parliament were using Irish tax-payers' money to enrich the city with public buildings. The leading fixer was John Beresford, Commissioner of the Revenue, and adviser to a succession of viceroys who ruled Ireland for Britain in partnership with the Irish Parliament. Beresford persuaded a young English architect, James Gandon, to come over to Dublin and design the new Custom House on reclaimed slobland just north of the river. Gandon favoured a modified form of neoclassicism. In turn he designed three of Dublin's grandest public buildings: the Custom House to the east, the Four Courts to the west and additions to the early 18th-century Parliament on College Green. Opposite Parliament was the elegant college itself, Trinity, partly designed by Gandon's patron, Sir William Chambers.

By 1800 the main lines of Georgian Dublin were complete – although two new squares were to be added. Then came catastrophe: the abortive United Irish rebellion of 1798. At the time, Dublin survived well enough, although the rebels had planned to begin their rising there. But when the smoke had cleared in 1800, Dublin paid the price. The British government imposed the Union and abolished the Dublin Parliament, buying out the fixers and jobbers, and the old Parliament became, appropriately enough, a bank.

In the succeeding two centuries Dublin has had its troubles – including the Rising of 1916, the War of Independence of 1919–21 and the Civil

War of 1922. Two of Gandon's masterpieces, the Custom House and Four Courts, were gutted in the fighting. But the government of the new Free State behaved generously, and those wounds to the city were soon mended.

Today, following two decades of dazzling economic success – the years of the Celtic Tiger – the self-inflicted wounds look more permanent. Coarse commercial developments vie with pushy office blocks hopelessly out of scale with the streets around them. But if you wander in the Georgian squares and terraces you will find much that is intact. Stand in the south side of Merrion Square and let your eye run up the rippling line of brickwork, stonework and ironwork to St Stephen's Church at Mount Street bridge. Wander in Lower Fitzwilliam Street and let your eye be carried in a great leap to the blue line of the Dublin mountains. Or exchange the hurly-burly of College Green for the calm of Trinity College itself, an 18th-century oasis of cobbled squares and limestone pediments miraculously preserved in the heart of the city.

# COPENHAGEN

## and Nordic Neoclassicism

### COLIN AMERY

*I did not know a living soul anywhere in the big city; with a small bundle of clothes I walked in through the West Gate; some of the travellers put up at 'Gardergaarden' in Vestergade street – I went there too, acquired a small room … and now – it seemed to me – I had reached the goal of my desires.*

HANS CHRISTIAN ANDERSEN, 1855

Despite the clichéd song there is indeed something wonderful about Denmark's model capital. It is the human scale, the presence of the sea, the Nordic light and the civilized way that traffic is kept in its place, that all make Copenhagen such an agreeable city. It is also the stability given by the long-standing presence of one the world's oldest monarchies. The present queen and her family, descended from the Vikings, live today at the very heart of the city in the royal quarter, Frederickstadt, commissioned in the 18th century by Frederick V. The four urban palaces he built, known as the Amalienborg, stand neatly around a square still guarded by soldiers in toy-town uniforms. Somehow those soldiers evoke the nursery world of Hans Christian Andersen (1805–75) – regarded as Denmark's most famous writer, who lived in and was always inspired by this city.

It was during the 60-year reign of Christian IV (1588–1648) that Copenhagen was first transformed into a great city. Tall towers and magnificent buildings were erected – the first stock exchange, Rosenborg Palace and the Round Tower gave the place an international flavour. Trade had moved on from herrings and was booming with faraway countries

THE EARLY MODERN WORLD

– there was even a colony in India. The city grew to match Christian IV's great vision for his expanding country.

The atmosphere of Copenhagen is still that of a well-heeled merchant city, where many of the finest quarters date from the 17th and 18th centuries. The city suffered three great fires in 1794, 1795 and 1807, the last following the brutal bombardment by the British navy at the battle of Copenhagen. The subsequent construction boom was the greatest the city had ever experienced. Artistically this period of rebuilding coincided with what became known as the Golden Age, when neoclassical art and architecture reached their aesthetic height in the city.

Although the style was international, neoclassical architecture seems particularly to suit the austere tastes of the Nordic countries and was eminently appropriate for Copenhagen. It is characterized by simplicity, symmetry and a preoccupation with archaeology and antiquity. In Copenhagen, C. F. Harsdorff and his accomplished protégé C. F. Hansen masterminded many of the city's grand neoclassical designs. Hansen's exceptional talent is most evident in the reconstruction of the Christiansborg Palace, of which only the Palace Church remains. He also reconstructed the Cathedral Church of Our Lady, on the ruins of the medieval cathedral destroyed during the battle of Copenhagen. Hansen was the chief arbiter in matters of taste and architecture in the city from 1784 until 1844. At the same time the great Danish sculptor Bertel Thorvaldsen was producing wonders, and his museum in Copenhagen (where his body lies) remains a moving shrine to a Scandinavian talent nourished by long periods spent in the southern climate of Rome.

Copenhagen also flourished during the 1890s, a time when Paris was seen by many Danish architects as their ideal. Monumental buildings such as the Marble Church, the Danish National Gallery and the Royal Theatre were all built as magnificent examples of Scandinavian historicism, a style that featured a unique eclectic blend of styles, such as Gothic, Classicism, Renaissance and baroque. An especially fluent example of historicism, the

Town Hall and its square were designed by the Danish architect Martin Nyrop and inspired by the late medieval town hall of Siena.

In the 1890s, Copenhagen had already extended far beyond the boundaries of the city ramparts, and in a civilized way typical of the city, the decision was made to replace all the old ramparts and fortification by a ring of public parks, such as Ørstedsparken, Kastellet, Østre Anlæg and the Botanical Gardens.

Functionalist architecture entered the capital in the 1920s and 1930s, when well-known buildings such as the Radio House, the central police station and the highly original Grundtvig Church were erected. Most recently an engineering marvel has been built, the magnificent Øresunds Bridge linking Copenhagen with Malmö in Sweden, which will undoubtedly make the city the leading urban centre for the entire Baltic region.

# ST PETERSBURG

## Russia's Window on the West

COLIN AMERY

*And here a city by our labour*
*Founded, shall gall our haughty neighbour;*
*'Here cut' – so Nature gives command – /*
*Your window through on Europe; stand*
*Firm-footed by the sea, unchanging!*
ALEXANDER PUSHKIN, 1833

A little more than 300 years ago in May 1703, Tsar Peter the Great seized a halberd from a young soldier. On a desolate spot on the north bank of the river Neva he scored a mark into the earth and declared, 'Here will be a city'. A hundred years later his successor Tsar Nicholas I would say to the critic and chronicler the Marquis de Custine: 'St Petersburg is Russian but St Petersburg is not Russia'. And that was really the point of this extraordinary city – the creation of absolute monarchy: it was to be as unlike the Russian cities of Moscow, Kiev and Novgorod as possible.

Peter the Great conceived his new capital as an elegant European paradise forged from the swamps and frozen wastes of northern Russia. It was to be the new Amsterdam or the new Venice, and was to act for Russia as a window on the West. Today that window has opened wider again after the fall of communism and the collapse of the Soviet empire. St Petersburg has been described as an epic city. The story of its foundation and construction is something which seems hardly credible. It was named after the apostle St Peter, whose task was to found the universal church. The founders of St Petersburg had almost as great a task: to create a city that would house an enlightened autocracy charged with the transformation of the whole of Russia.

There is something about the megalomaniac achievement of the construction of this city that is almost sublimely indifferent to the lives of mere mortals. Even today the scale of the infinite vistas of the main streets and the repetition of the classical rhythms of the architecture feel daunting. This is the city where communism took hold. Here the revolution began and from here autocratic rulers were imprisoned, exiled and shot in 1917.

As the window opened in the 18th century to the winds of Enlightenment from Europe, the city was designed by architects and artists trained and experienced in other lands. Peter had travelled a great deal in Europe, and he appreciated the calm efficiency of Amsterdam set around its canals. He wanted his churches to look Italian; his architects had learnt their skills in Rome and Paris. The dark shadows of the ultra-Orthodox world were to be banished and light allowed into the gloomiest corners of the Russian soul.

How was the miracle achieved, considering the harsh climate and the reluctance of so many to adapt to their enforced move to the new capital? It was built with ruthless brutality, and without serfdom it could never have happened. Canals were dug by hand, materials transported over the ice and there is no doubt that countless lives were lost. Underlying St Petersburg is always the sense of a city created and surviving against the odds. Its genesis and the climate have made the inhabitants of this city very tough. They survived the siege that lasted 900 days in the Second World War when over a million civilians and half a million soldiers died, blockaded in their own city. The trinity of values imposed by the Romanovs – autocracy, orthodoxy and nationalism – did not altogether encourage a sense of liberty and freedom of expression.

The actual layout of the city – the great avenues like the Nevsky Prospect all terminating at the golden spire of the Admiralty – seems to have been planned for the movement of large numbers of troops, not for the quiet strolling of its citizens. Not for nothing is one of the great open spaces in the city called the Field of Mars – a setting for the great military parades and drills that kept the populace firmly under control. And yet the visitor to St Petersburg who has read the novels of Fyodor Dostoyevsky or the poems of Alexander Pushkin and Anna Akhmatova will sense the undercurrent of cultural and political revolution that is fundamental to the story of the city.

At intervals along Nevsky Prospect are milestones and telegraph-signalling towers that linked the city centre to the ring of palaces that surround it. The Romanov rulers enjoyed St Petersburg, but perhaps they felt safer and more expansive at Peterhof or Pavlovsk and out at the Tsar's Village – Tsarskoe Selo, 26 km (16 miles) to the south. It was Catherine the Great in the late 18th century who saw the point of Tsarskoe and encouraged its development as an expanding group of palaces – almost a family compound. Her own choice of the Scottish architect Charles Cameron and English landscape gardeners created an Arcadian paradise that was both grand and informal. It was at Tsarskoe that Nicholas II and his empress Alexandra lived in the Alexander Palace, where they were to be incarcerated under house arrest until in 1917 they and all their children were sent by train to their deaths in Ekaterinburg.

Today it is the astonishing and immaculate restoration of the palaces that is so extraordinary and impressive. National pride after the appalling siege in the Second World War made Stalin and his government determined to restore the Russian people's heritage. The palaces were almost all burnt by the Nazis, and the work of the curators in rescuing the contents and applying their academic skills to accurate restoration has been exceptional.

What always amazes about St Petersburg is the miracle of what has survived after war, siege and communism. The Hermitage remains one of the greatest museums of the world. The collections are so large that six palaces are needed to show only a small part of them and a large proportion is in storage. The city owns the library of Voltaire, the bizarre ethnological and natural history collection of Peter the Great and, in the Academy of Fine Arts, the original architectural models of many of the city's finest buildings. The churches of the city having been converted into swimming pools and gymnasia and, in the case of the Kazan Cathedral, a museum to promote atheism, now resound again to the strong male voices singing the Orthodox liturgy.

Glasnost has arrived in the city that elected to change its name from the hero city of Leningrad back to its founding name of St Petersburg. Gradually prosperity is spreading, but behind the grand façades there is still poverty. The tercentenary celebrations in 2003 may have improved the paint and gilding of the city and Vladimir Putin may have restored the Constantine Palace at Strelna on the Baltic for government use, but there is a great deal to be done to heal the wounds of communism and the corruptions of rampant capitalism. St Petersburg has always fascinated its visitors – a city where the long dark winters and the sufferings of its recent past are relieved by the anticipation of the White Nights in the short summer, when darkness is entirely banished and beauty and optimism reign. This is the city where philosophers, writers and poets met on a weekly basis in the Hermitage to discuss how to preserve the values of civilization throughout the 900-day siege. Many of them perished; but they passed on the flame of civilized life to the city that celebrates its rejuvenation today.

# VIENNA

## and the Habsburg Emperors

MISHA GLENNY

*All in all, it was like a boiling bubble inside a pot made of the durable*
*stuff of buildings, laws, regulations and historical traditions.*
ROBERT MUSIL, 1930

By the beginning of the 18th century, the Ottoman empire had begun the great retreat from Europe that would end in its dissolution some two centuries later. When the tired Turkish caravan left central Hungary for the south, Vienna breathed a huge sigh of relief. Until this point, it was not only on the edge of the Habsburg territories, it was also considered one of the furthest outposts of Christian Europe.

As such, the place bore no relation to the popular image of gaiety and charm or artistic and intellectual daring associated with its golden period in the late 19th and early 20th centuries. Vienna was a fortress town where life was tough. Its role is reflected to this day in the name of some of its most famous streets such as am Graben, the Moat. The Ring, which encircles the city centre, corresponds roughly to the inner defensive walls that kept the Turks at bay during the two great sieges of 1529 and 1683.

With the Turkish threat now in the past, Vienna could develop as the centre of Habsburg power. The heart of imperial might was the Hofburg, the palatial complex which had begun life as a medieval fortress but was expanded over the centuries until it resembled a city within a city. This was the geographical starting point for the impressive expansion of Vienna which took place under the empress Maria Theresa and her son, Joseph II. The 'Theatre by the Castle', the Hofburgtheater, was founded as the first

'German National Theatre', on the Michaeler Platz at the very entrance to the Hofburg. Just over a century later its name contracted to the Burgtheater, as it moved a few hundred yards to its present location on the Karl-Lueger Ring opposite Vienna's city hall. It remains the largest auditorium in the German-speaking world and is still a centre of dramatic excellence.

Between the Ring and the suburbs was a large belt of open parkland that simultaneously accommodated baroque aesthetics and kept invading armies and the *hoi polloi* from the imperial centre. The 18th century saw the development of the Linienwall, the outer ring where the parkland ended, and which corresponds roughly to today's Gürtel or Belt. Its primary function was as a customs barrier for goods entering the city, and as such the ordinary Viennese and traders from outside regarded it with contempt and even loathing.

Just beyond these border posts, the Habsburgs built their magnificent summer residence, Schönbrunn. Modelled on Versailles, Schönbrunn came to symbolize the pomp of the imperial family that would steadily elevate its members to the status of the quasi-divine for some of their citizens – and of the diabolical for others. By the end of the 19th century, a sceptical Henry Wickham Steed, *The Times*'s man in Vienna, observed how 'at the apex of the social structure stood the Emperor, the Imperial family and the Court, so far removed from the common run of mortals and so hedged about by an old Spanish etiquette that they could, on occasion, afford to move as demi-gods among the crowd.'

If the 18th century saw Vienna transformed, the 19th century witnessed the creation of a spectacular mythology, the Empire of Illusions, with the capital at the very centre. The century started badly with Napoleon occupying the city twice. The second occasion, in 1809, followed the Austrian defeat at Deutsch-Wagram just outside Vienna. The large swathes of territory conceded by the Habsburgs and the huge financial indemnity they were forced to pay were severe punishment. But to watch Napoleon turn Schönbrunn into his temporary residence was the ultimate humiliation.

Revenge came six years later with the Congress of Vienna, when the master of statecraft and diplomacy, Prince Metternich, sought to castrate Napoleonic power at the Palais am Ballhausplatz, today the office of the Austrian Chancellor. By this time Mozart and Haydn had already ensured that the locus of European music had shifted from Saxony to Austria. More than a political turning point, the Congress of Vienna was the unmissable social event of the era. For almost a year, Vienna was transformed into the capital of Europe, swamped by heads of state, government, armed forces and civil services.

Metternich believed that the outcome of the Congress would both secure Austria's status as a major power and guarantee the victory of conservatism in Europe. But it was not long before the ungrateful citizens of the empire – Czechs, Ukrainians, Magyars, Ruthenes, Jews, Germans, Serbs, Italians, Croats, Slovenes and more – were muttering that Austria was nothing more than the 'prison of peoples', and in 1848 nationalism administered a huge shock to the smug assumptions of Vienna's court.

If you stroll away from the great gate of the Hofburg up the Herrengasse, with its elegant palaces and ministries, it is hard to imagine the street being anything other than serene. Today the coffee houses, including the magisterial Café Central, are as quiet as libraries. But in February and March 1848, they were alive with excitement as the middle classes and artisans, suffering from a prolonged economic downturn, exchanged the latest news and rumours about the revolution in Paris.

On 13 March, a horde of impassioned students made its way from the old university on Bäckerstrasse, past the cathedral on Stefansplatz before entering the Herrengasse to storm the Lower Austrian government building. Within hours, soldiers were firing into the crowds charging through the inner city's narrow streets. Not far away, workers from the railways and factories in the outlying districts were demolishing the hated tax offices on the Linienwall. As the fighting intensified, the workers broke through the locked gate at Schottentor and poured into the inner city to support the students, artisans and the revolutionary middle class. For two days, Vienna became a battlefield.

Metternich, the despised symbol of reaction, resigned, while the emperor and his court scuttled from the capital to the bracing Alpine air of Innsbruck. Huge ramshackle barricades, symbolizing the revolutionary spirit of liberalism, overshadowed Vienna's baroque façades. This extraordinary transformation of the city lasted for six months before coming to an abrupt end when Count Windischgrätz, a notoriously ruthless commander of the imperial army, pummelled his way into the inner city. Although, like the revolutionaries, he was careful to avoid damaging the centre, the suburbs were less fortunate: the Linienwall was destroyed at several key points.

The conservatives believed they had inflicted a decisive blow upon liberalism in Austria, but just 12 years later, worn down by foreign defeats and economic stagnation, Franz Joseph I finally conceded a modestly liberal constitution, and despite being the symbol of the Habsburgs, Vienna was the triumphant centre of German liberalism for four decades, reflected in an ambitious expansion that would see the Ringstrasse, begun by Franz Joseph, eclipse the emperor's political and architectural supremacy.

The newly confident families of the industrial bourgeoisie forced both the dismantling of the city's military fortifications and its modernization (including a high standard of public health, canalization, street lighting and flood defences). The Parliament, the Rathaus, the University, the Burgtheater and the great museums, that is the grand institutions of the liberal state (not to mention the splendid office and apartment buildings) on the Ring, built in a variety of architectural styles, stood in marked contrast to the baroque façades of the old imperial centre – the Ring was eclipsing the Hofburg.

By the 1890s, Otto Wagner, a gifted architect who had played a part in constructing the aesthetic monumentalism of *Ringstrassestil*, had undergone a fundamental change of heart. As technological developments pressed upon the city's ageing infrastructure and its population outgrew its infrastructural capacity, Wagner laid out his vision of the inner city as a centre and the Ring as the first of several radial semicircles spreading out but connected by arterial roads and the nascent metro system. Influenced by the Secessionists, Wagner laid the urban foundations for the Viennese school of Art Nouveau that embraced most media, creating in the crumbling ruins of the Habsburg empire a glittering burst of artistic endeavour which has rarely been matched. Away from Vienna, the paintings of Gustav Klimt are the most familiar representatives of the Secession. But in the city itself, Wagner's wonderful functional modernism is everywhere. Ironically, the empire's ultimate greatest artistic achievement is one which its supporters regarded at best with contempt and at worst with real loathing. Still, there are few empires whose final spasm, whether understood or not, was as magnificent as Vienna 1900.

# EDINBURGH

## and the Scottish Enlightenment

MAGNUS LINKLATER

*No situation could be more commanding for the head city
of a kingdom; none better chosen for noble prospects.*
ROBERT LOUIS STEVENSON, 1878

The Edinburgh that Stevenson described in 1878, with its broad boulevards, its handsome squares and grand neoclassical houses, was very different from the cramped, insanitary, smoke-enveloped, provincial town that most travellers had encountered in the previous century. Following the Union Treaty of 1707, Edinburgh was no longer home to a parliament, and when that went, it lost its status as the capital city of an independent nation. Its physical condition was just as dilapidated as its politics. Bounded by a stinking marsh on one side and a rabbit-warren of dangerous-looking wynds and closes on the other, it struck many visitors as an urban health hazard. Describing a night spent in Edinburgh in the 1720s, an English surveyor, Edward Burt, remembered principally the smell. He said that he was 'forced to hide my Head between the Sheets; for the Smell of the Filth, thrown out by the Neighbours on the Back-side of the House, came pouring into the Room.' In the narrow streets of the Old Town, waste ran through open gutters, pigs and other animals rooted for food, slops were heaved unceremoniously from tenement windows. It was, in short, a medieval city.

Within 50 years, however, Edinburgh had undergone a remarkable transformation. It had become the centre of an intellectual movement, so influential, so wide-ranging, so eclectic and so widely admired that some spoke of it as the capital of the new Enlightenment. Philosophers, historians and economists such as David Hume, Adam Ferguson, Adam Smith, Lord Kames and William Robertson, as well as architects, including Robert Adam, the geologist James Hutton, and the poets Robert Fergusson and Robert Burns flourished in an atmosphere so open, cosmopolitan, and above all enjoyable, that it became a byword for what a modern, civilized city should be. From lawyers and merchants to clergymen and bankers, its citizens were caught up in the spirit of debate, conducted in the many clubs and societies that sprang up around the city, irrigated by prodigious quantities of claret, brought in through the newly prosperous port of Leith.

That new-found confidence was to translate into a civic renaissance every bit as impressive. In 1763, the four times Lord Provost of Edinburgh, George Drummond, who had helped man the defences at Edinburgh Castle against Bonnie Prince Charlie and his Jacobite troops in 1745, stood looking out across the noisome North Loch which lay as an implacable barrier to the city's expansion. Turning to a young companion, he said: 'You, Mr Somerville, are a young man, and may probably live, though I will not, to see all those fields covered with houses, forming a splendid and magnificent city.' He was right. Within 20 years, the North Loch had been drained, and an architectural competition had been won by an unknown 21-year-old called James Craig, who produced a grand but simple gridiron plan based on three principal streets running east to west, with two great squares at either end.

As it developed, new crescents and circuses were commissioned and built, the jewel in their crown being Charlotte Square, designed by Robert Adam, and possibly the finest manifestation of neoclassical splendour in Europe. The New Town has been described by the historian Christopher Smout as 'the cold, clear and beautiful expression of the rational confidence of the eighteenth-century middle class', but for most modern visitors it is the balance between its neoclassical elegance, and the stark backcloth of the Castle and the Old Town that makes the city unique.

How was all this achieved in so short a span? There is no single answer. Edinburgh's renaissance took place against a background of remarkable economic expansion in the aftermath of the Union, when a nation with a keen instinct for trade began creating wealth on an unprecedented scale. The city's institutions – political, legal and religious – were already in place, as well as an education system which was the most liberal in Europe. The much-maligned Presbyterian Church, far from being a barrier to the great debates that took place in the Age of Reason, was a frequent participant in them. And into this rich and tolerant atmosphere was sprinkled the genius of a few individuals who, for a brief and heady period, set Europe ablaze. For that there is no rational explanation except, perhaps for what one observer described as 'a sort of enchantment'.

# THE AGE OF THE MODERN CITY

By the beginning of the 19th century the industrial revolution was well under way. The world was already changing fast, and is still continuing to do so at an ever-increasing speed. This constant acceleration of progress means, of course, that the final section of our book embraces a far wider field than did any of its predecessors. The world around us can nowadays be expected to show more change in a decade than it used to show in a century: whereas our survey of 'The Ancient World' extended across three millennia, in 'The Age of the Modern City' we are hard put to cover a couple of hundred years.

In these two centuries the capitals of England and France, in particular, were transformed: the London of Charles Dickens was a very different place from the London of Samuel Johnson, and Paris after the ministrations of Napoleon III and Baron Haussmann would have been unrecognizable to Voltaire. Elsewhere in Europe, Berlin – until the days of Frederick the Great just the chief city of one of the small German states – became, thanks to Bismarck, an imperial capital (though Bismarck would have been horrified to see it in the 1920s, as immortalized by Christopher Isherwood). Budapest at much the same time found itself to be, with Vienna, the joint axis of another empire, the Austro–Hungarian. Moscow, after the destruction of the Napoleonic campaign, was forging a new identity, European in some ways perhaps, but also distinctively Russian. Similarly, Barcelona has always maintained both a Catalan and Spanish character.

In the United States, too – which, it should be remembered, in 1800 was only a quarter of a century old – the changes were dramatic, owing in large measure to the vast immigration of Europeans, which increased almost annually as the century pursued its course. Of the five North American cities discussed in the following pages, only Washington, New York and Montreal would have been heard of in Europe before 1800. Chicago owed its meteoric rise to the railways, of which it became the principal junction for the entire continent, and to the development of shipping on the Great Lakes, which made it effectively an oceanic port. Los Angeles, the city of dreams, though much older, was transformed by Hollywood.

Latin America presented a somewhat different picture. The old pre-Columbian civilizations were long since gone – though many superb monuments have fortunately survived. Two of the leading – and very different – South American cities are now Buenos Aires, in Argentina, and, in Brazil, São Paulo, now the largest metropolitan area in South America.

The past two decades have seen the astonishing increase in prosperity – and consequently in economic clout – of Asia, and in particular of India and China. Where India is concerned, our choice fell on New Delhi. A planned city, built for the projection of power, it is not only Sir Edwin Lutyens's inspired symbol in stone of the last chapter of the British Raj, but it also remains, still today, the seat of the government of India.

By the same token, when we turned our attention to China, we might once more have selected Beijing rather than Shanghai; but I believe that anyone who has recently visited Shanghai will agree that it is nothing less than a phenomenon, pulsating with an energy and drive which none of us could have predicted even a quarter of a century ago. Much the same could be said of Singapore, the outstanding example of what has now become a rarity – the self-contained city state. Here again, the whole island throbs with life; the skyscrapers seem to rise as you watch them. Japan has already enjoyed its economic miracle, but to be in Tokyo is to know that one is in one of the great cities of the world.

Finally, Sydney. Once again, booming as it is, it may not be quite a Shanghai; but I doubt whether any of its inhabitants wish it were. If I were banned from London, and if Australia were not quite so far away from Europe, it is in Sydney that I should wish to live.

# MOSCOW

## Capital Without a Court

ORLANDO FIGES

*Moscow may be wild and dissolute but there is no point*
*in trying to change it. For there is a part of Moscow in us all,*
*and no Russian can expunge Moscow.*

F. F. VIGEL, 1864

With the building of St Petersburg (p. 242), Moscow's fortunes declined rapidly. It was reduced to a provincial capital. Pushkin compared Moscow to a faded dowager queen in purple mourning clothes obliged to curtsy before a new king. Until the middle of the 19th century it retained the character of a sleepy hollow. With its little wooden houses and narrow winding lanes, its mansions with their stables and enclosed courtyards, Moscow had a distinct rural feel. It was called 'the big village' – a nickname it has retained to this day. Catherine the Great, who despised it even more than Peter the Great had, thought to clear the lot when the Black Death swept the city in the early 1770s and several thousand houses needed to be burnt. As she saw it, Moscow was 'the seat of sloth' whose vast size encouraged the nobility to live in 'idleness and luxury'. It was the incarnation of the old medieval Russia which the empress aimed to sweep away. Plans were drawn up to rebuild the city in the European image of St Petersburg. The architects Bazhenov and Kazakov persuaded her to replace the greater part of the medieval Kremlin with new classical structures. Some demolition did take place. But the project was postponed for lack of cash.

After 1812 the centre of the city was finally rebuilt in the European style. The fires sparked by Napoleon's invasion had cleared space for the expansive principles of classicism. Red Square was opened up by removing the old trading stalls that had given it the feeling of an enclosed market rather than an open public space. Three new avenues were laid out in a fan shape from the square. Twisting little lanes were flattened to make room for broad straight lines. Theatre Square, the first of several planned ensembles, with the Bolshoi Theatre at its centre, was completed in 1824, followed by the Boulevard and Garden Rings (still today the city's main ring roads) and the Alexander Gardens, laid out by the Kremlin's western walls. Private money poured into the building of the city, which became a standard of the national revival after 1812, and it was not long before the central avenues were lined by graceful mansions and Palladian palaces.

Yet in all this frenzy of construction there was never slavish imitation of the West. Moscow always mixed the European with its own distinctive style. Classical façades were softened by the use of warm pastel colours, large round bulky forms and Russian ornament. The overall effect was to radiate an easy-going charm that was entirely absent from the cold austerity and imperial grandeur of St Petersburg. Petersburg's style was dictated by the court and by European fashion; Moscow's was set more by the provinces. But oriental customs and colours and motifs were also to be seen on Moscow's streets. Writing in the 1830s, the Marquis de Custine thought that Moscow's cupolas were 'like oriental domes that transport you to Delhi, while donjon-keeps and turrets bring you back to Europe at the time of the crusades'.

Moscow's semi-oriental nature was given full expression in the so-called neo-Byzantine style of architecture that dominated its reconstruction in the 1830s and 1840s. The term was fostered by Nicholas I and his ideologists to signal Russia's cultural turning away from the West. The Tsar sympathized with a Slavophile world-view that associated Russia with the eastern traditions of Byzantium. Churches, such as the Cathedral of Christ the Saviour, built near the Kremlin as a monument to the war against Napoleon of 1812, combined elements of the Greek-Byzantine and medieval Russian styles, with its onion domes and bell-towers, its tent roofs and *kokoshnik* pediments. With buildings such as this, Moscow's rebirth was soon mythologized as a national renaissance, a conscious rejection of the European culture of St Petersburg in favour of a return to the ancient native traditions of Muscovy.

Moscow was a place of down-to-earth pursuits. With the rise of Petersburg, it became the centre of the good life for the nobility. Pushkin said that it attracted 'rascals and eccentrics' – independent noblemen who 'shunned the court and lived without a care, devoting all their passions to harmless scandal-mongering and hospitality'. Moscow was a capital without a court – and without a court, its grandees gave themselves up to sensual amusement. It was famous for its epicureans, its restaurants and clubs, its sumptuous balls and lavish entertainments – in sum for everything that Petersburg was not. Petersburgers despised Moscow for its sinful idleness. 'Moscow is an abyss of hedonistic pleasure', wrote the poet Nikolai Turgenev. 'All its people do is eat, drink, sleep, go to parties and play cards – and all at the expense of the suffering of their serfs.' Yet no one could deny its Russian character.

In the 19th century Moscow grew into a great commercial centre. Within 60 years the peaceful nest of gentlefolk Napoleon had found was transformed into a bustling metropolis of shops and offices, theatres and museums, with sprawling industrial suburbs that every year drew hordes of immigrants. By 1900, Moscow, with New York, was the fastest-growing city in the world. Of its population of 1 million, three-quarters had been born elsewhere.

The railways held the key to Moscow's growth. All the major lines converged on the city, the geographic centre between east and west, the agricultural south and the new industrial regions of the north. The railways opened new markets for Moscow's trade and linked its industries with provincial sources of labour and raw materials. Thousands of commuters came in every day by train to Moscow. The cheap boarding houses in the areas around the city's nine main stations were always overcrowded with casual labourers from the countryside. Moscow, then, emerged as the metropolis of capitalist Russia – a position it still occupies today. Provincial towns such as Tver, Kaluga and Riazan, all brought into Moscow's orbit by the train, fell into decay as Moscow's manufacturers sent their goods by rail directly to the local rural markets, and shoppers came themselves to buy in Moscow, where prices were cheaper than in district towns. Moscow's rise meant the demise of its own provincial satellites, which spelt ruin for those gentry farmers, like the Raevskys in Chekhov's *The Cherry Orchard*, who depended on these towns as consumers of their grain.

Moscow had a growing 'middle' class of merchants and a group of fabulously wealthy merchant dynasties – many far richer than the aristocracy – that had branched out from their family businesses to form vast conglomerates. The Riabushinskys added glass and paper, publishing and banking, and later motor cars, to their textile factories in Moscow; the Mamontovs had an immense empire of railways and iron foundries that financed their investments in the arts (Savva Mamontov's private opera, established in 1885, fostered many of the artistic talents of the Ballets Russes); the Morozovs were factory owners and financiers who, with the Stanislavskys put their money into the foundation of the Moscow Art Theatre (where most of Chekhov's plays were premiered); and the Tretiakovs were textile barons and philanthropists – Pavel Tretiakov collected Russian art and left it all to Moscow as the Tretiakov Museum, the largest collection of its kind, with an astonishing 1,276 easel paintings, in 1892.

On a trip to Moscow in the 1900s, the founder of the Ballets Russes, Sergei Diaghilev, remarked that in the visual arts Moscow produced everything worth looking at. Moscow was the centre of the avant-garde – Petersburg 'a city of artistic gossiping, academic professors and Friday watercolour classes'. Coming as it did from the arch-patriot of Petrine culture, this was a remarkable acknowledgment. But Moscow really was the place to be in 1900, when the Russian avant-garde first burst onto the scene. Along with Paris, Berlin and Milan, it became a major centre in the world of art, and its extraordinary collection of avant-garde artists were as much influenced by trends in Europe as they were by Moscow's heritage. Its progressive politics, its relaxed atmosphere, its noisy modern ways and new technologies – there was so much in Moscow's cultural milieu to inspire artists in experimental forms. The poet Mikhail Kuzmin, another patriot of Petersburg, noted on a trip to Moscow at this time:

> *The loud Moscow accent, the peculiar words, the way they clicked their heels as they walked along, the Tatar cheekbones and eyes, the moustaches twirled upwards, the shocking neckties, brightly coloured waistcoats and jackets, the sheer bravado and implacability of their ideas and judgments – all this made me think: new people have come forward.*

# PARIS

## in the Time of Napoleon III and Baron Haussmann

PHILIP MANSEL

*Everything is so truly regal, so large, so grand, so comprehensive, it*
*makes me jealous that our great country and particularly our great*
*metropolis should have nothing of the same kind to show!*
QUEEN VICTORIA, 22 AUGUST 1855

Like Versailles under Louis XIV, Paris under Napoleon III dominated Europe
both by arms and by the arts. Memories of Napoleon I's victories helped his
nephew to be elected President of the Republic in 1848, to seize absolute
power through a military coup on 2 December 1851 and to be proclaimed
Emperor of the French a year later. Napoleon III soon won victories of
his own. The French army helped defeat Russia in the Crimean War and
Austria in the war of 1859 in Italy. France became a world power, acquiring
new territory in Europe (by the annexation of Nice and Savoy), Africa and
Asia, sending armies as far as Mexico and China, providing the drive and
finance for the Suez Canal. Paris under Napoleon III, in keeping with the
emperor's military origins, was a city of soldiers, parading, playing music,
setting off for war.

Even more than conquest, however, culture made all eyes turn to Paris.
Paris contained the best cafés, theatres and – with the Louvre – the finest
museum in the world. London, Vienna and Rome could not compete. In
a way almost forgotten today, the French language helped the hegemony
of Paris. French was the second, or first, language of the educated elites
of Europe, from Lisbon to St Petersburg. By 1850 France was also making
new conquests in Latin America and the Levant. Visitors from as far away

as Brazil, Egypt and Russia enjoyed Paris more than other cities, since they already spoke French.

Paris was also the capital of science, medicine and literature. Young Turks were told: 'If you have not been to Paris, you have not come into the world.' Since it was stimulating and welcoming, and they spoke the language, foreign writers such as Heinrich Heine, Ivan Turgenev and Alessandro Manzoni chose to live in Paris.

To Paris's military and cultural supremacy, Napoleon III added the excitement of a court and an urban revolution. He needed a court to bolster his regime and help the luxury trades of Paris. His wife, the beautiful Spanish-born Empress Eugénie, could entertain better than any other crowned head – although she had an unfortunate tendency to intervene in politics and to dress as Marie Antoinette at balls. In addition to the state balls in winter during the carnival season, she held private balls in the spring for a few hundred guests, known as *'les lundis de l'impératrice'*. Every woman invited had to wear a new dress. The empress's dress-maker, Charles Worth, dominated world fashion: in its size and luxury his shop on the Rue de la Paix resembled an embassy.

Ministers also had a duty to entertain. Even its enemies admired the regime's pursuit of pleasure – though they sometimes complained that the court was *'le rendez-vous des grisettes'* and Paris 'the foreigners' brothel'. So many monarchs visited Paris under Napoleon III that the writer Prosper Mérimée, a childhood friend of the empress who spent weeks at her court, wrote that they were treating the Tuileries palace as a railway station.

The emperor himself was one of the most complex figures in his capital. Although he had received a European education during his exile from France after 1815 – it was said that he spoke French with a Swiss accent – he was also a nationalist. Confident that he was a 'man of destiny', he was determined to redraw the map of Paris. In September 1848 he had returned with plans for new streets, drawn on a map in different colours, in order to improve the appearance, salubrity and accessibility of the capital. In 1853 he gave a copy of his map to his new prefect Baron Haussmann. Helped by an economic boom, emperor and prefect worked together, with little government restraint, to make Paris what Haussmann called 'the imperial Rome of our time'.

Paris became a city of demolition men, stonemasons and carpenters, as well as soldiers. Between 1852 and 1869 20,000 houses (including many historic *hôtels* and churches) were demolished, and 43,000 new ones built. Some 70 schools, 15 churches and synagogues and 9 barracks were constructed. The filthy alleys around the Halles and the Ile de la Cité were replaced by straight new boulevards (de Sebastopol, Saint-Germain, the Rue de Rennes, the Avenue de l'Opéra and many others) designed, it was said, with the subtlety and intelligence of a cannonball. They had a political as well as an architectural purpose. They were intended to bring not only light and traffic into the heart of the city, but also troops in case of riots.

Napoleon III also completed the wing linking the Louvre and his principal residence, the Tuileries palace, along the Rue de Rivoli. A statue of Napoleon III as protector of the arts can still be seen above an entrance to the Louvre. Paris had become a model of modernity. Hence the admiring phrases, coined at this time, calling new capitals such as Buenos Aires or Bucharest, the Paris of Latin America or the Balkans.

The emperor's foreign policy, however, was less successful than his town planning. The Universal Exhibition of 1867 was the apogee of Paris's role as a world city. The Ottoman sultan came with his sons, as did the emperors of Russia and Austria, and the king of Prussia, who asked for a map of the city to help him replan Berlin. But on the day the prizes were given out, 19 June, news arrived of the execution of the emperor's protégé, the emperor Maximilian of Mexico.

Prematurely aged, in July 1870 Napoleon III was pushed into war with Prussia and the other German states. The actual cause was trivial – simply the wording of a Prussian prince's renunciation of his candidature for the throne of Spain; but public opinion and the emperor's desire for prestige made it inevitable. Paris boulevards echoed with cries of *Au Rhin! A Berlin!* Mérimée wrote that this war was more popular than all the emperor's previous wars. Anyone advocating peace would have been murdered on the spot.

The Second Empire had risen by the sword, and it fell by the sword. The main French army was soon defeated; on 2 September Napoleon III was taken prisoner. On a radiant autumn day, 4 September, Paris switched roles, yet again, from court city to revolutionary capital. Shouting *A bas l'Empire! Vive la République!* crowds surged into the Corps Legislatif and threatened the Tuileries palace. The Republic was proclaimed at the Hôtel de Ville. The empress fled from the Tuileries down the corridors of the Louvre and hailed a cab, arriving in England a few days later with the help of her American dentist Dr Evans.

The war led to the siege of Paris, the burning of the Tuileries and the Hôtel de Ville, and the proclamation of the German empire in the Galérie des Glaces of Versailles – at once a tribute to, and the end of, the hegemony of Paris. Europe had exchanged a mistress for a master – a catastrophe from which it took a hundred years to recover. And yet, the Second Empire had cast so great a spell that for many years thereafter visitors to Paris, without the Tuileries palace and the emperor's guards outside it, felt that it was no longer a capital.

# LONDON

## from Queen Victoria to 'Big Bang'

A. N. WILSON

*The first shock of a great earthquake had just, at that period,
rent the whole neighbourhood to its centre. Traces of its course
were visible on every side. Houses were knocked down;
streets broken through and stopped ... Everywhere were bridges
that led nowhere; thoroughfares that were wholly impassable.*

CHARLES DICKENS, 1848

You cannot exaggerate the Victorian hatred of the past – but especially of their recent past, in the 18th and late 17th centuries. They had absolutely no concept of Georgian London, or Wren's London, as being part of their heritage, as we would – having seen London attacked and all but destroyed by the combined efforts of the Luftwaffe and the 'plansters', as John Betjeman called them. Far more Wren churches were removed by Victorian speculative builders than by German air-raids. In 1881, *The Builder* announced, 'the church has to give way to commerce, vested interests in narrow streets are bought out and wide thoroughfares flanked by new structures to take their place'.

St Dionis Backchurch, St Benet Gracechurch, St Bartholomew Exchange (that was a medieval church, not a Wren one), St George Botolph Lane, were all pulled down to make the roads wider or to make space for a bank. When St Benet Gracechurch was demolished in 1867, the *Illustrated London News* rejoiced at the disappearance of its 'ugly spire'. A similar confidence in their own times allowed the Victorians to pull down St Olave Old Jewry, St Michael Wood Street, St Michael Bassishaw, St Matthew Friday Street,

St Martin's Outwich – the list goes on. If we had walked about Victorian London we should have had muddy boots, since it was a permanent building site, attempting to accommodate its exploding population and its exploding prosperity.

The greatest cause of demolition, in the early and middle Victorian periods, was the expansion of the railways. Between 1859 and 1867 some 37,000 people were moved out of central London in clearances caused by railway construction. The Midland Railway alone had to raze a whole slum, Agar Town, to make St Pancras Station, which is now, as the gateway to the European rail networks, reborn as one of the great monuments of Victorian engineering and Victorian neo-Gothic aesthetic, but which in the modernist period of taste was itself under threat as an 'eyesore'.

The railway stations of London are among the greatest of the Victorian achievements – Paddington, Victoria, Charing Cross, Cannon Street, Ludgate Hill. With the railway also came that great Victorian phenomenon, the hotel. If you were of gentle birth and came up to London for the Season, then you would have taken a house and brought your own staff. For the socially mobile Victorians there were many reasons to come up to town – business, primarily. But you might come up for entertainment at one of the new theatres built in such profusion near Piccadilly Circus. Or you might be drawn by self-improvement: a chance, for example, to see the new museums of the Albertopolis of South Kensington – the area where, in the wake of, and with money raised by, the Great Exhibition of 1851, the Victoria and Albert Museum, the Science Museum and the Natural History Museum were constructed through the inspiration and to the memory of Queen Victoria's polymathic young husband. If you came to London for these reasons, and/or for a little discreet adultery, the hotel was there to accommodate you. By 1888, Charles Eyre Pascoe could write, 'London has become a pleasure lounge for the idlers of the globe. Americans, French, Germans, Indians, Colonials and persons of leisure and wealth from all parts of the world flock to the capital city during the season.'

Because London has always run to extremes, the contrast between rich and poor, obvious in any of the great Victorian cities, would have been overwhelming for any of those visitors who chose to leave the spacious and well-planted parks, the new-built department stores, the theatres and hotels of the West End, and head east. Henry Mayhew, one of the founders of *Punch*, wrote a series of articles on those who strove to make a living: he entitled it *London Labour and the London Poor*. The journalist and popular dramatist who wrote 'It is Christmas Day in the Workhouse', George R. Sims, did for the late Victorian poor what Mayhew had done for their Dickensian predecessors. He gave them a voice, not merely in his comic monologues but also in his articles in such papers as the *Sunday Dispatch* – 'The Theatre of Life', 'How the Poor Live' and 'Horrible London'.

It *was* horrible, and stinking and unhealthy. When Victoria came to the throne, the river Thames was an open sewer and the excrement of 1,945,000 people (according to the 1841 census) found its way into the waters. Disraeli described the Thames as 'a Stygian pool reeking with ineffable and unbearable horror'. Water-borne disease was rife. Cholera epidemics killed 18,000 Londoners in 1849 and 20,000 in 1865. The heroes who brought this deplorable state of things to an end included the man who was inadvertently responsible for the Thames becoming even filthier: Edwin Chadwick, who, in order to purge the streets, had advocated flushing the drains into the river. Chadwick did not initially know what was demonstrated by Dr John Snow, that cholera was a water-borne disease.

The Victorians, with all their resourcefulness, did something about their own plight. Chadwick's successors on the Metropolitan Commission of Sewers enlisted great engineers – notably Joseph Bazalgette – to build a network of huge brick tunnel sewers and an efficient pumping system, which survived two wars in which Londoners were aerially bombarded. But the London poor continued very poor indeed until after the Second World War; and until the rebuilding after the Blitz, London was in essence the same city that the Victorians had left.

Two enormous changes happened in the second half of the 20th century. One was the introduction of brutalist modernist architecture, both for offices and for housing. The skyline was wrecked. St Paul's Cathedral, which had loomed above the city, a reassuring mother's breast, until the Second World War, was now dwarfed by nondescript new building.

The second big change was in ethnic mixing. London had been the first port of call for immigrants since the Roman emperor Claudius pitched camp on the Thames in AD 43. But the Huguenots, Jews and others who had settled had done so in tiny numbers in proportion to the indigenous population. By 1981 there were 945,000 Londoners of Afro-Caribbean or Asian descent – 20 per cent of the population of Inner London. The period of the immigrations coincided – and it was a pure coincidence – with London ceasing to be one of Britain's great manufacturing cities.

In the midst of this period of transformation, which saw the greatest changes in the city's 2,000 or so years of history, another revolution occurred. The Square Mile, the City of London, had always been the financial hub of the nation, but there were many other places in Britain bubbling with money – Manchester, Birmingham, Glasgow, for example. During Margaret Thatcher's monetarist revolution, while manufacturing industry in the provinces declined, London became even richer. On 27 October 1986 the London Stock Market was deregulated. 'Big Bang' made the London Stock Market the International Stock Exchange and for the next 20 years, London, an exclusively British city no longer, became one of the great financial centres of the world.

The rest of Britain limped along. In many places the decline was catastrophic. London had a new life. It had become, in a way, a city-state that financed and carried Britain but had little in common with it.

Like Victorian London, 21st-century London is architecturally merciless to its past, commercially successful and bursting at its seams. The life of the poor remains wretched, and some people living in Tower Hamlets in the east of the city, for example, are among the poorest in Britain. Yet for all the wretchedness of young drug addicts sleeping in cold doorways and disconsolate Asian hill-people huddling in the urine-marinaded concrete blocks of Dagenham and Tooting, London retains its cruel vitality. Its almost boundless capacity to resurrect and reinvent itself – seen after the plagues of the 17th century, the Fire of 1666, the destruction wrought by the Victorian railways and the German air force – has shown itself once again, in the time of Big Bang and mass immigration.

The Monument built after the Fire of 1666 traduced the Roman Catholics and accused them – quite falsely – of having started the Fire. The 21st-century Muslim Londoners live with comparable slanders, and create some of them – fears which remind us of the old days of Popish Plots. But it would be a pessimist who did not see in modern London one of the most extraordinary and successful examples of collective civic genius in the world.

# BUDAPEST

## Bridging the Danube

MISHA GLENNY

*If you come from Paris to Budapest you think you are in Moscow.*
*But if you go from Moscow to Budapest you think you are in Paris.*
GYÖRGY LIGETI, 1987

Budapest is a quintessentially 19th-century city, not least because until 1873 it did not exist. The final fusing of Buda and Obuda on the western side of the Danube with the town of Pest on the opposite bank was the culmination of an arduous process, but one which would have been even harder without the ingenuity of a Scottish engineer who built the first bridge over the Danube. The Chain Bridge still stands as a symbol of 19th-century Hungarian nationalism and the country's determination to assert its separateness within the Austro-Hungarian empire.

Since the early 16th century, Buda and Pest had languished under Ottoman rule. The number of Hungarian speakers dwindled as the Ottomans populated the two towns with people drawn from across the empire. Even when the Habsburgs drove out the Ottomans in 1686, the imperial army virtually obliterated Buda and Pest in the process.

The capital of Austrian Hungary was many hours ride away in Pressburg (now the Slovak capital Bratislava). Hungary's national movement, which had emerged in the first half of the 19th century, had two powerful weapons in its arsenal. The first was its language: one of the few major non-Indo-European languages on the continent, it was incomprehensible to the Slav, Romance and Teutonic speakers who surrounded the Hungarians, contributing hugely to the growth of a separate national consciousness.

The second was the dream of a capital built around the throne of Hungary's medieval monarchs in Buda, which was a predominantly residential area. Stretching out over several hills, it was dominated by the castle, which looks down upon the Danube. But like the Hungarians, the castle had enjoyed a chequered history – it was razed during the siege of 1686 when the Ottomans were pushed out, and took another battering in the great revolutionary year of 1848 as Hungary's liberals and aristocrats tried to force the young Franz Joseph I into major political concessions.

Across the Danube, Pest was the perfect complement to Buda – a thriving market district with small streets and a lively social life. It was the commercial engine of the region and together the two communities represented the soul of Hungary's economic and political existence. The challenge for the national movement was simple – how to join the two together to create a specifically Hungarian metropolis in opposition to the imperial capital, Vienna?

Crossing the Danube from Buda to Pest was a hazardous business. In winter the river often froze and could be easily traversed. In the summer a pontoon bridge was laid, but there were many drawbacks to this system. The bridge blocked river traffic, so it was dismantled and reassembled at different hours of the day. As the water froze or thawed, ice floes made the passage of small boats an uncertain affair.

After many years of lobbying, Istvan Szechenyi, a Hungarian noble who became infected with liberal and national ideas, finally received permission in the 1830s to construct a bridge linking the two. Apart from the countless difficulties in raising capital for the venture, Szechenyi faced one overwhelming problem – Hungarians were no engineers.

So began the story of Hungary's two Clarks: William Tierney Clark, the architect responsible for the original Hammersmith Bridge across the Thames in London, who designed the suspension bridge; and the engineer, Adam Clark, who would become the only Scot to have a square in Budapest named in his honour. Adam Clark brought with him Scottish workers who established a Church and then later a school for young ladies – favoured by the city's large Jewish community. It was to enjoy an illustrious history before being closed by the communists.

Building the bridge was fraught with difficulties. As it neared completion in 1848, revolution broke out in Hungary as the liberals led by Lajos Kossuth attempted to rid the country of the Habsburg monarchy. Vienna was to seek its revenge in 1849 when it reasserted its full control over its Hungarian domain in a period characterized by the brutality of the Austrian commander, General von Haynau. Mercifully, however, the bridge remained intact – although it did come perilously close to being bombed.

And so the two towns were physically linked just at the moment when it seemed that all was lost for the Hungarian national movement. In fact, the victory in 1849 contained the seeds of ultimate defeat for the Habsburgs, and in 1867 Franz Joseph was compelled to grant Hungary a greatly improved status in the empire. Six years later, Buda, Obuda and Pest became Pest-Buda – later inverted to Budapest – and six years after that, the National Assembly approved the construction of the imposing Orszaghaz or Parliament (modelled in part on the Houses of Parliament in London) that stares grandly across the Danube towards the Castle. Henceforth, there was no stopping the builders of Budapest. The city was transformed by the grand boulevards which swing around and across Pest towards the magnificent Eastern railway station. By the time the Habsburg empire collapsed at the end of the First World War, Budapest had become one of Europe's most elegant and exciting capitals.

# MONTREAL

## The Defiance that Made Canada

RORY MACLEAN

*Vive le Québec libre!*
CHARLES DE GAULLE, MONTREAL 1967

Canada was first coveted for its fish and its furs. Cod lured English, French and Spanish fishing smacks to Newfoundland's Grand Banks. Then the European fashion for wide-brimmed felt hats opened the continent's interior, and for more than a century Montreal was the centre of the wildly lucrative fur trade. This in turn encouraged the exploration of much of North America.

In 1534 the Breton seaman Jacques Cartier entered the Gulf of St Lawrence and claimed possession of 'New France' for King Francis I. Samuel de Champlain followed him, pushing a thousand kilometres up river in the service of fur-trading monopolies to establish settlements at Quebec and La Place Royale. The latter was a domed island at the confluence of the St Lawrence and Ottawa rivers. By 1642, when the first missionaries arrived on the island 'to convert the savages', the word 'Montreal' had become the general name for this isolated and unknown district.

The energy and faith of the early French *habitants* – a mere 196 intrepid souls in Montreal in 1650 – was remarkable: surviving extreme seclusion and bitter cold, nurturing a savage love for the land. The adventurous *voyageurs* among them canoed as far as the Mississippi, and probably Lake Winnipeg, long before the Virginia colonists had crossed the Alleghenies. Their discoveries laid the basis for the fur trade and gave Britain and France another reason to go to war.

After 1701 Montreal prospered, as the Compagnie des Habitants, the Compagnie d'Occident and – following the French defeat in the Seven Years War (1756–63), when France lost most of its territories in North America – the North West Company paddled further into the *pays d'en haut*. Every spring with the break up of the ice, the great birch-bark *canots de maître* raced from Montreal to the western tip of Lake Superior to rendezvous with the beaver-laden *canots du nord* from the interior. Millions of pelts were shipped to Europe from Montreal's fine natural harbour. When the Nor'Westers eventually amalgamated with their arch-rival the Hudson's Bay Company they created a fur-trade empire – based in nearby Lachine – which encompassed a vast territory, spanning the continent from Labrador in the east to Nootka Sound in the far north.

The people of the province of Québec set themselves apart from British latecomers. In 1775 when American Revolutionaries briefly captured Montreal, they tried to turn that defiance to their advantage. Benjamin Franklin himself moved to the city, attempting to convince its residents to join the Revolutionary cause (he failed, escaping just ahead of the returning British forces). But Franklin's failure did not reflect any acceptance of the status quo. The enduring differences between French and English settlers made Montreal a centre for agitation and open violence, casting the die for the nation of 'two solitudes'.

When the felt hat fell out of fashion in Europe, British entrepreneurs – most of them Scots – redirected the search towards other natural resources. Steam navigation assured Montreal's ascendancy over Quebec City, as did the opening of the Lachine Canal, which linked the Great Lakes to the Atlantic. The economy boomed and by the 1890s over half the nation's wealth was owned by a hundred anglophone Montrealers. They built so many banks, universities, hospitals and places of worship that Mark Twain observed that theirs was a city where a boy could not throw a stone without breaking a church window. Montreal became the largest city in British North America and the undisputed economic and cultural centre of Canada. Throughout those years the French were excluded from the boardrooms and clubs of the elite.

Québécois resentment endured into the 20th century. The francophone majority feared the loss of their culture and language. In response to their concerns, wide-ranging social and political changes shifted the balance of power. Many Anglo mansions – symbols of English privilege – were razed by the long-serving mayor Jean Drapeau. The 1970 October Crisis, triggered by kidnappings by the *Front de libération du Québec* and the election of the separatist political party, the *Parti Québécois*, deepened linguistic divisions. Within only a few years Toronto had become Canada's largest metropolis, stimulated in part by the exodus of Montrealers escaping the uncertain political climate.

Yet Montreal remains the only Canadian city where English and French have always coexisted, the collision of cultures defining its vibrant, independent spirit. Paradoxically, that defiance has assured Canada's own distinct identity. At no time was this more true than during the hard, isolated, historic years of the fur trade. Without the whim of European fashion, and the ardent, adventurous *voyageurs*, Canada would almost certainly have been absorbed into the United States.

# WASHINGTON DC

## Ideology Made Visible

SIMON SCHAMA

*It is sometimes called the City of Magnificent Distances, but it might with greater propriety be termed the City of Magnificent Intentions.*
CHARLES DICKENS, 1842

Are any city avenues more inhumanly broad than those of Washington DC? They are not really boulevards at all, these immense expanses at the centre of the institutional city. The engineer who drew up the first plan, Pierre Charles L'Enfant, prescribed avenues not less than 160 ft wide. That's what you get when you hire a French classicist: someone who doesn't notice that the place gets broiling in the summer and that narrower, tree-shaded streets might have been a kinder idea and encouraged some ease of street life.

Washington does have its true neighbourhoods where the beehive hums – Adams Morgan, for instance, or around U Street where African-American Washington comes alive near the Duke Ellington Theater. And the sense of a vast bureaucratic-punditocratic savannah is broken by Washington's bosky places, the parks and gardens laid out after 1900. But most of the young people who frequent them aren't there because of the romance of the city but because they need to live in an idea made architecturally visible: the idea of democratic government. That is at the beating heart of the place, the pulse of its body politic; but that same notion is also why 'Washington' in some quarters of American life is not so much an actual city as a byword for remote bureaucracy and self-importance.

Its problems and its many genuine splendours are both products of the original split personality of the American Republic. For Thomas

Jefferson, the true America lay in the myriad farms where the yeomen citizens were building a truly new society and polity. George Washington was more ambiguous. He hated empty pomp, but it mattered deeply to him that the United States should hold its head high in a world of vainglorious monarchies; that a capital city should be the visible expression of the superiority of a democratic constitution. Washington the city is in fact very much the vision of Washington the man.

The very characteristics of which many complain – the artificiality of the city, its detachment from anything resembling a self-sustaining commercial economy – were precisely what George Washington sought. Metropolitan wens like London and Paris were, he and Jefferson thought, the breeding places of idle fashion, vice and corruption. But a nation founded on the majesty of the people needed a city custom-designed as a residence for democratic institutions. The relationship between the independent legislature and the governing executive, for example, ought to be made visible by their mile-long separation at opposite ends of Pennsylvania Avenue; the two, however, always in each other's sight.

The very notion of a federal city originally came from necessity as much as ideology. Because of the moving theatre of peril during the Revolutionary War, the itinerant Congress had shifted no fewer than eight times. To have a single, defensible site was obviously essential to the integrity and efficiency of government. A decision was taken almost as soon as the war was over in 1783, but a protracted debate then ensued as to where that site should be. Ultimately it was George Washington himself who decided the matter: his firm preference was for a city on the Potomac.

For a detailed plan he turned in 1790 to L'Enfant, a French military engineer. Not surprisingly, L'Enfant's vision was formed by classical French urbanism: central *grandes places* from which broad radial avenues would extend, lined with the edifices of government. The Potomac and its Great Falls outside the city would provide a series of watercourses, so that Washington would resemble not just classical Paris but a little of Venice and Rome for good measure. Though L'Enfant ran foul of Congress, and a much modified plan was executed by the less grandiose Andrew Ellicott, much of his essential vision survived: the emblematic separation and connection of executive and legislature – the eminence of the latter, the gentility of the former – and those immense avenues. It was the other great Enlightenment mind, that of Jefferson, who made sure that both L'Enfant and Ellicott were supplied with plans of all the great European cities.

By 1800, when Jefferson moved into the President's House, there were just 3,000 inhabitants of the federal district, of whom a third were slaves and free blacks. The House itself already had its little colonnade and modest park and its East Room planned for state receptions, but most of it was unfinished. The Capitol was being built by the Boston architect Charles Bulfinch, who provided for the nation's legislature a dome flanked by two pavilions. The ensemble when built was grand by American standards, but as the Republic grew, not ceremonious enough, resembling, as one wag put it, 'an upside down sugar bowl between two tea chests'.

After the British burnt Washington in the summer of 1814, it took time for rebuilding to begin, and for decades Washington was jeered at as a place of 'streets without buildings', while its neighbour, the busy port of Georgetown, had 'buildings without streets'. The climate was more brutal than the First President had imagined: mosquitoes devoured the population in the fetid summer; and rather than the graceful torrents and limpid basins that L'Enfant had envisioned, the water supply was foul and prone to delivering cholera to the city. Hogs wandered the Mall, and rickety taverns and disorderly houses contributed to the city's peculiar mix of solemnity and squalor, the emblems of liberty and the reality of slavery.

And then in the early 1850s, there arrived in town one of the most prodigious and still relatively unknown American heroes, the army engineer who as quartermaster general of the Union would win the Civil War for the North quite as decisively as Lincoln, Grant and Sherman. Montgomery Meigs was first and foremost a builder. His spectacular brick Romanesque temple-like structure for the Pensions Building (now the National Building Museum) is one of the most extraordinary architectural achievements in the country. It was he who created the aqueduct that carried, at last, a decent supply of fresh water (also imperative for the extinguishing of fires) from the Great Falls of the Potomac to Washington. It was he too who presided over the rebuilding of the Capitol, replacing the Bulfinch sugar bowl with something taken from Brunelleschi, Michelangelo and Wren, but with an iron fabric just in case the British decided to set fire to it again.

Modern Washington, though, came into being around the turn of the century. It was then that the old federal government buildings were replaced by the masonry-faced piles that house the Treasury, the Department of State and the rest. Every so often there were wonderful, eccentric exceptions like the Gothic Smithsonian 'castle', the result of a legacy offered (and accepted by Congress in 1846) by the English scientist James Smithson as an 'establishment for the increase of knowledge among men'. The Corcoran Gallery, designed by one of the city's mavericks, James Renwick, and the Freer were home to spectacular collections (it was only in the 1930s that the immense National Gallery was finally established). And the great memorial monuments that bookend the axis of the Mall – of Washington, Lincoln and Jefferson – were a long time coming. Washington's great obelisk and the Lincoln Memorial, with its seated figure sculpted by Daniel Chester French, were both creations of the second half of the 19th century. In the 20th, Maya Lin's profoundly eloquent Vietnam memorial, a basalt wall in a cut trench that rises and falls with the body count and the grief of the century, transcends its own materials to become a place of true communing.

It is these, with the Capitol and the White House, that make Washington the control room of the nation. But for the ordinary residents of the city, when the cherry blossom is doing its shameless thing and the streets of Adams Morgan are warming to the kids on the block, it's entirely possible to see Washington as not just DC, not just ideology made visible, but as an American community, and a good one at that.

# BARCELONA

## The Catalan Phoenix

FELIPE FERNANDEZ-ARMESTO

*Barcelona has seen more fighting on the barricades
than any other city in the world.*
KARL MARX AND FRIEDRICH ENGELS, 1864

'If I was you,' said an English yokel to a passing motorist who stopped to ask for directions, 'I wouldn't start from here.' Hemmed to landward by mountains, restricted to seaward by unserviceable currents, Barcelona seems the wrong place to start creating a great city. Yet the place has defied its own geography. In the Middle Ages, Barcelona became the centre of a maritime empire without possessing a natural harbour: ships too big to beach stood out in the roads and communicated with the port by boat. In modern times, industrialization made Barcelona rich, without natural resources and without direct access to major markets.

Barcelona has also defied its own history, transcending structural difficulties, rebounding from repeated disasters. The industrial take-off in the 19th century happened amid civil disorders that in any other city would have made long-term investment unthinkable. The foundations of manufacturing prosperity were laid when Barcelona was a conquered and occupied victim of a long period of war and defeat. From the 1820s Spain's struggles between absolutists and constitutionalists, together with the loss of American markets as a result of revolutions in the colonies, threatened the city's economy. In 1834, the first of a series of cholera outbreaks killed liberals and constitutionalists alike. In 1842–43, General Espartero bombarded Barcelona republicans into submission.

RIGHT Vienna c. 1890: a photograph from the tower of the inner city's town hall shows the new Burgtheater, one of the great public buildings erected along the Ringstrasse between 1874 and 1888.

BELOW A section from Robert Barker's panorama of Edinburgh from Calton Hill, 1792. Struck by the all-round view here, he invented and trademarked the idea of reproducing it inside a rotunda, where visitors could admire the illusion of reality. It became a popular form of entertainment in the 19th century and is said to have heralded the advent of cinema.

ABOVE The people of Paris carry on their daily lives as the city is rebuilt around them in Adolf Menzel's painting of 1869. Buildings are being demolished on the left, while in the centre is one of the new, more elaborate stone-faced blocks.

BELOW Parade of the Home Guard, Budapest, on the Bridge of Chains, 1840s. Built in 1839–49 by an Englishman and a Scot, both called Clark, it was the first permanent bridge to link old Buda with newer Pest across the Danube. Destroyed in 1945, it has been rebuilt in replica.

ABOVE The National Mall in Washington throngs with crowds come to witness Barack Obama's swearing in as the 44th President of the United States on Inauguration Day, 20 January 2009.

BELOW In New Delhi, Herbert Baker's Parliament House rises above the cliff-like walls of red sandstone, standing proud on either side of the approach to the Rashtrapati Bhavan. Today these buildings are the city's government offices.

ABOVE  Chicago, c. 1909: a tangle of horse-drawn vehicles and streetcars in the Loop shows the rapidly growing city's need for Daniel Burnham's *Plan of Chicago*, published on 4 July 1909. He aimed to improve transport, impose order and create a 'well-ordered and convenient city'.

OPPOSITE ABOVE  The Berlin Wall passes under the shadow of the Brandenburg Gate. With the fall of the Wall and the collapse of Communism, Germany was finally free from totalitarian rule – fascist or communist – and had the opportunity to embrace liberal democracy again.

OPPOSITE BELOW  Downtown Los Angeles, serviced by a triumphant network of freeways, had by the 21st century achieved an iconic skyline suggestive of its status as the second most populous city in the United States and a capital of the Pacific Rim. A paradigm of urban self-invention, the Great Gatsby of American cities, Los Angeles was now fully what it had always known itself to be, a global metropolis.

OPPOSITE Singapore – from commercial entrepôt to corporate capital and city-state. The high-rise towers of the financial district now mock the heavily restored and Wedgwood-shaded shophouses of Tanjong Pagar.

ABOVE Ellis Island, just off the tip of Manhattan, was the gateway to the United States until 1954. Over 40 per cent of Americans are estimated to have an ancestor who passed through this island.

LEFT Sydney Opera House under construction, 1966: a series of landmark projects showed the power of architecture to enhance and transform a city.

OVERLEAF Mount Fuji looms behind the Tokyo skyline. Kenzo Tange's Metropolitan Government Office dominates to the right; at the left edge is the Park Hyatt Hotel, where much of the film Lost in Translation takes place.

Yet the Renaixença – the rebirth of Catalan arts and letters – flowered, while great factories multiplied, breathing, according to the poet Zorrilla, 'fire and smoke like the volcanoes'. The building of the Eixample – the rational grid of modern streets in which the ancient city is encased – followed a bloody insurrection by Luddite workers and bourgeois radicals in 1854. In the late 19th century, Barcelona became 'the city of bombs', riven with industrial unrest and stalked by incendiary anarchists, while the bourgeoisie led the gilded life described in Narcís Oller's novel, *La febre d'or* (*Gold Fever*) in a brittle world of numerous companies with huge capital and few, nervy subscribers. The Spanish–American War of 1898–1902 and the drain and strain of wars in Morocco exacerbated tensions, while great architects such as Gaudí and Puig i Cadafalch adorned the city with modernist marvels of 'creative bad taste'. Ramon Casas and Santiago Rusiñol painted genre scenes in bourgeois interiors and savage versions of violence in the streets. In 1909 smouldering social resentment ignited the flames of 'Tragic Week', when anarchist rioters burnt 80 buildings – mostly church schools and churches. Joan Maragall, the leading poet writing in Catalan, trod the embers in his 'Nova Oda a Barcelona', celebrating 'the spirit of Catalonia' embodied in a city that was 'ours, warts and all'. The spires of Gaudí's Sagrada Família soared in defiance. Even the extinction of Catalan institutions under General Primo de Rivera's dictatorship in 1924 did nothing to interrupt a brilliant era in the arts or a period of dynamic growth for the city. By the time Barcelona hosted the International Exposition of 1929, the population exceeded a million. The 'Catalan Phoenix' seemed irrepressible.

The plumage of the Phoenix was unique. Builders of factories archly quoted or brazenly trumped churches, castles, artists' studios, and, above all, palaces, which, said a newspaper of 1855, 'house no pharaohs, no orgies, but are a means of life for hundreds of families' – the first palaces of production in a history of palaces of consumption. Architects searching for a 'national' style scattered the city with Mauresque fantasies and angular Gothic allusions to the mythic Middle Ages, when princes of the House of

Barcelona ruled much of the western Mediterranean and enclaves as far afield as Greece. The architects Rogent, Domènech and Puig i Cadafalch pierced battlemented skylines with fairytale towers. By the early years of the 20th century, however, the prevailing style was modernist. Gaudí took his aversion to the straight line to wild extremes in the Casa Batlló, where interior ceilings swirl like ridged whipped cream, or the Casa Milá, designed for an 'unbuilt' look, an illusion of organic growth, decoratively barnacled, like a *cathédrale engloutie* eroded into curves. By 1929, when modernism no longer looked modern, progressives visiting the Expo goggled at the effortless rationalism of Mies van de Rohe's German Pavilion and clamoured to demolish the Barcelona of the previous generation. Rationalists competed to replace slums with clean-lined, starkly functional, plate-glass utopias. Few of their projects came to fulfilment – some workers' housing, the Antituberculosis Clinic and a jewellers' shop on the Gran Via, where utopia is accessible beyond a threshold crossed only by the rich.

Barcelona was so preponderant in Catalonia – economically, demographically, culturally and politically – that it was easy for the city to identify with the region. With Spain, however, Barcelona's relationship was equivocal. The city was the nearest thing Spain had to a city-state or medieval Italian-style commune. In the 16th century, ambassadors represented Barcelona at Spain's royal court. After 1640, when Catalan rebels repudiated Spanish rule, 'the trouble with Barcelona', as a distinguished Spanish statesman once said, off the record, 'is that once or twice a century we have to send an army from Castile to conquer it'. In the 19th century, Barcelona's wealth and sophistication made it a classic 'second city'. It vied with Madrid for the admiration of the world, and civic rivalry became confused with contending levels of nationalism, as Madrid embodied centralization within a Spanish state, while Barcelona was the hearthstone of Catalanist sentiments. In the hundred years before Catalan autonomy was secured in the constitution of 1978, rebels had proclaimed it unilaterally four times from the balcony of the old parliament building in Barcelona.

F.C. Barcelona lent a whole new meaning to the term 'political football'. 'Long live Catalonia!' cried Frank Rijkaard, the Dutch manager, when his team won the European Champions League in 2006.

The last 'conquest' came in 1939 in the course of the Spanish Civil War, which – *inter alia* – pitched centralists against devolutionists and separatists. Into the bomb-blasted city Franco's troops marched with the cry, 'Spain has arrived!' They were only the spearhead. Over the next 40 years Spain arrived in a potentially more transmutative form, as hundreds of thousands of immigrants poured into the city from poorer parts of the country, swelling its official population to 1.75 million by 1981, with over 3 million in the metropolitan area, and threatening Barcelona's Catalan character with immersion. Yet when the dictator died in 1975, the President of the Catalan government-in-exile returned to the cheers of natives and immigrants alike.

Since then, Barcelona's working class has voted consistently for Catalan autonomy and broadly Catalanist cultural policies. The Spanish-speaking proletariat has been extraordinarily amenable to the sensibilities of the Catalan-speaking bourgeoisie. Embourgeoisement has been more or less commensurate with Catalanization. In the European Union, Barcelona has acquired a role as Spain's European face and bridgehead, and a possible future beyond Spain as the metropolis of the western Mediterranean. The city's essential character, detected by a Castilian visitor 500 years ago, seems intact in Barcelona today: 'Oh, God of grace, I now behold a city securely placed ... and her citizens, triumphant despite their dearth of natural resources, and her people possessed of all worldly prosperity, thanks to their own efforts alone.'

# NEW DELHI

## Symbol in Stone

JANE RIDLEY

*The Rome of Hindostan lies on a scorched and windswept plain,
historied with tumbledown memorials of the Mahommedan
conquerors. Across this plain glitters now an eighth, an English,
Delhi, a vision of domes and towers, pink and cream against
the morning blue and the new green trees below.*

ROBERT BYRON, 1931

New Delhi is a planned city, an administrative capital like Washington DC (p. 276) or Canberra. It was built as the seat of government, and designed for the projection of power. But the new city rose upon the ruins of former settlements and was situated close to Old Delhi, one of the oldest continually occupied sites in the world. Its location in the Gangetic plains, on the banks of the Yamuna river, places it at the head of the trade routes from northwest India, well positioned to resist the waves of invaders who swept into India from the north. Seven cities have risen and fallen on this site. New Delhi is the eighth.

In the 1640s, the Mughal emperor Shah Jahan had moved the capital of his empire from Agra (p. 188) to Delhi, creating the city of Shahjahanabad, usually known as Old Delhi. Shah Jahan's Red Fort was the grandest and most gorgeous of Mughal palaces. The notables of Old Delhi lived in splendid *havelis*, town houses arranged around an internal courtyard. As Mughal power crumbled in the 18th century, Old Delhi sank into decay. In 1739, the city was sacked and 150,000 people massacred by the Persian Nadir Shah, who looted the Peacock Throne from the Red Fort. By the end of the century Delhi was ruined and impoverished. Some of the bitterest fighting of the Indian Rebellion of 1857 took place there. Delhi was captured by the British after fierce fighting; the atrocities which followed are still remembered by Indians today.

New Delhi was founded as the capital of India at the moment when the British empire was at the height of its power and prestige. In 1911, King George V visited India and held a durbar at Delhi, at which he announced the transfer of the capital of British India from Calcutta and laid the foundation stone of the new city. The new capital was intended to express the splendour and might of the Raj. It was also a response to the Indian nationalists, whose growing influence challenged British authority.

The decision to move the capital from Calcutta to Delhi was prompted by political problems in Bengal. The Viceroy, Lord Curzon, had partitioned Bengal in 1905, provoking bitter cries of betrayal from the Hindu Bengalis, who saw this as a deliberate attempt to undermine their power by creating a Muslim-dominated province of East Bengal. Terrorist activity meant that Calcutta was no longer considered a safe place for the capital to be. In 1911 the British reversed the partition, thus appeasing the Hindus. To please the Muslims they moved the capital to Delhi, the historic capital of the Muslim Mughal empire.

The new city was largely the creation of one architect: Edwin Lutyens. His collaborator and rival, Herbert Baker, has now been largely forgotten, as have the other members of the architects' team. Lutyens was invited to decide a site for the new foundation, and he received the commission to build New Delhi in 1913. The work took some 20 years.

New Delhi's plan is designed to impress. The focus of the city is a ridge or acropolis, known as Raisina Hill. Here stand the proud prestige buildings – the Viceroy's House, now the Rashtrapati Bhavan, and the Secretariats or government offices. They are approached by a long, straight processional avenue, the Rajpath, formerly King's Way. This central part of the city recalls the boulevards and vistas of Haussmann's Paris (p. 261).

Wide avenues march through the triumphal arch of India Gate, and converge on a grand climax – the dome of the Rashtrapati Bhavan. But New Delhi's classical triumphalism is tempered by space and shade. The avenues of the Indian capital are lined not by hot masonry, but by trees, grass and canals.

Superimposed upon the rectangular grid of the classical city is a geometrical system composed of two overlapping hexagons. Filling the leafy, shady streets are bungalows, each with its own grass compound – an oasis of cool and space in the parched, overpopulated metropolis. New Delhi is India's version of an English Edwardian garden city.

The long processional avenue from the All-India Memorial arch (India Gate) starts with a vista of the gleaming dome of the Rashtrapati Bhavan, but half-way up the dome vanishes, only to reappear further on. This optical trick was not intended by Lutyens. It was imposed upon him by Herbert Baker, his collaborator, who needed to raise the gradient in order to place the Secretariat buildings, which he had designed, on the acropolis. The gradient caused a furious quarrel between the two architects which Lutyens lost, and ever afterwards he referred to it as his Bakerloo.

The architectural style of the new city, especially of the Viceroy's House, was fiercely disputed. For political reasons, the Viceroy, Lord Hardinge, demanded the style known as Indo-Saracenic, a synthesis of western Gothic and Indian Muslim pointed arches. Lutyens stubbornly resisted. More than anything he abhorred the pointed arch. His first drawings show a palace inspired by Rome. Pressed to orientalize his design, he developed an architectural language which combines western planning and geometry with Indian elements, such as the Buddhist dome or *stupa* and the long horizontals, wide projecting cornice or *chujjah* and rooftop pavilions or *chattris* of Mughal architecture. The rhubarb-red and creamy sandstone was quarried from Dholpar, which had supplied the stone for the Mughals centuries before.

The building was acclaimed by critics as an architectural masterpiece. That this fairy-tale palace, bigger than the palace of Versailles, was commissioned and built by British imperialists during the last days of the Raj was an extraordinary feat. It owed much to Lutyens's determination to resist the bureaucrats' attempts to cut costs. He saw the new city as a permanent legacy for India.

There is an ancient Persian prophecy that whoever builds a new city in Delhi is bound to lose it. To guard against this, Lutyens adorned his columns with his design for what he called the Delhi Order – stone bells, which can never ring to toll the end of a dynasty.

Two days after the Viceroy's House was formally inaugurated in 1931, Mahatma Gandhi, the leader of the Indian Congress Party, visited the Viceroy, Lord Irwin. His presence on the steps of the Viceroy's House angered the British at the time, but Gandhi was the man of the future. In 1947, Lord Mountbatten, the last Viceroy of British India, negotiated the transfer of power and signed the Partition of India in the Viceroy's House. Within 16 years of the completion of the new city, the British had lost their Indian empire.

Throughout its history Delhi has been repeatedly destroyed, but it has always risen again. William Dalrymple, the modern historian, called it the City of Djinns, after the fable of the spirits who love Delhi so much that they cannot bear to see it deserted. After each cycle of violence and destruction the city appears in a new incarnation, so that in Delhi, the different ages of the city lie 'suspended side by side as in aspic'.

The Partition brought violence to Delhi once more. Most of the Muslim population fled the city, but they were more than replaced by the influx of Hindus and Sikhs from West Punjab and Sindh. New Delhi was not destroyed, nor was it left to go to ruin. On the contrary, it became the capital of the new republic. The Viceroy's House became the Rashtrapati Bhavan, the President's House, and power shifted down the hill, to the parliament building designed by Herbert Baker. The British civil servants went home, and Lutyens's bungalows were occupied by the officials of independent India.

The years after Independence, when a socialist republic was grafted on to the remains of the Raj, were a golden age for Delhi. The water was clean, the power worked and the streets of the mosquito-free city were sprinkled daily to keep down the dust. New Delhi was integrated into Old Delhi, functioning as a single city, and to the new elite New Delhi seemed 'like paradise on earth'. The greatest challenge since has been demographic. Delhi is the migrant city of the north, and since 1946 its population has swollen from under 1 million to 12 million, creating acute environmental and social pressures.

# BERLIN

## Dancing on the Edge of a Volcano

RORY MACLEAN

*Berlin was transformed into the Babylon of the world – bars,
amusement parks, honky-tonks sprang up like mushrooms … Even
the Rome of Suetonius had never known such orgies as the balls of
Berlin, where hundreds of men costumed as women and hundreds
of women as men danced under the benevolent eyes of the police.
In the collapse of all values a kind of madness gained hold.*

STEFAN ZWEIG, 1930S

In the 'Golden Twenties' Berlin was the world's most exciting city. Europe's most talented artists, its most flamboyant showmen and its most decadent hedonists were lured to the capital by a strange, sparkling and complex fusion of events. Walter Gropius conceived the Bauhaus, Kurt Weill penned "The Ballad of Mack the Knife' and Christopher Isherwood invented Sally Bowles. George Grosz satirized German society's ills, while Otto Dix portrayed its brutality. At Babelsberg Film Studios, Fritz Lang conjured *Metropolis*, while von Sternberg and Dietrich created *The Blue Angel*. For ten breathless years, the intellectuals and elite of the city danced on the edge of a volcano. When their vision of a new world was rejected by Germans in 1933, the year Hitler became Chancellor, Berlin's exiles carried their new modernity abroad.

Situated in a long plain of marshes that stretches as far as Warsaw, medieval Berlin was an uncultured spot. Christianity did not take root here until the 12th century. Robber barons and the plague besieged the primitive outpost as late as the 15th century. It was the Hohenzollern princes who wrested a capital from the swamps by hard work and determination.

But their obsession with military power also laid the foundations for the bullish force of Prussia, the 'army within a state' which aspired to European domination. In 1871, Berlin became capital of the German empire, or Reich, a grandiose city dominated by pomp, parades and overbearing buildings of immense ugliness.

The outbreak of the First World War initially delighted Berliners. 'Groups of people everywhere, and in addition, soldiers marching out of the city, showered with blossoms as they went. Every face looks happy: We have war!' cheered the actress Tilla Durieux in 1914. But within a year, disillusionment had set in and, by 1918, some 350,000 young Berliners had been killed in action. The ignominy of defeat and the vindictive Versailles Treaty made the returning troops ideal candidates for radicals on both the left and right. Revolution, insurrection and political assassinations characterized the next few desperate years and – along with the wild inflation of 1922/23 – completed the destruction of the old imperial system.

Then, in 1924, the American-led Dawes Plan stabilized the German mark, fuelling a bubble of prosperity and stimulating a remarkable cultural flowering that bridged east and west and transformed Berlin into the international capital of modernism. Almost overnight the population boomed, industrial output soared above pre-war levels and Germany became second only to the US in value of world exports. The city pulsated with life and easy money.

Hungry for experimentation, artists from Britain, France, America and Russia were drawn to Berlin, attracted by creative and sexual freedom, as well as by the least repressive censorship laws in Europe. In the painting studios and cabarets, on the drafting tables and film sets, the avant-garde embraced the *Neue Sachlichkeit*, or 'New Objectivity', an art movement that rejected sentimentality and expressionism in favour of dispassionate rationalism and function. New building schemes reflected the belief that technology could help create a new society. Visionary architectural fantasies – the horseshoe-shaped Britz estate, the gracefully curved Shell House, the soaring Karstadt department store in Neukölln – rose above the dark, ubiquitous Wilhelmine *Hinterhöfe* slums. Every night in literally hundreds of revues, young – and not-so-young – women stepped on to the stage, stripped off their clothes and danced.

Heinrich Mann called Berlin of the Twenties 'a city of excitement and hope'. But for all its frenzied, prodigious output, the decade was golden for only a small minority, many of whom were immigrants or outsiders. The city's great cultural renaissance in fact touched few of its residents, for all its visibility. For them, life on the factory floor and in the workshops remained hard and unchanging. Like Berlin's growing band of white-collar workers – most of whom came from poor backgrounds – they wanted hit songs, escapist American-style musicals and *völkisch* culture. The intellectual elite did not provide them with popular entertainment, nor address Weimar's desperate political problems. On the contrary, many artists, among them Bertolt Brecht and Kurt Tucholsky, went to great lengths to undermine the Republic which had facilitated their success.

In 1926, a young Joseph Goebbels – another of many ambitious outsiders – arrived at the Anhalter Bahnhof, determined to 'take the city' for an aspirant Hitler. At the time, there were fewer than 200 Nazi Party members in Berlin, while the communists boasted a membership of 250,000. In an audacious move Goebbels cast the communists – along with the Jews – as the scapegoats for society's ills. He orchestrated hundreds of street battles against them to gain publicity. He took advantage of the resurgent financial crisis and, after 1929, of mass unemployment (one-third of the city's labour force was out of work towards the end of the Great Depression). His Machiavellian mastery of propaganda exploited the suffering of Berlin's majority; like most Germans they embraced the Nazis' radical solutions in response. In the month following Hitler's accession to power over 50,000 Berliners joined the Party.

The minority left-wing avant-garde was easily destroyed in 1933. 'Un-German' books were banned by the new Reich Centre for the

Advancement of German Literature. Artists with 'cosmopolitan and Bolshevist symptoms' were branded as degenerate. Lang, Dietrich, Weill, Einstein, Mies van der Rohe and thousands of others left – or had already left – the country. With the Nazis' arrogant triumph, Hitler proposed rebuilding Berlin as 'Germania', the new capital of the populist, nationalistic 'Thousand-Year Reich'. 'In ten years no one will recognize the city', he boasted. By 1945 his words came true: 70 per cent of the city lay in ruins.

At the end of the Second World War the victorious Allies divided Berlin into four sectors. Stalin's secret intention was to draw Berlin – and then the whole of Germany – into the communist orbit. In 1948 he blockaded the city as a means of driving the Americans out of Europe, but the Allies retaliated by launching the Berlin Airlift to sustain its freedom. The Soviets were forced to back down, the Cold War turned hot and Berlin became the 'Flashpoint of the World'. Nuclear war was expected to erupt there at any time. In 1961 the Soviets built a heinous 156-km (97-mile) long barrier – 'die Mauer' – to encircle the Western sectors completely. Over the 28 years of its existence as many as 200 people were shot trying to flee across it from East to West Berlin. In 1989, with the loosening of Soviet hegemony, the Wall was opened and – within a few years – almost all traces of it removed, some of it chipped away by souvenir hunters. Until then, few could have imagined that today Berlin would once again be the vibrant capital of a united and prosperous German state.

# CHICAGO

## The Engine of America

JAMES CUNO

*Here hungry men, raw from the shops and fields, idyls and romances
in their minds, builded them an empire crying glory in the mud.*
THEODORE DREISER, 1914

Chicago was all but destroyed in a day, on 8–9 October 1871. A fire began
in a barn on a ramshackle street on the city's southwest side. A hot, dry
wind whipped the flames furiously and within minutes a thousand framed
buildings were destroyed; on average the fire burnt 26 ha (65 acres) an
hour. In the end, it consumed some 9 sq. km (3.5 sq. miles) in the centre
of the city, destroying more than 18,000 structures and causing damage to
property worth $7.5 million. One-third of the 300,000 residents lost their
homes, and at least 300 died.

The city had been a city for only three decades by the time it was
destroyed. It had been settled two centuries earlier, when French traders
favoured its portage as a means of linking the waters and forests of the north
with the Mississippi river. In 1673, Louis Jolliet proposed that a canal be
built between Lake Michigan and what was then called the St Louis river
(now the Illinois river).

The city's location held the key to its future. By 1850, it had become
the centre of nearly all lines of transportation entering the American
West. Plank roads were laid, steamboats and schooners swarmed on the
lake, and the earliest trains brought wheat in from the plains. By 1856, 58
passenger and 38 freight trains arrived and departed daily. And as many as
300 vessels arrived in a single 12-hour period, bringing a total of 3 million

tons of produce in 1869. Timber and grain were the principal commodities; and then of course animals: some 75,000 hogs, 20,000 cattle and 20,000 sheep in pens on a single square mile of the Union Stock Yards. All of this booming economic activity brought spectacular increases in population, from 30,000 in 1850 to 300,000 in 1870.

Such rapid growth engendered social hardship. More than 200,000 residents, many of them new arrivals from abroad, lived in squalor in modest pine cottages amid tanneries, packing houses and distilleries on small lots without paved streets or sewers. It was here, in Patrick O'Leary's barn, that the fire started that evening in 1871. All the city's development and promise were suddenly destroyed. Or so it seemed. But with destruction came the chance for reconstruction.

The rebirth of Chicago coincided with dramatic advances in building, in foundation engineering, metal-frame construction, lighting, steam-heating and fireproofing, as well as faster, safer elevators. Soaring land values demanded the intensive use of downtown lots. And innovative architects were attracted to Chicago from across the country. Among the leading firms working in the city were Adler and Sullivan, Burnham and Root, and Holabird and Roche, and all were attracted to the possibilities of the tall building. The distinction of being the 'tallest' building passed quickly from one to the next: 10 storeys in 1882, 13 in 1885, 16 in 1890 and 21 in 1890. Such dramatic vertical development was matched by rampant lateral growth and annexation. In 1889, residents of burgeoning neighbouring communities voted to join Chicago, quadrupling the city's territory in one day and increasing its population to 1 million. Despite the devastating fire, the city that had only 50 residents in 1830 grew into a fully fledged metropolis within 50 years.

The ambitions of the city's leaders were not satisfied, however. Following the success of London's Great Exhibition of 1851, Paris's in 1867 and 1889, and Philadelphia's in 1876, Chicago offered itself up as the site for an exhibition in 1892 marking the 400th anniversary of Columbus's arrival in the New World. In this Chicago had to compete with other cities, including New York and Washington DC, and it was up to the US Congress to decide.

Driven by competition, Chicago's capitalists raised pledges of more than $15 million, including more than $5 million in stock certificates from ordinary citizens. To the horror of the New York bankers, the city was awarded the exposition, which opened in 1893. The World's Columbian Exposition was an extraordinary success, attracting more than 750,000 visitors a day, and inspired the construction of the city's first elevated railway line to carry them from the many new downtown hotels.

Now the omnivorous city was in desperate need of a plan. So in 1906, the Merchants' and Commercial clubs commissioned Daniel Burnham, the lead architect and planner of the Exposition, to draw up a *Plan of Chicago*. Extraordinary in sweep, the plan would reserve the lakefront for public recreation, create an efficient system of broad streets and arterials for better crosstown travel, concentrate railway facilities in outlying areas and demonstrate how public spaces could be made magnificent and uplifting for civic life. By 1910, the planned city boasted a transportation system, elevated and surface, that delivered over three-quarters of a million people a day into Chicago's commercial centre – its famed Loop. To relieve the burden on and above ground, the city dug miles of tunnels beneath the city, with more than 100 locomotives carrying goods and workers throughout the business district.

There were, however, social problems attendant on such success. It was suggested that if all of Chicago were as densely populated as its average slum (270 persons per acre) the city's population would be 32 million. The social reformer Jane Addams believed that the best way to address the problem was to create a semi-public space, the settlement house, offering a variety of services and instruction. Her most famous and enduring contribution was Hull House, which ultimately expanded to cover a city block and provided child care, physical education, a bank, a library, and instruction in the arts and domestic science. Its success spawned numerous similar facilities across the city, helping thousands of people in desperate need in a metropolis that was famously described by the novelist Upton Sinclair as *The Jungle*.

The stock market collapse of 1929 hit the city hard. By 1933, employment in the city's industry had been cut in half, foreclosures quintupled in four years and homeless people were left to fend for themselves. And yet, once again, the city picked itself up by means of a World's Fair – the Century of Progress – in 1933–34. It was a demonstration of the capacity of the city's leaders to envision the future. Designed by the modernist architect Joseph Urban, the lakefront festival of the newest architecture, technology and entertainment was a voice for the return of prosperity through science, industry and business. In all, over 39 million people attended the fair. Its success, however, was at best a psychological boost. The city was still in dire straits in the midst of the Great Depression, which was relieved only by the Second World War and greater economic development during the 1950s and 1960s.

Once again, the city's location and visionary understanding of the role of transportation in securing its future served it well. Improvements to the St Lawrence Seaway increased water traffic through the Great Lakes to Chicago. The city's second airport, O'Hare, expanded significantly, providing the region with an air-traffic hub equal in national importance to the city's railway connections.

As after the fire, the resurgent economy attracted leading architects who produced innovative buildings, led by the recently arrived Mies van der Rohe; he had emigrated from Germany in 1937 to head the School of Architecture at the Armour Institute of Technology (now the Illinois Institute of Technology – IIT). One of his projects was a new campus for the Institute, the most famous building of which is the School of Architecture (Crown Hall), and a series of apartment buildings that set a new standard for high-rise construction internationally.

Chicago has long been a literary city, producing authors from Theodore Dreiser and Upton Sinclair to Saul Bellow and David Mamet. Nelson Algren, in *Chicago, City on the Make*, wrote of the city: 'It's always been an artist's town ... a writer's town and it's always been a fighter's town.' Among the other arts most associated with Chicago, in addition to the visual arts, theatre and classical music – all of which have international standing – are the African-American music of gospel, blues and jazz. African-Americans have long been a substantial presence in Chicago. The first black newspaper was established in 1878; in 1895 Ida B. Wells moved to Chicago, married the newspaper's publisher, continued her anti-lynching campaign, joined the Women's Suffrage and Settlement House movements and played a key role in founding the National Association for the Advancement of Colored People (NAACP). Steady migration from the US South increased Chicago's black population, but despite their early arrival and great numbers, African-American integration in the city was not easy. By 1910, 78 per cent of black Chicagoans lived on the city's South Side, which soon became – and still is – the centre of the city's African-American residential and cultural life.

Gospel music, which combines evangelical Christian texts with early American folk and spiritual melodies, is said to have begun in Chicago under the direction of Thomas Dorsey (not to be confused with the band leader Tommy Dorsey) in the 1920s. Dorsey had come north from a small town in the state of Georgia in the early years of the Great Migration of blacks from the South. In 1931, he and other musicians formed the first gospel choir in Chicago at Ebenezer Baptist Church. He would go on to direct the gospel choir at Pilgrim Baptist Church for 60 years and set the standard for gospel music nationwide.

The blues emerged alongside gospel music. Among the early, great Chicago blues men was Willie Dixon, a Mississippi-born singer/guitarist who moved to Chicago in 1936 and became the model for blues musicians who would flourish with the establishment of Chess Records. Founded in 1950 by two Polish immigrants, this recording company captured the particularly urban sound of Chicago blues and would influence every rock-and-roll pioneer from Chuck Berry to the Rolling Stones. Chicago jazz prospered with new arrivals from New Orleans and the Mississippi Delta, including King Oliver and Louis Armstrong, establishing the city as a jazz centre. Especially during the radical 1960s, it became a hub of experimentation led by the innovative Art Ensemble of Chicago.

Chicago's culture and history are marked by its immigrants; and, despite all the problems of integrating different waves over the years, the city is proud of its polyglot history. From the early arrivals of the Irish (by 1860 Chicago was the fourth largest Irish city in America), Germans (in 1900, one out of every four Chicagoans had either been born in Germany or had a parent born there), and Italians (73,960 by 1930) until today, when the city boasts 26 ethnic groups of at least 25,000 members each and more than 100 languages spoken in its public schools, Chicago has thrived on new arrivals, diversity and innovation. Those qualities, together with its geographical location and the entrepreneurship, civic spirit and philanthropy of its social, commercial and civic leaders has made Chicago the most important city in the US after New York.

With the decline of so many US Midwestern cities, Chicago's success over the years stands out all the more. Chicago was one of four international cities, with Madrid, Rio de Janeiro and Tokyo, selected as finalists in the competition for the 2016 Olympics. If successful on another occasion, Chicago will once again, as in 1893 and 1933, demonstrate its capacity to host the world and exploit that fact to its great and enduring advantage. A city of famously broad shoulders, Chicago has always inspired big dreamers and those willing to start afresh.

# LOS ANGELES

## The Culture of the Imagination

KEVIN STARR

*Los Angeles, give me some of you! Los Angeles, come to me*
*the way I came to you, my feet over your streets, you pretty town*
*I loved you so much, you sad flower in the sand, you pretty town.*
JOHN FANTE, 1939

Since its foundation by Spain in September 1781 at the bend of the Los
Angeles river near the ancient Native American village of Yang-na, the city
of Los Angeles has acquired a variety of identities and designations. The
Spanish founders of the pueblo called it *El Pueblo de Nuestra Señora La Reina*
*de Los Angeles de Portiuncula* in honour of the Virgin Mary, the angels and a
chapel in Italy where St Francis of Assisi, founder of the Franciscan order
responsible for the evangelization of Alta California, exercised his ministry
in the early 13th century. This formal designation, however beautiful, quite
naturally attracted briefer sobriquets. Almost immediately, the Spanish, who
governed Alta California until 1822, followed by the Republic of Mexico,
which held jurisdiction until 1846, shortened the name to Los Angeles.

In the early American era, which began in 1846 when the United
States navy and army seized California during the Mexican War, Los Angeles
emerged as the violent epicentre of the southern California cattle industry,
whose cowboys – particularly the El Monte gang – had a habit of shooting
up the place on a more or less regular basis. Then came respectability,
starting in the 1860s and 1870s, with the construction of business blocks,
the Pico House (1870) – the finest hotel in the American Southwest – and
St Vibiana's Cathedral (1876), which still stands.

Despite the settling down and physical improvement of the city through the 1870s, including a railroad connection to San Francisco by 1876, and the influx of middle-class health seekers in the 1880s and 1890s when a direct railroad connection was established with the Midwest and East, Los Angeles remained a relatively small town – barely 100,000 residents by 1900 – in comparison with the city of San Francisco to the north, a maritime colony and instant metropolis that by 1870 had become the 10th largest city in the United States. Indeed, by the end of the first decade of the 20th century, nearly 60 per cent of the total population of California was living in the San Francisco Bay area.

All that, however, was destined to change in the course of the 20th century. Like F. Scott Fitzgerald's Great Gatsby, Los Angeles reinvented itself in this era. Being 96 km (60 miles) inland, Los Angeles had no port; and so, starting in 1899, with federal funds, it dynamited Dead Man's Island and other obstructions and created for itself a deep-water port at Wilmington-San Pedro, which it annexed in 1909. Located on a semi-arid plain, with a water-table seriously depleted by 19th-century usage, Los Angeles had little fresh water; and so, between 1907 and 1913, under the guidance of its engineer William Mulholland, the city built an aqueduct to bring the water of the Owens river to the city.

Using this water as leverage, Los Angeles began to metropolitanize itself by the annexation of local townships. Hollywood had already been annexed in 1910. It was followed in 1915 by the San Fernando valley, adding 435 sq. km (168 sq. miles) to the city. The resort city of Venice on the shores of Santa Monica Bay was annexed in 1925, followed by Watts in 1926. All in all, there were more than 300 annexations, bringing the total area of the city to 943 sq. km (364 sq. miles) by 1920 (and 1,205 sq. km/465 sq. miles by 1970), transforming Los Angeles into a city-state, complete with its own port and agricultural zone.

In the early years of the 20th century, Los Angeles made the transition from overgrown town to city and regional capital. Thanks to the invention of the electric streetcar in the 1880s, the city spread out across its plain, with the Big Red Cars of the Pacific Electric Railway and the Yellow Cars of Los Angeles Railway moving west to Santa Monica and the sea, northwest into the San Fernando valley, south to Wilmington-San Pedro, northeast to Pasadena. Following the pathways of Native American trails that had become American cattle trails in the frontier era, these inter-urban streetcar lines would soon be transformed into streets and boulevards when the automobile, starting in the 1920s, began to compete with the inter-urban electrics as a primary mode of transportation.

In 1909, the film director David Wark Griffith brought his Biograph Players out to Mission San Gabriel to film *Ramon*. Cecil B. DeMille arrived in the city in 1913, took a lease out on a barn at Vine and Selma, and filmed *The Squaw Man*. By the 1920s a network of studios were producing films enjoyed by millions around the world and, in the process, projecting an image of the city and its hinterlands to an admiring population, many of whom decided to move west. A population boom – energized by movie imagery, by a growing tourist culture centred in a number of first-rate hotels, by the search by snow-bound Midwesterners for sunshine and health, by surplus populations no longer needed in the agricultural Midwest, and, of equal importance, by the sheer exuberance of the 1910s and 1920s – brought more than 1 million people into Los Angeles and another 2 million into its hinterlands in the first three decades of the 20th century.

Thus was created 1930s Los Angeles, which is to say, art deco Los Angeles, extending westwards to Santa Monica on the sea via Wilshire and Sunset boulevards. The Miracle Mile on Wilshire helped define Beverly Hills – so recently fields of lima beans, now an epicentre of luxurious living, focused around the famed Beverly Hills Hotel and its Polo Lounge. Running along the base of the Santa Monica mountains, Sunset Boulevard passed through Hollywood before reaching Bel-Air and the newly established UCLA campus and Pacific Palisades overlooking the ocean. English actor Charles Laughton and his wife Elsa Lanchester lived on the Palisades, where they were frequently visited by Bertolt Brecht. Another German émigré, Thomas Mann, also had a home nearby, on San Remo Drive, and was putting the finishing touches to his tetralogy *Joseph and His Brothers*. He was also starting to meditate a novel, *Doctor Faustus*, at which Arnold Schoenberg, also a German émigré, who was teaching at UCLA, was to take great offence.

Mann himself, Igor Stravinsky, Man Ray, Otto Preminger, Franz Werfel, Hedy Lamarr, Aldous Huxley, Christopher Isherwood, and all the other émigrés, were transforming Los Angeles, internationalizing it, during the Golden Age of the Hollywood studio. An oil executive by the name of Raymond Chandler, meanwhile, was beginning a career in fiction that would send his protagonist, private detective Philip Marlowe, into the mean and dark places of the city to uncover its secrets, or to drive by night down its neon-lit boulevards – Wilshire, Sunset, Venice, Pico, Sepulveda, Santa Monica – that seemed never to end, just like Los Angeles never seemed to end either, but to go on forever into an indefinite future.

The Los Angeles of the 1920s was the Great Gatsby of American cities, a figment of its own imagination. The Los Angeles of the 1930s was the George Gershwin of American cities, for George Gershwin was here, he and his brother Ira, playing with the Los Angeles Philharmonic at the Hollywood Bowl and writing those gorgeous late last songs for Sam Goldwyn's *Follies of* 1937: 'Love Walked In', 'Embraceable You', 'Love Is Here To Stay'. You can still experience this Los Angeles – so crisp, so modern, so debonair – in the beautiful homes by Richard Neutra and Rudolph Schindler on the Westside, or the Ovitz Building in the downtown, or in the neon signs along the major boulevards: celestial fires of green, gold, ruby red, electric blue, up and down along the Wilshire Corridor, up through Hollywood and out along Sunset Boulevard running east and west.

Driving down these neon corridors by night, writers such as James M. Cain, Horace McCoy, John O'Hara, F. Scott Fitzgerald, Nathanael West, William Faulkner, Christopher Isherwood, Budd Schulberg and Raymond

Chandler felt themselves in the presence, as Fitzgerald put it, of a vast and meretricious beauty: a city in the borderlands of fact and fantasy, dream and desire, corruption and innocence. For Raymond Chandler especially, the neon-lit hotels, apartment houses, stores, bars, restaurants and theatres of Los Angeles offered by night a landscape literally electric with subliminal power. 'The lights were wonderful,' noted Philip Marlowe, driving through the city in Chandler's novel *The Little Sister*. 'There ought to be a monument to the man who invented neon lights fifteen stories high ... there's a boy who really made something out of nothing.'

During the Second World War, Los Angeles had a new role, thanks to an aviation industry that had already been established there by such pioneers as Donald Douglas, the Lockheed Brothers and Jack Northrop, together with the endless supply of electricity now being brought in from Boulder Dam on the Colorado river. Millions of service- men and women took their training in the region or passed through the City of Angels en route to the Pacific, spending time, if possible, at the Hollywood Canteen on Sunset Boulevard or the many bars and bistros of the city. When the war was over and they were released from service, veterans remembered the city with pleasure and returned there, boosting further growth.

Now ensued an epic of freeway construction and further metropolitanization. To police the city, Chief William Parker refashioned the Los Angeles Police Department into an up-to-date praetorian guard, efficient but also, increasingly, the dominant public entity in the city, celebrated each week on national television on *Dragnet*, which opened with a long shot of City Hall and unforgettable theme music. In 1958, the Dodgers baseball team moved from Brooklyn and Los Angeles became, officially, a Big League town. An impressive Music Center and Museum of Art were constructed in the early 1960s.

By the mid-1960s, Los Angeles, so recently the City of Folks from the Midwest, had become a much more varied place. To its Anglo, Mexican, and Asian mix was added a significant African-American presence – there from the beginning (indeed there from September 1781 in the Afro-Latino founders of the city), but augmented in great numbers during the war by African-American workers coming west for employment in the shipyards. The reform of American immigration law in 1965, adjusting upwards quotas for Asian and other previously restricted immigrants, transformed the city even further. By the millennium, Los Angeles, city and county, was the second largest Mexican city on the planet, the second largest Korean city, and a ranking Iranian, Armenian, Ethiopian, Vietnamese and Native American metropolis. It was also the second most populous city in the United States, the Big Orange to New York's Big Apple.

And here, finally, today Los Angeles has emerged as World City, as Ecumenical City, as Global Polis. This is the Los Angeles of multiple cultures and multiple identities, somehow, mysteriously, holding to a centre, sustaining a common identity amid some 80 languages and the world's great cultures and religions. And still it remains the City of Angels, the City of Dreams, the Great Gatsby of American cities, a figment of its own imagination, the result – in its port, its water system, its freeways, its film studios – of its own fierce will, its determination to declare itself a city, to fill in the surrounding plain with Oz, with Tinsel Town, with America – with the world!

# BUENOS AIRES

## City of Permanent Promise

FELIPE FERNANDEZ-ARMESTO

*Hard to believe Buenos Aires had any beginning.*
*I feel it to be as eternal as air and water.*
JORGE LUIS BORGES, 1929

'The most aristocratic faubourg of the future' – according to a cartoon of 1909 – featured a shack made of flattened oil cans, amid scrub strewn with rubbish, where smoke and effluent rose from a distant factory chimney. In another satire on realtors' patter, a man with seven-league boots took 'one step to the railway station' from a suburban development in the same city.

Buenos Aires was booming. The image of miraculously lengthening strides seemed appropriate. On the eve of the take-off, in the 1870s, when the population was around 200,000, the city seemed to teeter on the edge of civilization. Argentina was an estuary, and the pampa a palatinate. Every view was limitless, along the sea-wide river, across the ocean-wide sea, into the apparently endless plain. A ride away lived people the citizens called savages. In the 1880s, General Roca machine-gunned the Indians of the pampa into submission and the conversion of the wilderness into ranchland and farmland began. From being a net importer of grain, Argentina exported a hundred million bushels by 1899. Refrigeration, introduced in 1883, made possible a similar take-off in beef exports. Argentina's trade almost trebled in the last three decades of the century. Rates of increase in population and production were scarcely equalled anywhere else in the world. By 1914 there were 2.5 million people in Buenos Aires – about a third of the population of the country.

It was a city of immigrants. Nearly half were Italian, nearly a third Spanish, communicating in the Italo-Spanish argot of the dockland. An even more cosmopolitan population thronged the brothels of 'sin city'. In the lurid demi-monde, where tales of white slavery were rife, nearly a fifth of the prostitutes registered in 1899–1901 were subjects of the Russian empire; more than a third came from Europe east of the Rhine. A louche image seemed inescapable in a frontier town suddenly transformed into a gimcrack metropolis. Ambitions were indistinguishable from pretensions. The parvenu swagger for which Argentina became notorious was symbolized in the woodcocks stuffed with foie gras served to 1,200 guests at a senator's golden wedding in 1906, and reached down to the customers of the housing developers and the children in school. According to the oath to the flag introduced in 1909, the Argentine Republic was simply 'the finest country on earth'. Argentinians were encouraged to believe that they would 'know no history without a triumph'.

Buenos Aires never fully emerged from the disappointments that followed. The voices of outrage can be heard in 1930s' tango lyrics – ironic paeans to filth and money sung by Discepolín, for whom 'Jesus was worth the same as the thief', or, in a song by Caledonio Flores, 'the anger of strong men, helpless with hunger.' Writers blamed foreign capitalists and 'beef barons' who supposedly mortgaged the people's food to British imperialists; but the economy recovered from the reversals of the thirties. The real 'lost moment' came after the Second World War. Chasing markets in Europe, the US decreed that Marshall Aid could not be spent on Argentine produce. Average wages fell by 20 per cent from 1948 to 1952. Government policies of industrialization and import-substitution failed. In the 1960s, Argentina was a land of ageing automobiles, where only half the school-age population completed primary school. A mould-growth of shanties enclosed the decayed gentility of Buenos Aires. At Harrods in the calle Florida, steam-lifts, operated by flunkies in threadbare uniforms, swished shoppers between floors of shoddy goods. The city bred a disproportionate share of the world's great novelists, partly because there was little investment for costlier arts, though cinema flickered sporadically and music never fell silent.

Towards the end of the 20th century, democracy, Chicago-economics and globalization restored the city's cosmopolitan vibrancy. The old hubris returned when the government pegged the peso to the US dollar as the economy stuttered. In 2002, the collapse of the banking system provoked riots so severe that security staff at one bank opened fire on the crowd. Buenos Aires remains a city of permanent promise, repeatedly postponed.

# SINGAPORE

## The Lion City

JOHN KEAY

*Our object is not territory but trade, a great commercial emporium*
*and fulcrum whence we may extend our influence politically …*
*what Malta is in the West, that may Singapore become in the East.*
THOMAS STAMFORD RAFFLES, 1819

When on 29 January 1819 Thomas Stamford Raffles first set foot on Singapore island – a statue of him on North Quay Road marks the spot – the chances of the place hosting a nation-state were not promising. Dense rainforest blanketed the entire island; the humidity, a day's sailing from the equator, stood at around 100 per cent, the only habitations were rattan huts, the only trade piracy. But a screen of lesser islands held the promise of a harbour, its frontage on the Malacca Strait being rich in strategic and commercial potential. Indeed, nearly a century earlier, a passing sea-captain had pinpointed the island as 'a proper place for a company to settle a colony on'. With a township hastily conjured from the jungle, shipping and shopping – those mainstays of a free port – could be anticipated. But not even the visionary Raffles foresaw the island's potential as a dynamic city-state.

In Europe the sovereign city-state has become an anachronism: Monaco and the Vatican barely qualify as sovereign; Malta and Gibraltar barely qualify as cities. For the equivalent of ancient Athens or medieval Venice, one must look to Asia, to the Gulf (Dubai, Bahrain) and above all to Singapore. Nowhere else does a nation of 3.7 million occupy an area of just 704 sq. km (270 sq. miles) 'at low tide'. Singapore's population density of over 6,000 per sq. km is easily the highest of any country in the world; and though thanks to reclamation, the land area is growing, so too is the number of people, inflated by a million non-residents. Literacy at 95 per cent is probably the highest in Asia; life expectancy, at around 80 years, the longest.

In 1885 the naturalist William Hornaday declared it 'the handiest city I ever saw'. He likened the already booming entrepôt to 'a big desk, full of drawers and pigeon-holes, where everything has its place, and can always be found in it'. Raffles, also an indefatigable collector, had ordained it so. Immigrants were located according to their ethnicity and professional skills. You could tell where you were – and still largely can – by the people in the street. Custom-built, as well as customs-free, Singapore had a drawer for everyone.

A planner's paradise, then; yet a nation-builder's nightmare. Other multi-ethnic 'emporia' – Malacca, Penang, Shanghai, Hong Kong – abandoned their sovereign pretensions as their colonial sponsors withdrew. Singapore nearly followed suit; it was one of the Straits Settlements under British rule and part of the Malaysian Federation from 1963 to 1965. Survival and eventual success came courtesy of events in mid-century. Though not the city's finest hour, it was then that its distinct identity was forged.

Immigration had rocketed. Labour had been needed for processing and shipping the tin and rubber hauled from the neighbouring Malay peninsula; and though some indentured workers were shipped from India, the vast majority came from Fujian and Guangdong. Singapore's ethnic mix became overwhelmingly Chinese. Tile-roofed shop-houses now constituted its architectural stereotype. Their frontages gaped with street-level warehouses while overhead, deep verandahs linked the office-cum-accommodation of each to its neighbour. Examples may still be seen, over-restored in Tanjong Pagar, unregarded around Serangoon Road.

To the British, the city's economic and strategic importance had become second to none. The stately façades of courthouse, city-hall and museum graced the streets of the European town; colonnades bestrode the pavements and royal palms soared to a majestic maturity. Dockyards were being expanded, fortunes made. 'You felt that all those vessels, their activity for the moment suspended, were waiting for some event of peculiar significance,' observed a Somerset Maugham character. In airy Raffles Hotel, the band played on. The threat of war brought such massive military investment that the city became comfortingly known as 'Fortress Singapore'.

Japan's invasion of mainland China in 1937 sounded a warning. The Singapore Chinese, with return to their homeland now precluded, stayed put. So did the imperturbable British. Then the Second World War engulfed Europe (1939), the Japanese extended their operations into Indo-China (1941), and still the British remained sublimely confident. Enormous shore batteries now commanded the harbour. Singapore felt so impregnable that any old aircraft seemed adequate for reconnaissance; tanks were supposed ineffective in jungle; and where the island's north shore nearly brushed the mainland, even barbed-wire defences were deemed an unnecessary strain on civilian morale. When, in February 1942, after a landing on the Malay coast and a lightning advance, Japanese forces reached the narrows, not even the causeway had been properly blown. The island held out for just over a week, the city itself for just under a week.

Churchill called the fall of Singapore 'the worst disaster ... in British history'; it was also the most ignominious. Cameras caught every move – the hapless CO trudging to the surrender under a white flag, Japanese tanks rumbling past bomb-blasted oil depots, the long crocodile of Allied prisoners winding its way out to Changi. Now the site of the international airport, Changi hosted the most brutal of Japanese prison camps. Nearby were shot some of the 50,000 Singapore Chinese gratuitously massacred during the occupation.

Forty-two months later the nightmare was all over. Mountbatten took the surrender at City Hall; 300 Japanese servicemen committed suicide in Raffles Hotel; and in its five-star rival, the Goodwood Park, a war crimes tribunal assembled. Infrastructure was restored, insurgency quelled and representational government introduced. But British protection – the ultimate sanction for colonial rule – had been irrevocably discredited. The Union Jack flew limply over the city only until 1963 and over the naval dockyard until 1971. Admitted to the UN in 1965, Singapore now went it alone. With no incentive to return to a Maoist China, Singapore Chinese completed their long transition into Chinese Singaporeans. Fiscal incentives, regimented politics, responsible alliances and above all the creation of a highly educated and industrious workforce drew heavy international investment. The city-state cynics were silenced; a city-nation was born. Purring with high growth rates, *Singha-pura*, literally 'the Lion City', joined the Asian tigers round the Pacific rim.

# NEW YORK

## The Prospect of the Future

JAN MORRIS

*One belongs to New York instantly. One belongs to it
as much in five minutes as in five years.*
THOMAS WOLFE, 1939

Probably no metropolis of the modern era has been more pre-eminent among
its peers than the city of New York in the years immediately after the Second
World War. As a whole the sprawling metropolis offered no particular image
to the world at large: but it was almost mythically exemplified by its own
epitome, the offshore island borough of Manhattan.

This was not a large island – 20 km (12.5 miles) from end to end,
nowhere more than 4 km (2.5 miles) wide, and connected to the civic
mainland by many bridges and tunnels – but it was packed with 1.9 million
people of countless ethnic origins. Its proudest boast was still expressed
in the exhortatory poem on the Statue of Liberty, at the entrance to its
harbour – 'Bring me your tired, your poor, your huddled masses yearning
to breathe free' – but by the early 1940s its function as a haven had been
supplanted by its status as the richest, most vibrant and most confident
metropolis of the most powerful nation on earth.

Much of the rest of the world was still ruined or impoverished by the
effects of war, not least the majestic capitals of Europe which had for so
long presided over western civilization. On the other hand, Manhattan,
untouched by bomb or battle, had been greatly enriched by the conflict, and
the combined effect was a fundamental shift in global power. Its financial
institutions were fast becoming the world's prime movers, its intellectual

life was wonderfully energetic, its already legendary skyline stood at the head of its bay like a frieze of destiny.

Manhattan's inhabitants were seldom modest about their new dominance, and their pride was enhanced rather than diminished by the fact that New York was not the capital of the United States. In Washington DC the tired, cynical mechanisms of diplomacy revolved as always, and pompous 18th-century structures represented the meaning of the nation. Manhattan was overwhelmingly new, and young – it was already a hackneyed joke that it would be a great place when it was finished – and the city was alive with the promise of fresh starts. The old world, London to Tokyo, looked at the past with sad regret: New York, the very symbol of the new, buzzed with prospects of the future.

From abroad, of course, this gleaming phenomenon seemed magically enviable. Everywhere on the globe people rich and poor marvelled at it, and wished they too could step ashore in the shadow of the skyscrapers. But it seemed hardly less wonderful to its own citizens. They thought of Manhattan not only as the physical gateway to America, through which their conquering armies were returning from the battlefields of Europe, but as a metaphysical gateway to Progress.

Publicists liked to call it the Wonder City, or the City of Tomorrow. Economists foresaw it providing unimaginable prosperity for all. Technological marvels abounded, and set the everyday style of the city with pocket radios, Scotch tape, decaffeinated coffee, behemoth automobiles, fax machines, elevators travelling at two floors a second and telephones in limousines – astonishments almost unknown to the rest of mankind (or even, for that matter, to the rest of America). The Empire State Building, looming over Manhattan's epicentre, was the tallest building ever made, and they called it the Cathedral of the Skies.

For the island had spiritual aspirations too – and brilliant cultural credentials. Bertolt Brecht, Arthur Miller, John Steinbeck, e. e. cummings, Tennessee Williams, W. H. Auden were all Manhattan residents. The

New York School of Art, with practitioners such as Jackson Pollock and Mark Rothko, was already challenging Parisian supremacies, and the Museum of Modern Art was the precursor of clones everywhere. Several universities thrived, four symphony orchestras, two great newspapers and the seminal *New Yorker*. Broadway was a prodigious entertainment factory, dedicated above all to that archetypal American art form, the stage musical, Even the fearful slums of Manhattan were full of cosmopolitan energy and talent, and the poorest of tenement-dwellers, the most hopeless of drunken down-and-outs, were famously pleased to be members of the same community as the Rockefellers or Toscanini.

Yet materially and socially dazzling as it was, artistically fertile, rich in fun and buoyancy, the fundamental element of Manhattan was Power. The messages it gave mankind were not illusory. This really was the City of the Future. All that fizz, wealth, ingenuity and complacency were manifesting the potential of America itself, just realizing its own immensity.

Mills, mines and factories of Illinois and Ohio, vast grain-prairies of the west, the fleets and armies, the mammoth corporations, the plots and purposes of Washington DC, the awful atom bomb itself – at this victorious moment all found their ultimate display in the island of Manhattan, just over 12 miles long from tip to toe, where King Kong stood on the summit of the Cathedral of the Skies, and hotel waiters loved to boast that in this city there was nothing, absolutely nothing, that they could not serve you for your dinner – 'just ask, lady, we got it …'.

# AN AGE OF LEAD TO AN AGE OF GOLD

ALEXANDER BLOOM

For a young writer or intellectual the best time to have arrived in New York always seems to have been in the previous generation. Older New Yorkers always speak of the great days of the city, just past. During the 1930s, the pre-First World War Greenwich Village scene of radical politics and avant-garde culture became the stuff of folk mythology. In the post-Second World War years, writers lamented the passing of the Village of the twenties, as one described it, 'with its great crusade for personal and sexual freedom.' But as long-time New York resident and journalist Murray Kempton observed, 'If you live in New York long enough, what you thought was an age of lead will look like an age of gold.'

New York in the post-Second World War years was once thought of as an 'age of lead', with the Cold War, McCarthyism, anti-intellectualism and the emergence of suburban America. It has, however, turned into an age of gold. Celebrations of the era abound. Critic Anatole Broyard's posthumous memoir begins, 'I think there's a great nostalgia for life in New York City, especially in Greenwich Village in the period just after World War II ... a good time – perhaps the best time – in the twentieth century.' Novelist Dan Wakefield's reminiscences recall: 'we started out in the most exciting city of its era, a Mecca that, like Paris in the twenties, exists now only in memory. Its naming now seems legendary: New York in the fifties.'

New York teemed with the tangible signs of cultural and intellectual activity. To Columbia sociologist Daniel Bell, New York was like an iceberg. 'The visible portions are the theatres, art galleries, museums, universities, publishing houses, restaurants, night clubs, espresso cafés, smart stores – all the activities that give the city its peculiar glittering place as the metropolis of America.' Intellectuals and artists came into new prominence in the post-war years, and nowhere more than in New York. The 'New York School' identified the reigning lights of modern art – Jackson Pollock, Willem de Kooning, Mark Rothko and others. The 'New York intellectuals' – Lionel Trilling, Sidney Hook, Clement Greenberg, Irving Howe and more – emerged as the leading literary critics, social thinkers and political analysts of the time. Institutions such as Columbia University and the Museum of Modern Art shaped social and cultural attitudes across the nation, if not around the world.

At the same time, New York still attracted the cultural renegades. Allen Ginsberg, once a student of Trilling's at Columbia, joined with other young, avant-garde writers such as Jack Kerouac and William Burroughs, to found the Beats in the late 1940s. Although they would not become famous until the late 1950s, the Beats considered New York a hospitable place for their countercultural lifestyle. Photographer and *Village Voice* editor Fred McDarrah recalls Beat life in New York:

> Rents were cheap. I lived on the edge of the Village and paid $46.68 a month. I earned about $50 a week but we could eat out for two bucks.... On weekends everybody from the neighborhood went to Washington Square Park to be part of the action.

Clearly a generational divide was growing, however. The Village that drew and excited so many of the young no longer seemed the province of the avant-garde – at least to an older intellectual such as NYU philosopher William Barrett. He found the Village of 1954 to have 'gone bourgeois'. Instead of those who led 'lives of great moment', as in his youth, Barrett found the Village filled with young marrieds, and he missed the 'action' Fred McDarrah found. 'The real centers of social intrigues,' Barrett observed, 'are the play pens in Washington Square where the mothers visit each other while the kids romp.'

By the early 1960s, the stage was being set for yet another generational shift. Some of the post-war rebels would merge with the developing youth movement and counter-culture, Allen Ginsberg notably among them. Still others would find it just as hard to connect fifties' avant-garde sensibility with the sixties, as thirties' intellectuals had had trouble connecting with fifties' culture. The political and social thinker Michael Harrington observed that the Village he knew ended 'the night a gawky kid named Bob Dylan showed up ... I heard the future and I didn't like it.' Among the newer generation, of course, Dylan would be hailed as its poet. If the best time to be in the Village or to be in New York seems to be with the last generation, the worst time is with the next.

In his famous essay of 1949, 'Here is New York', E. B. White separated New Yorkers into three groups: commuters, who 'give the city its tidal restlessness'; natives, who provide 'its solidity and continuity'; and settlers. They 'give it passion'. This is especially true if it is youthful passion, making it more of the moment, more fulsome, more intense – a modern version of the folk tale of the young man from the provinces making his way in the larger world. And as Lionel Trilling himself noted of this ancient parable, through it 'runs the thread of legendary romance, even downright magic'. In New York City in the 1950s we can again see the alchemy of the young, embracing the world with fresh enthusiasm, ever able to turn lead into gold.

# SÃO PAULO

## Coffee and Commerce

ELIZABETH JOHNSON

*Rio is a beauty. But São Paulo – São Paulo is a city.*
MARLENE DIETRICH

In the 450 years since São Paulo was founded, it has gone from being a quiet backwater of the Portuguese empire to the largest metropolitan area in South America and the fourth largest in the world. At present, the population of greater São Paulo is fast approaching 20 million.

São Paulo was founded in 1554 by Jesuit missionaries Manuel da Nóbrega and José de Anchieta. At the time, it was one of the few cities in colonial Portuguese America located away from the coast. Several aspects of São Paulo's inland topography attracted the Jesuits to the site. Most important among these was its location at the convergence of the Tietê, Pinheiros, Anhangabaú and Tamanduateí rivers. Access to these waterways greatly facilitated trade between the Jesuits and the Indian groups who populated Brazil's vast interior. And not long after São Paulo was founded, it became a melting pot of ethnicities, as Indians began to settle in the area and live together with the Jesuits; the town also attracted Portuguese immigrants and their mixed-race descendants.

The four rivers that converge on São Paulo – particularly the Tietê – ultimately helped shape the geography of Brazil. São Paulo residents, known as Paulistas, followed these waterways deep into the interior of the new continent in search of precious metals and Indian labourers for their farms. The Paulistas' lust for gold led them further and further into the backlands, where they carved out more and more territory for the Portuguese crown.

While the residents of São Paulo were active explorers who continued to branch out into new parts of Brazil, São Paulo itself remained relatively unimportant until the end of the 19th century. It was in this period that Paulista farmers began to cultivate coffee. The São Paulo coffee boom unleashed a flood of foreign investment in Brazilian infrastructure, and this in turn led to the construction of key transportation links, such as the railway that climbs the steep coastal escarpment from the port city of Santos to the São Paulo plateau. The new railway facilitated not only the export of coffee but also the influx of more than 5 million new immigrants from regions all over the globe. And unlike Rio de Janeiro, its more important colonial neighbour, São Paulo became, and remains, one of Brazil's most ethnically diverse cities, with significant Japanese and Lebanese as well as various European populations.

São Paulo expanded rapidly with the coffee economy and soon eclipsed Rio de Janeiro as the most important metropolis in Brazil. A new class of wealthy Paulistas, known as the coffee barons, emerged during this period, and they invested heavily in the urban landscape. Some of São Paulo's most impressive architecture was initiated during this period, most designed by architect Francisco de Paula Ramos de Azevedo.

A Paulista by birth, Ramos de Azevedo returned to his native city in 1879 following a period of study in Belgium. Back in São Paulo, he teamed up with the local aristocracy to bring a taste of Europe to Brazil. His most important works include the Luz train station, the Municipal Theatre, the Municipal Market and the Liceu de Artes. He was also instrumental in the design and construction of a grand new boulevard which would eventually eclipse the city centre as the true heart of São Paulo. Avenida Paulista was inaugurated in 1891, the result of an initiative led by Uruguayan architect Joaquim Eugenio de Lima. De Lima envisioned a long boulevard, 28 m (92 ft) wide, where residents would have ample space to build their mansions. Flush with capital, the coffee barons were eager to move to the new area of town.

Avenida Paulista soon became the focus of São Paulo society. In 1894, under pressure from the avenue's elite residents, the city council prohibited the construction of factories along it, in effect passing one of São Paulo's first zoning laws. The council also forbade cattle herds arriving from rural areas to pass along the majestic boulevard.

In the 20 years following Avenida Paulista's inauguration, Ramos de Azevedo and other local and European architects erected dozens of mansions along the tree-lined boulevard. The Trianon Belvedere, a terraced garden where the elite gathered to admire a spectacular view of the Anhangabaú river valley, was also built during this period. One of São Paulo's first major engineering projects, the 9 de Julho tunnel, was built under the Trianon to connect the new residential areas to the city centre. The fate of the Trianon Belvedere is emblematic of São Paulo's readiness to renovate and its thirst for perpetual change. In 1957, the expansive green space was demolished and the São Paulo Art Museum, or MASP – a symbol of Paulista modernity – was built in its place. The same destroy-to-build mentality sealed the fate of all but five of the mansions originally built by the coffee barons. Starting in the 1950s, Avenida Paulista became increasingly commercial. Today its landscape is dominated by banks and shopping centres.

Not only Avenida Paulista but São Paulo as a whole underwent a significant transformation after the coffee-boom period. In the 1920s, after a steep decline in coffee prices, a new class of urban entrepreneurs increasingly turned their attention to industry. As immigration from overseas waned in the 1930s, a growing number of migrants began to arrive in São Paulo from Brazil's impoverished northeast. Fleeing poverty and drought in their home states and seeking urban opportunity and wealth, millions of rural subsistence farmers from northeastern Brazil flocked to São Paulo. The influx accelerated in the 1950s, satisfying local industry's hunger for cheap labour but exacerbating the explosion of urban poverty.

Like Avenida Paulista, São Paulo as a whole has a somewhat uneasy relationship with the past. Within the limits of the municipality, the past and present strain against one another, forever trying to strike a balance. Avenida Paulista is home to over 200,000 apartment dwellers and hundreds of businesses, and nearly 2 million pedestrians and more than 100,000 vehicles pass along the boulevard each day. In contrast, the city centre is a landscape of once-grand-but-now-gritty architecture. And in the southernmost district of the city, a group of Krukutu Guarani Indians continues to live, despite the proximity of the ever-encroaching megalopolis.

In its juxtaposition of the ultramodern and the traditional, São Paulo is a complex and diverse reflection of both the future and the past. New commercial areas have sprung up in recent decades to rival the primacy of Avenida Paulista, but the historic boulevard remains the true heart of the city.

# SYDNEY

## Shanty Town to Global City

ELIZABETH FARRELLY

*Sydney derives its name ultimately from Dionysus,*
*youthful god of wine, vegetation and wild pleasure.*
PETER TONKIN, 2000

In January 1788, as revolution rumbled in France's empty stomach and Massachusetts' yeoman farmers haggled over the proposed 'aristocratickal' Constitution, Captain Arthur Phillip shepherded the first, ragtag transport of Britain's convict-settlers safely between two jagged headlands on the underside of the world. After eight months at sea even the convicts cheered for joy. This fjord-like space, cut into the misty eastern edge of the fabled southern continent, walled in honey-coloured sandstone and fringed with gnarly, pink-barked angophora, forms Sydney Harbour.

Since then, Sydney has grown up quickly. Too quickly, perhaps, from shanty town to global city in just over two centuries. And yet this meeting of sea and sandstone still flavours the city's physical nature – a seductive mix of salt and terracotta – just as surely as the governance of that newborn penal settlement by the corrupt, red-coat 'Rum Corps' still shapes its topsy-turvy political culture, and the chiaroscuro of inky shadow and brilliant sunlight seems to manifest its moral texture.

It is this confluence – the salty physicality, the tangled politics, the heightened contrast of good and institutionalized evil – that makes the ten-year reign of New South Wales Premier Robert Askin (1965–75), Sydney's heyday. Not necessarily its best moment, which, for so young a city, should be yet to come. But that interval between the helplessness of infancy and the blandness of globalism when – like the blessed moment in the Australian bush between the flies of the day and the mosquitoes of dusk – Sydney was most intensely, most hedonistically, most subversively itself.

The Askin decade, or 'Green Light years' as they are known, is not, on the face of it, everyone's idea of a heyday. It was a time of speakeasies, protection rackets and illegal casinos, of development free-for-all, organized crime, police brutality and entrenched government corruption. Askin, reputedly a former illegal bookmaker, earning him the nickname Slippery Sam, was bankrolled into office by media magnate Sir Frank Packer, and knighted, on his own recommendation, in 1972, the year Gough Whitlam became Prime Minister. On the night of the election in 1965, Askin is said to have exulted, 'we're in the tart shop now, boys!'

Askin came to power as Sydney struggled from its swaddling-wraps of post-war austerity, forelock-tugging colonialism and the crippling anglocentrism of the White Australia policy (which restricted non-white immigration). At federal level, the anglophile Robert Menzies was nearing the end of his 17-year reign, while in city hall a long-term dedication to the principles of 'graft, corruption, nepotism and general chicanery' had left a governance culture all but incapable of action. Just a few years out from under its 50-year statutory ban on skyscrapers and from the famed 'six o'clock swill' – the spectacular response to early pub-closing by this alcohol-and-testosterone-fuelled culture – Sydney was in the grip of what is known, even now, as 'rissole culture'.

Struggling to blow it apart, however, was an exuberant mix of baby-boomer energy, anti-apartheid sentiment, Vietnam protest and 1960s rock culture. From an upstairs back room in the Royal George, the libertarian drinking club known as the Sydney Push had been disseminating its heady intellectual permissiveness since the 1940s, thus obliging the next, incandescent generation of writers and thinkers – including Germaine Greer, Clive James, Robert Hughes and Geoffrey Robertson – to outshine and outshock before moving on to wider, groovier pastures.

In 1967, the first US marines arrived in Sydney on R&R, streaming up from the Garden Island navy base through Sydney's Kings Cross club and red-light district, bringing an instant market in music, drugs, sex and blue jeans, as well as the rumoured involvement of the CIA and international Mafiosi. *Oz* magazine was in its third year of life under Richard Neville and Martin Sharp, before the notorious Privy Council obscenity trial of 1971.

A similar clash of cultures began to be felt in Sydney's built fabric. In 1965, downtown Sydney was a huddled matrix of polite if provincial street buildings, up to the permitted 12 storeys high, their central light-wells and cell-like offices maintaining appearances but enjoying little natural light. From this uniform field, after the removal of the 12-storey legal limit in 1957, a single skyscraper soared heavenwards: the elegant AMP tower at Circular Quay. A few blocks away, Sydney's second tower, the heroic Australia Square, was half-built. Designed by Harry Seidler with his 'shiny American ideas' and built by Dutch immigrant Dick Dusseldorp on the sites of some 20 earlier buildings (plus the odd laneway), Australia Square represented an entirely new world: radiant, self-centred and obsessed by the sparkling view.

A few blocks the other way, its ribbed shells bristling with scaffolds and reinforcing steel, the Opera House was also half-built, but already bedevilled by politics and cost overruns. As ex-Prime Minister Paul Keating noted recently, 'The city got tapped on the shoulder by a rainbow. The odds of Sydney picking up the building of the 20th century must have been millions to one.' In 1957, the profession had put Jørn Utzon's competition scheme in the bin. It took visiting guru Eero Saarinen, arriving late, to spot the genius.

But by 1965 the same profession, including immigrant stars such as Seidler, took to the streets against Utzon's effective sacking by Askin's Public Works Minister, Davis Hughes, who happily accepted Utzon's resignation rather than pay him what he was owed. Universities might curry favour, giving honorary doctorates to the powerful, as the University of New South Wales did to Askin in 1966, but their students turned out en masse to support Utzon.

The heritage movement was just beginning. Even as most Sydneysiders pursued the great suburban dream, many of the same fierce modernists who had supported Utzon were returning to the centre, renovating century-old terrace houses in the hope of creating a more urban and European lifestyle. In 1971, the first of Sydney's famous 'Green Bans' was imposed, when Unionist Jack Mundey mobilized his Builders' Labourers' Federation to save Kelly's Bush, a small suburban bush-remnant. It was a technique that was later applied to much of inner Sydney. The same dichotomy was apparent in the simultaneous publication of two official (but diametrically opposed) city plans. One, presuming a sprawling Los Angeles city model, slated much of old inner Sydney for motorway construction, while the other, emphasizing pedestrian priority, tree-planting and street-furniture, earmarked these same areas as heritage precincts.

This culture war culminated in the battle over the bohemian and working-class neighbourhood of Victoria Street, Kings Cross. A vast redevelopment proposal, supported by Askin's government, had been fiercely controversial for some years before a Green Ban was imposed in 1972. The controversy continued until the mysterious 1975 disappearance – still unsolved – of the development's most vocal opponent, local writer and publisher, Juanita Nielsen.

Since then, Sydney has cleaned up its act. Although corruption, poverty, organized crime and racial tension still surface now and then, Sydney has leapt at global-city status with its 2000 Olympics, its immense wealth and its frantic yuppification. As the Mayor of Bogotá recently told a large gathering concerned at Sydney's public transport and environmental performance, 'Sydney's problems are problems we would love to have.' And on a summer's evening, as commuters throng the streets and bats fly home across a frangipani sky, Sydney can still seem the most seductive city on earth.

# TOKYO

## City of Constant Change

LESLEY DOWNER

*For a century now Tokyo has been known as the 'city of contrasts'*
*or 'capital of the old and the new'. Ever since its opening to the*
*outside world in the middle of the last century, Japan has with*
*increasing skill and style combined East and West, present and past.*
DONALD RICHIE, 1987

Tokyo is the most effervescent of cities. Constantly in the process of change, it is a city in which – at first sight at least – there is little that is old. This sense of impermanence has been part of the city's fabric since the beginning.

In 1590, the warlord Tokugawa Ieyasu chose the village of Edo, on the cusp of the undeveloped northern part of the island of Honshu, as his base. With mountains behind, a river running along one side and an easily defended bay in front, it satisfied both geomantic and practical requirements. A wily general and brilliant administrator, Ieyasu soon became shogun and master of all Japan. Under his command, Edo grew into an enormous city. Land was reclaimed from the sea, dykes built, canals dug; early visitors described it as the Venice of the East. Dominating the city was Edo Castle, a monumental edifice surrounded by moats and waterways. Around its massive granite walls 260 subject warlords maintained splendid mansions, while commoners populated warrens of alleys to the east, along the river. Earthquakes and fires – 'flowers of Edo' – regularly laid waste the wooden city, which was rebuilt again and again, bigger and better. There the 'floating world' – the evanescent culture of merchants and prostitutes depicted in woodblock prints – reached its zenith.

In 1868 the shogun was defeated. The emperor moved from Kyoto (p. 201) to Edo, now renamed Tokyo, the 'Eastern Capital'. Edo Castle became the Imperial Palace. A bright new city grew up with railways, electric lights and western-style stone and brick buildings. A few, such as the imposing brick façade of Tokyo station's west entrance, still remain.

Then, in 1923, earthquake reduced the city to rubble. In the Second World War it was flattened again. When the Americans arrived in 1945, Tokyo was a sea of ash. Painfully the people of Tokyo set to work to rebuild. A great deal was to change; though some things remained the same. The emperor renounced his divinity. But the Imperial Palace in which he lived in majestic seclusion remained the hub of the city, a vast impenetrable oasis of green beneath which subway lines were forbidden to pass and above which aeroplanes could not fly.

Edo had been planned as a spiral, a maze so convoluted that no enemy would ever reach the castle at the centre. With the city in ruins there was a chance to develop a more orderly street plan, perhaps a grid as in Kyoto. But in fact the layout of the city remained as labyrinthine as ever.

The east end of the city, Asakusa, where the commoners had lived, was rebuilt. Once again visitors crowded to Tokyo's well-loved Buddhist temple, Sensoji, to pray to Kannon, the goddess of mercy. But while Asakusa remained the heart of traditional culture, it never regained its pre-war energy. Whereas once it had been the bustling heart of the city, it was now a repository of nostalgia. For the focus of the city moved elsewhere. As Tokyo came back to life, it spread west.

The Olympic Games of 1964 were held in Tokyo. It was Japan's chance to show the world how much had been achieved since the war. The first bullet train lines were laid down, linking Tokyo and Osaka. Many-laned highways appeared, flying over the city on stilts or shadowing the once-celebrated canals. A broad, tree-lined boulevard, dubbed 'the Champs-Elysées of Tokyo', swept up to Yoyogi, where the spectacular curves and jutting prow of the Olympic Stadium, designed by Kenzo Tange, dominated the skyline.

The Olympics were the turning point. By the 1970s Japan was on the brink of unprecedented prosperity. These were the years of the 'economic miracle' and Tokyo was at the heart of it. As wealth soared, skyscrapers mushroomed in west Shinjuku. Shinjuku embodied the energy and contradictions of Tokyo, where old and new Japan rubbed up against each other. It boasted the largest railway station in the world. The west exit led to broad empty streets dominated by ghostly skyscrapers. The east exit, conversely, spat the traveller out into streets seething with people, with ranks of blazing neon signs like the banners of a samurai army. In 1968 it was a ferment of creativity, the centre of student unrest, avant-garde art and anti-establishment protests. Many future cultural leaders of the new Japan spread their wings there. The fashion designer Issey Miyake, the artist Tadanori Yokoo, the dancer Tatsumi Hijikata, the theatre director Shuji Terayama and the writer Yukio Mishima were all associated with those early years in Shinjuku.

By the 1980s Tokyo had grown confident. Brash young western architects were invited to give the city a playful, post-modern edge. For a season Nigel Coates's Metropole restaurant, with its Greek pillars and Victorian drapes, was emblematic. But nothing lasted, not even the building, which has long since faded away. The most lasting monument to the era is Philippe Starck's building for Asahi Breweries, with its shiny black trapezoid walls and gaudy golden flame, which sprang up in the east end of the city, across the river from the venerable Sensoji temple.

These were the years of the $250 cup of coffee, when people dined on sushi sprinkled with gold leaf and indulged in gold massages. Novelists such as Haruki Murakami and performance arts such as *butoh* were known worldwide. People living in rabbit-hutch apartments several hours' commute from the city happily spent their wealth on designer fashion, and the Tiffany gold heart was what every young man bought for his girl.

In 1987 Yoshiaki Tsutsumi, a Japanese business magnate and owner of some of the most expensive real estate in the world, was named in

*Forbes* magazine as the world's wealthiest man. When in 1989 – the year of Emperor Hirohito's death – Kenzo Tange's cathedral-like Tokyo Metropolitan Government Office opened in Shinjuku, it marked the pinnacle of the decade.

The 1990s were marked by economic downturn. But by 2000, Tokyo was ready to begin reinventing itself again. Marunouchi – 'inside the citadel', where the mansions of warlords once stood and which had been home to office developments for decades – suddenly sprouted glamorous hotels. The Mandarin Oriental opened in 2005, the gold-fronted Peninsula in 2007. Along Omotesando Street – the Champs-Elysées built for the Tokyo Olympics – wonderfully light, curvaceous buildings sprang up, from the Dior building, which emulated ripples of silk, to Toyo Ito's Tod's building, a sinuous network of branches.

And in Roppongi, the splendid Midtown opened, encompassing luxury apartment blocks, a landscaped garden, shopping malls, art galleries and 21_21 Design Sight, an airy pavilion shaped like a bird in flight, created by Issey Miyake and the architect Tadao Ando to nurture avant-garde design. There was also a 54-storey tower, the tallest in Tokyo, whose top floors housed the luxurious Ritz-Carlton Hotel.

Tokyo's skyscrapers, of course, are theoretically earthquake-proof. Nevertheless, perhaps one factor behind the city's all-pervading flavour of living on the edge is the knowledge that an earthquake might strike at any time. Much of Tokyo is built on reclaimed land, which would simply turn to mush.

Tokyo has been called a dreamscape, an architect's paradise. But no matter how dazzling the neon, no matter how many glittering new buildings soar ever higher and higher into the stratosphere, at Sensoji temple the incense still burns and the crowds are as thick as ever. Tokyo is a city which embraces past and present as it reinvents itself to fit the future.

# SHANGHAI

## China's Super-City

JOHN GITTINGS

*He always looked forward to the evening drives through the centre of Shanghai, this electric and lurid city more exciting than any other in the world.*

J. G. BALLARD, 1984

From the rooftop terrace of the Peace Hotel – once the Cathay – the visitor looks east across the Huangpu river to a skyline of skyscrapers, and west down busy Nanjing Road to the People's Park – once the racecourse when pre-war Shanghai was under international control. The riverside Bund runs north past the notorious garden where the only Chinese allowed in semi-colonial times were nannies with their foreign wards. And it stretches south past the former headquarters of the Hong Kong and Shanghai Bank towards the original Chinese town, still huddled around a temple, lake and garden.

Shanghai is one of the few cities in China where rapid economic development has not yet completely obliterated the past, and where it is still possible to walk the streets through history. Its physical fabric, though constantly changing, is layered with memories and with the most amazing – and sometimes terrible – tales.

Halfway down Huashan Road on the edge of the former French Concession is the Lilac Garden, with tall camphor trees and a glazed dragon wall. A century ago this was home for the youngest concubine of Li Hongzhang, the Manchu dynasty official who handled China's relations with the foreign powers. During the Cultural Revolution (1966–76), it became the headquarters for Yao Wenyuan, one of the Gang of Four led by Madame

Mao. Across the road is a cluster of old villas where the beautiful opera singer Yan Huizhu was hounded by Red Guards until she committed suicide. The Lilac Garden now houses a retirement home for former communist cadres, and an expensive Cantonese restaurant.

The standard English guidebook of the 1930s described Shanghai as 'the Paris of the East', which until recently had been just a 'fishing village on a mudflat'. This disparaging view of Shanghai's past was widespread, but inaccurate. It was already a commercial port in the 13th century AD, controlling river traffic on the Huangpu with the delta towns south of the lower Yangtze. Shanghai's merchants grew rich brokering cotton from the hinterland.

The city's original name of *Hu* dates back two millennia and is still used in some written contexts today. It acquired the name of Shanghai in AD 1280; it means 'Above the Sea', since the Yangtze estuary is only a short distance downstream. Shanghai is often referred to as 'the mouth of the (Yangtze) dragon'.

When British warships captured Shanghai in 1842, after the first Opium War, they burnt down its public buildings and opened up its 'rich granaries' for the people. The Treaty of Nanjing established Shanghai and four other cities on the Chinese coast as 'treaty ports', where foreigners could reside, trade and over the years would acquire extra-territorial rights. By the end of the century the International and French Settlements, both administered by foreign-run councils, covered more than 30 sq. km (12 sq. miles). Foreign control crept outwards along 80 km (50 miles) of roads beyond the settlement boundaries.

In the first half of the 20th century, as China emerged from imperial rule to experience decades of revolution, Japanese aggression and civil war, Shanghai led a double existence as both the rich commercial centre of cosmopolitan hedonism and the focus of serious political struggle. The Chinese Communist Party held its first Congress there in 1921; the 30 May incident in 1925, when British-led police shot and killed students supporting a labour strike, led to nationwide protests. Two years later, as the Nationalist-led revolution freed China from warlord rule, Chiang Kai-shek occupied Shanghai, and with the support of the local criminal gangs turned on his communist allies in a bloody slaughter (described by André Malraux in *La Condition Humaine*).

In the same year Arthur Ransome caused great offence to the British 'Shanghai-landers', saying that they 'look on their magnificent buildings' and 'are surprised that China is not grateful to them for their gifts, forgetting that the money to build them came out of China.' Shanghai workers, refugees from civil unrest elsewhere, laboured in sweatshop conditions. Harold Timperley in the *Manchester Guardian* described how young factory apprentices 'worked from ten to twelve hours a day, undernourished, and suffering from eye troubles, poisoned arms and legs.'

Two famous photos span Shanghai's war years: the first, taken anonymously in August 1937, shows Chinese refugees streaming across the iron bridge to escape the Japanese; the second, taken by Henri Cartier-Bresson in December 1948, shows a desperate queue outside a bank as Chiang Kai-shek's Nationalist rule collapsed.

After Shanghai was 'liberated' by the victorious communists, Madame Soong Jingling, widow of China's first Nationalist leader, Sun Yat-sen, proclaimed that 'Shanghai's new day has dawned'. But the city's economy languished for several decades while the Beijing government encouraged development elsewhere.

During the Cultural Revolution, Shanghai became a hotbed of radicalism; thus, after Mao Zedong's death in 1976, it had to watch while the new 'special economic zones' further south enjoyed economic reform. The balance shifted in the city's favour only after the 1989 suppression of the Beijing students, when mayor Jiang Zemin became Communist Party leader and later president of China under his patron, Deng Xiaoping.

Shanghai has now regained its pre-war reputation as the brash, do-it-all, ultra-modern super-city of China. It is the first stop for foreign investors, the place of choice for Overseas Chinese to buy property and a serious rival to Hong Kong. Shanghai has more coffee bars than any other city in China, more high-rise buildings (over 3,000), more supermarkets and department stores. New housing developments have swept away most of the traditional Shanghai lanes (*lilong*), often against local opposition, and satellite towns are being built in the suburbs. A new eco-city is planned for Chongming Island in the mouth of the Yangtze, linked to Shanghai by bridge and tunnel.

By 2008, Shanghai's urban population had reached over 18 million – a 50 per cent increase in 15 years – including at least 3 million migrant workers whose labour provides the muscle power for the city's economic boom. Shanghai's traditional industries of steel and shipbuilding have been overtaken by electronics and financial services: some of the last shipyards have been demolished to provide a riverside site for the 2010 World Expo.

The district of Pudong, between the Huangpu river and the sea, is the fastest-growing urban landscape in China. Pudong's new industries have doubled the value of Shanghai's output in the past 12 years. The skyscrapers around the Jinmao Hotel, the world's third tallest building when it was constructed, house offices from 90 per cent of the top 500 world companies. Shanghai's splendid new Pudong airport is linked by the world's first MagLev (magnetic levitation) line into town.

'If you live in Shanghai', China's most famous modern writer Lu Xun wrote in 1933, 'it pays better to be smart than dowdy', and Shanghai once again rivals Paris for shopping and fashion. The migrant workers through whose labour the city has risen again are mostly out of sight, living in temporary barracks behind the new towers of glass and steel.

# List of Contributors

**John Julius Norwich** is the author of magisterial histories of Norman Sicily, Venice, Byzantium and the Mediterranean; he has also written on Mount Athos, the Sahara, English architecture, Shakespeare's histories, 19th-century Venice and the Papacy. His memoirs, *Trying to Please*, were published in 2008. From 1970 he compiled an annual pamphlet anthology, *A Christmas Cracker*. He has made some 30 historical documentaries for television and lectures regularly. Formerly Chairman of Colnaghi, the oldest fine art dealers in London, he is Honorary Chairman of the Venice in Peril Fund and Chairman Emeritus of World Monuments Fund Britain.

**Colin Amery** was the founding director of the World Monuments Fund Britain and now practises as an architectural writer and consultant. He was recently the main contributor to *St George's Bloomsbury* (2008), published to mark the restoration by WMFB of Nicholas Hawksmoor's church. He is the joint author of *Saint Petersburg* (2006) with Brian Curran.

**Brian S. Bauer** is Professor of Anthropology at the University of Illinois at Chicago. He has published a dozen books and monographs on Andean prehistory and is particularly well known for his work on Cuzco and the Inca. His best-known book is *Ancient Cuzco: Heartland of the Inca* (2004).

**Doris Behrens-Abouseif** has degrees from the American University in Cairo, the University of Hamburg and the University of Freiburg. Before joining the School of Oriental and African Studies in 2000, where she holds the Nasser D. Khalili Chair of Islamic Art and Archaeology, she taught Islamic Art at the American University in Cairo and at the universities of Freiburg and Munich. She was Visiting Professor at Harvard University, the universities of Berlin and Bamberg in Germany and the University of Leuven in Belgium, and was 'Distinguished Visiting Professor' at the American University in Cairo. She has published a number of books on Islamic art and cultural history, notably *Egypt's Adjustment to Ottoman Rule* (1994), *Beauty in Arabic Culture* (1999) and *Cairo of the Mamluks. A History of Architecture and its Culture* (2007).

**Stephen P. Blake** is Senior Research Fellow, Center for Early Modern History, University of Minnesota. He has published many articles on Mughal India and Safavid Iran. His books include *Shahjahanabad: The Sovereign City in Mughal India, 1639–1739* (1991) and *Half the World: The Social Architecture of Safavid Isfahan, 1590–1722* (1999).

**Alexander Bloom** is Jane Oxford Keiter Professor of History and American Studies at Wheaton College in Massachusetts. He is the author of *Prodigal Sons: The New York Intellectuals and Their World* (1986), 'The Social and Intellectual Life of the City', in *New York: Culture Capital of the World, 1940–1965* (1988), *"Takin' It to the Streets": A Sixties Reader* (1995), and *"Long Time Gone": Sixties America Then and Now* (2001). He is currently working on a book titled *The End of the Tunnel: The Vietnam Experience and the Shape of American Life*.

**Trevor Bryce** is a Fellow of the Australian Academy of the Humanities, Emeritus Professor of the University of New England (Australia) and Honorary Professor in the University of Queensland. He specializes in the history and civilization of the ancient Near East, particularly Turkey. Among his most recent books are *The Kingdom of the Hittites* (2005), *The World of the Neo-Hittite Kingdoms* (2012) and *Ancient Syria* (2014).

**Michael D. Coe** is Charles J. MacCurdy Professor of Anthropology, Emeritus, at Yale University, and author of *Angkor and the Khmer Civilization* (2004), as well as many books on Mesoamerican archaeology and writing systems, and his memoirs, *Final Report* (2006).

**Robin Coningham** is Professor of Archaeology and Pro-Vice-Chancellor at Durham University. He has conducted fieldwork throughout South Asia and Iran, directing major excavations at Anuradhapura in Sri Lanka, Charsadda in Pakistan and Tepe Pardis in Iran. He is currently co-directing a survey of the hinterland of Anuradhapura and a programme of survey and excavation in the Central Plateau of Iran.

**James Cuno** is President and Director of the Art Institute of Chicago. Previously he was Professor and Director of the Courtauld Institute of Art, University of London, and Professor and Director of the Harvard University Art Museums.

**Patrick Darling** was Senior Research Associate, School of Conservation Sciences, at the University of Bournemouth. He undertook extensive survey work on the earthworks of Benin and published widely on the subject. He was also a member of African Legacy, an organization formed to promote the positive and realistic aspects of African heritage to colleges and universities worldwide.

**Lesley Downer** is a writer, journalist and broadcaster who specializes in Japanese culture and history. Her books include *On the Narrow Road to the Deep North* (1989), *The Brothers* (1994), *Geisha: The Secret History of a Vanishing World* (2000), *Madame Sadayakko: The Geisha who Seduced the West* (2003) and three novels.

**Margarete van Ess** is scientific director of the Orient Department of the German Archaeological Institute, acting Director of its branch in Baghdad and responsible for the scientific research in Uruk. Her research focuses on the history of urbanism in, and the material culture of, ancient Mesopotamia. She sits on several committees for the preservation of the cultural heritage of the Near East and has published many papers, articles and books.

**Susan Toby Evans** is a Professor of Anthropology at Penn State University. She studies the cultures of ancient Mexico, particularly that of the Aztecs. Her book *Ancient Mexico: Archaeology and Culture History* (3rd ed., 2013) won the Society for American Archaeology's book award. Her research into Aztec palaces and courtly life was published in *Palaces of the Ancient New World* (2004), which she edited with Joanne Pillsbury.

**Elizabeth Farrelly** is a Sydney-based columnist and author who trained in architecture and philosophy, practised in London and Bristol and is now Adjunct Associate Professor, University of Sydney. She was formerly Assistant Editor of the *Architectural Review*, independent Sydney City Councillor and inaugural chair of the Australia Award for Urban Design. Her books include *Three Houses*, a monograph on Pritzker prizewinner Glenn Murcutt (1993), and *Blubberland: The Dangers of Happiness* (2007).

**Felipe Fernandez-Armesto** is a historian who taught at the University of Oxford before taking up the Chair of Global Environmental History at Queen Mary College, University of London, in 2000, followed by chairs at Tufts University, and the University of Notre Dame, Indiana. He has been awarded distinctions and won literary prizes for his many books, which include *The Americas: The History of a Hemisphere* (2003), *So You Think You're Human: A Brief History of Humankind* (2004), *Pathfinders: A Global History of Exploration* (2006) and *The World: A History* (2nd ed. 2009).

**Orlando Figes** is Professor of History at Birkbeck College, University of London, and was previously Lecturer in History and Fellow of Trinity College, Cambridge (1984–99). He is the author of many books on Russian history, including *A People's Tragedy: The Russian Revolution, 1891–1924* (1996), which won several prizes, *Natasha's Dance: A Cultural History of Russia* (2002), *The Whisperers: Private Life in Stalin's Russia* (2007), *Crimea* (2007) and *Just Send Me Word* (2012) His books have been translated into 15 languages.

**Charles FitzRoy** is an art historian who runs art tours in western Europe, specializing in Italy. He has led numerous tours to Florence and Rome, and also to Stockholm. He has written a number of books, including *Italy: A Grand Tour for the Modern Traveller* (1991) and *Italy Revealed* (1994). His most recent book is *The Rape of Europa: The Intriguing History of Titian's Masterpiece* (2015).

**John Gittings** first visited Shanghai in 1971 and later became the *Guardian's* China specialist and East Asia editor. In 2001 he opened the newspaper's first China mainland staff bureau in Shanghai. His latest book is *The Changing Face of China: From Mao to Market* (2012), and his website is www.johngittings.com.

**Misha Glenny** is a former BBC correspondent and the author of several books on eastern and southeastern Europe, including *The Balkans, 1804–1999: Nationalism, War and the Great Powers* (1999), *The Fall of Yugoslavia* (3rd ed. 1996) and the highly acclaimed *McMafia: A Journey through the Global Criminal Underworld* (2008).

**Martin Goodman** is Professor of Jewish Studies at the University of Oxford. He is a Fellow of the Oxford Centre of Hebrew and Jewish Studies. His many books include *Rome and Jerusalem: The Clash of Ancient Civilizations* (2007).

**Jason Goodwin** is the author of *Lords of the Horizons: A History of the Ottoman Empire* (1998) and of *The Janissary Tree*, a detective series set in 19th-century Istanbul, the latest of which is *The Baklava Club* (2014).

**Bettany Hughes** is an award-winning historian, author and broadcaster. A Research Fellow of King's College, London, she has devoted her professional life to the research and promotion of history and the classics. Her television series include Athens, The Spartans, Helen of Troy and When The Moors Ruled Europe. She is the author of the best-selling book *Helen of Troy: Goddess, Princess, Whore* (2005), translated into 10 languages, and the highly acclaimed *The Hemlock Cup: Socrates, Athens and the Search for the Good Life* (2010); she is currently working on a cultural history of Istanbul.

**Henry Hurst** is Reader Emeritus in Classical Archaeology at Cambridge University. He has a special interest in ancient cities and worked at Carthage for over 25 years from 1974, making an extended study of the city's port area. He has also excavated and published on Roman and medieval Gloucester and on central Rome.

**W. J. F. Jenner** is an academic, writer and translator who has written on Chinese history and culture for over fifty years. His books include *Memories of Loyang* (1981), *The Tyranny of History: The Roots of China's Crisis* (1992) and many translations.

**Elizabeth Johnson** is the head of Brazil Research for Trusted Sources and has written extensively on Brazil for a wide range of publications. Her doctoral dissertation at the Johns Hopkins University, entitled 'Ora et Labora: Labor Transitions on Benedictine and Carmelite Properties in Colonial São Paulo', focuses on slavery and coerced labour in Brazil.

**Chris Jones** is a senior lecturer in the Department of History at the University of Canterbury, New Zealand. He is a Fellow of the Royal Historical Society and his research focuses on medieval chronicles, concepts of identity and political thought. His publications include *Eclipse of Empire? Perceptions of the Western Empire and its Rulers in Late-Medieval France* (2007).

**John Keay** is the author of many works on Asian history, including *The Honourable Company* (1991), *Last Post: The End of Empire in the Far East* (1997) and *The Spice Route* (2005). He also writes on the history of exploration: he edited *The Royal Geographical Society History of World Exploration* (1991) and wrote *Mad About the Mekong: Exploration and Empire in South East Asia* (2005).

**Ebba Koch** is Professor at the Institute of Art History in Vienna and has been architectural advisor to the Taj Mahal Conservation Collaborative since 2001. Her books include *King of the World: The Padshanama* (1997), *Mughal Art and Imperial Ideology* (2001), *Mughal Architecture* (2002) and *The Complete Taj Mahal* (2006).

**Magnus Linklater**, a journalist and writer, has been editor of *The Scotsman* and Scotland Editor of *The Times*. He is the author of several books on current affairs and Scottish history, including *Massacre: The Story of Glencoe* (1982) and *Bonnie Dundee: John Graham of Claverhouse* (1992). He lives in Edinburgh.

**Alan B. Lloyd** is Research Professor in the Department of Classics, Ancient History and Egyptology, Swansea University. He was for many years Chair of the Egypt Exploration Society and editor of the *Journal of Egyptian Archaeology* (1979–85). He is the author of many publications on Egyptological and classical subjects with a particular emphasis on Late Period Egypt.

**Rory MacLean** is a travel writer whose books, including UK top-ten *Stalin's Nose* (1992) and *Under the Dragon* (1998), have challenged and invigorated the genre, and – according to the late John Fowles – are among works that 'marvellously explain why literature still lives'. He is a recipient of an Arts Council Writers' Award and was nominated for the International IMPAC Dublin Literary prize.

**Bill Manley** teaches Ancient Egyptian and Coptic at the University of Glasgow and Universidad Complutense, Madrid. He is Honorary Research Fellow at the University of Liverpool and was formerly Senior Curator for Ancient Egypt at National Museums, Scotland. His publications include *The Penguin Historical Atlas of Ancient Egypt* (1996), *How to Read Egyptian Hieroglyphs* (with

Mark Collier, 1998), *The Seventy Great Mysteries of Ancient Egypt* (as editor, 2003) and *Egyptian Hieroglyphs for Complete Beginners* (2012).

**Philip Mansel** is a historian and biographer who has written nine books, including *Paris Between Empires* (2001) and *Dressed to Rule: Royal and Court Costume from Louis XIV to Elizabeth II* (2005). He has also written numerous articles and reviews and lectures widely. He is a founder member of the Society for Court Studies and is a Fellow of the Royal Historical Society, the Institute of Historical Research and the Royal Asiatic Society.

**Simon Martin** is an Associate Curator in the American Section of the University of Pennsylvania Museum. He specializes in historical research and the integration of textual and archaeological sources. He is the author (with Nikolai Grube) of *Chronicle of the Maya Kings and Queens* (2nd ed., 2008).

**Robert Morkot** is Senior Lecturer in Archaeology at the University of Exeter. His research interests are based in the Mediterranean and northeast Africa, in particular Egypt, Nubia and Sudan, and Libya. His books include *The Black Pharaohs: Egypt's Nubian Rulers* (2000), *Historical Dictionary of Ancient Egyptian Warfare* (2003) and *The Egyptians: An Introduction* (2005)

**Jan Morris** is an Anglo-Welsh writer, born in 1926, who has published some 40 books of history, place, biography and memoir, including two concerning the city of New York. She lives on the northwest coast of Wales.

**Malyn Newitt** was Deputy Vice-Chancellor of Exeter University and the first Charles Boxer Professor of History at King's College London. He retired in 2005. He is the author of 12 books including *History of Mozambique* (1995) and *A History of Portuguese Overseas Expansion* (2004).

**Joan Oates** is an archaeologist who has worked in Iraq and Syria for over 50 years. She is now a Senior Research Fellow at the McDonald Institute for Archaeological Research, University of Cambridge. Her many books include *The Rise of Civilization* (1976), *Babylon* (2005) and *Nimrud, An Assyrian City Revealed* (2001); she has also published a number of excavation reports as well

as over 100 papers on the archaeology and history of Mesopotamia. She is a Fellow of the British Academy.

**Thomas Pakenham** is the author of *Meetings with Remarkable Trees* (1997) and *Remarkable Trees of the World* (2002), as well as *The Boer War* (1979), *The Year of Liberty: The Story of the Great Irish Rebellion of 1798* (rev. ed. 1997), *The Mountains of Rasselas* (1998; 1st ed. 1959) and the critically acclaimed *The Scramble for Africa* (1991). He is chairman of the Irish Tree Society and plants trees both for profit and ornament.

**Nigel Pollard** lectures in Roman history and archaeology at Swansea University. The main focus of his research is the Roman empire, especially the eastern provinces and the role of the Roman army. His publications include *Soldiers, Cities and Civilians in Roman Syria* (2000) and *The Complete Roman Legions* (with Joanne Berry, 2012).

**Julian Reade** is Honorary Professor in Near Eastern Studies at the University of Copenhagen, and was formerly Wainwright Fellow at the University of Oxford and Assistant Keeper in the British Museum, London. He has directed excavations in Iraq and Oman, and has written extensively on the history, geography, ideology, art and architecture of the Middle East, including *Assyrian Sculpture* (2nd ed., 1996), on its connections with Greece and India, and on the evolution of modern historical research and attitudes to antiquity.

**Jane Ridley** is Professor of History at the University of Buckingham. She has written numerous articles and books, and her biography of Lutyens, *The Architect and his Wife: A Life of Edwin Lutyens*, won the Duff Cooper Prize in 2003.

**Barnaby Rogerson** has travelled widely from an early age. He is the author of *The Prophet Muhammad* (2003), *The Heirs of the Prophet Muhammad* (2006), *A Traveller's History of North Africa: From Carthage to Casablanca* (new ed., 2008) and *The Last Crusaders* (2009), plus guidebooks to Morocco, Cyprus, Istanbul and Tunisia. He runs Eland with his wife Rose Baring, publishing classic books of travel literature (www.travelbooks.co.uk).

**Simon Schama** is University Professor of Art History and History at Columbia University. His 15 books, including *The Embarrassment of Riches: An Interpretation of Dutch Culture in the Golden Age* (1987), *Citizens, a Chronicle of the French Revolution* (1989), *Landscape and Memory* (1995), *Rough Crossings: Britain, the Slaves and the American Revolution* (2005) and most recently *The American Future: A History* (2008), have won awards on both sides of the Atlantic. He won the National Magazine Award for his art criticism in the *New Yorker* in 1996 and an International Emmy for his film on Bernini in *The Power of Art*. He is the writer-presenter of more than 30 films for the BBC and his *The American Future: A History* won the Broadcast Press Guild award for best documentary series of 2008. He also writes regularly for the *Guardian* on politics, art, popular music and food, and his BBC Radio 4 programmes *Baseball and Me* were broadcast in 2009.

**Ian Shaw** is Professor of Archaeology at the School of Archaeology, Classics and Egyptology, University of Liverpool. He has excavated and surveyed at the ancient Egyptian cities of Amarna and Memphis, and is currently excavating at Gurob in the Faiyum. His publications include *Ancient Egypt: A Very Short Introduction* (2004) and *Ancient Egyptian Technology and Innovation* (2012).

**Kevin Starr** is University Professor and Professor of History at the University of Southern California in Los Angeles and the California state librarian emeritus. His 7-volume *Americans and the California Dream* series has won him a Guggenheim fellowship, membership of the Society of American Historians, the National Humanities Medal and the Centennial Medal of the Graduate School of Arts and Sciences of Harvard University.

**Colin Thubron** is a travel writer and novelist. His journeys and books have mainly focused on Russia, Central Asia and China: 'the lands my generation was brought up to fear'. His best-known works include *Behind the Wall* (1987), *In Siberia* (1999) and *Shadow of the Silk Road* (2006). He has won many prizes and awards.

**William L. Urban** is the Lee L. Morgan Professor of History and International Studies at Monmouth College in Monmouth, Illinois. He is an expert in Baltic studies, particularly the northern crusades and the Teutonic Order, on which he has written many articles and books.

**A. N. Wilson**, writer and journalist, is a fellow of the Royal Society of Literature and former literary editor of *The Spectator* and the *Evening Standard*. An award-winning biographer and a celebrated novelist, his books include the highly acclaimed *The Victorians* (2002), *London: A Short History* (new ed., 2005), *Dante in Love* (2011), *The Elizabethans* (2011) and, his most recent, *Victoria: A Life* (2014).

**Frances Wood** was curator of the Chinese collections in the British Library 1977–2013. She studied Chinese at the universities of Cambridge, Peking and London and has written many books on Chinese history and culture, including *The Forbidden City* (2005) and *The First Emperor of China* (2007). Her recent publications include two articles in *Sir Aurel Stein: Colleagues and Collections* (ed. Helen Wang, 2012) and, with Mark Barnard, *The Diamond Sutra: The Story of the World's Earliest Dated Printed Book* (2010).

**Victor C. Xiong** is professor of Chinese history at Western Michigan University. He has published numerous articles on medieval China, and served as editor of the academic journals *Early Medieval China* (1994–99) and *Chinese Historians* (1995–99). He is also the author of *Sui-Tang Chang'an: A Study in the Urban History of Medieval China* (2000), *Emperor Yang of the Sui Dynasty: His Life, Times, and Legacy* (2006) and *A Historical Dictionary of Medieval China* (2009).

**Adam Zamoyski** is a freelance historian who has published three biographies and several books on European history. His works include *Rites of Peace: The Fall of Napoleon and the Congress of Vienna* (2007), *Warsaw 1920: Lenin's Failed Conquest of Europe* (2008), *Poland: A History* (2009) and *Phantom Terror: The Threat of Revolution and the Repression of Liberty 1789–1848*.

# Further Reading

## The Ancient World

### URUK

Crüsemann, N., M. van Ess, M. Hilgert & B. Salje, *Uruk. 5000 Jahre Megacity* (Petersberg, 2013)
George, A. R., *The Epic of Gilgamesh* (London, 1999)
Liverani, M. et al., *Uruk: The First City* (London, 2006)
Nissen, H. J., *The Early History of the Ancient Near East, 9000–2000 BC* (Chicago & London, 1988)
Nissen, H. J., P. Damerow & R. K. Englund, *Archaic Bookkeeping. Early Writing and Techniques of Economic Administration in the Ancient Near East* (Chicago & London, 1993)
Roaf, M., *Cultural Atlas of Mesopotamia and the Ancient Near East* (Oxford, 1996)

### MOHENJO-DARO

Coningham, R. A. E., 'South Asia: From Early Villages to Buddhism', in C. J. Scarre (ed.), *The Human Past* (2nd ed., New York & London, 2009) 518–551
Jansen, M., *Mohenjo-Daro: Stadt der Brunnen und Kanäle: Wasserluxus vor 4500 Jahren* (Bergisch Gladbach, 1993)
Kenoyer, J. M., *Ancient Cities of the Indus Valley Civilization* (Oxford, 1998)
Marshall, J. H., *Mohenjo-Daro and the Indus Civilisation* (London, 1931)
Possehl, G. L., *The Indus Civilization: A Contemporary Perspective* (Walnut Creek, CA, 2002)

### MEMPHIS

Anthes, R., *Mit Rahineh, 1956* (Philadelphia, PA, 1965)
Giddy, L., *Kom Rabi'a: The New Kingdom and Post-New Kingdom Objects* (London, 1999)
Jeffreys, D. G., *The Survey of Memphis, I: The Archaeological Report* (London, 1985)
Jeffreys, D. G., *The Survey of Memphis, V: Kom Rabia: The New Kingdom Settlement (levels II–V)* (London, 2006)
Petrie, W. M. F. & J. H. Walker, *Memphis I* (London, 1909)
Petrie, W. M. F. & J. H. Walker, *The Palace of Apries (Memphis II)* (London, 1909)
Porter, B. & R. L. B. Moss, *Topographical Bibliography of Ancient Egyptian Hieroglyphic Texts, Statues, Reliefs, and Paintings*, Vol. III, Part 2 (Oxford, 1978) 830–75

### THEBES

Hornung, E., *The Valley of the Kings: Horizon of Eternity* (New York, 1990)
Lacovara, P., *The New Kingdom Royal City* (London & New York, 1997)
Nims, C. F. & W. Swaan, *Thebes of the Pharaohs: Pattern for Every City* (London, 1965)
Reeves, N. & R. H. Wilkinson, *The Complete Valley of the Kings* (London & New York, 1996)
Rhind, A. H., *Thebes: Its Tombs and their Tenants* (London, 1862)
Romer, J., *Valley of the Kings* (London, 1981)
Strudwick, H. & N., *Thebes in Egypt: A Guide to the Tombs and Temples of Ancient Luxor* (London & Ithaca, NY, 1999)
Weeks, K., *Atlas of the Valley of the Kings: The Theban Mapping Project* (Cairo, 2000)
Wente, E. F., *Late Ramesside Letters* (Chicago, 1967)
Wilkinson, R. H., *The Complete Temples of Ancient Egypt* (London & New York, 2000)

### HATTUSA

Bryce, T. R., *Life and Society in the Hittite World* (Oxford & New York, 2002) 230–56
Bryce, T. R., *The Trojans and their Neighbours* (London & New York, 2006)
Latacz, J., *Troy and Homer* (Oxford & New York, 2004)
Neve, P., *Hattuša Stadt der Götter und Tempel* (Mainz, 1993)
Seeher, J., *Hattusha Guide: A Day in the Hittite Capital* (Istanbul, 2002)

### BABYLON

Bergamini, G., 'Levels of Babylon reconsidered', *Mesopotamia* 12 (1977) 111–52
Finkel, I. L. & M. J. Seymour, *Babylon* (London, 2008)
George, A. R., 'Babylon revisited: archaeology and philology in harness', *Antiquity* 67 (1993) 734–46
Koldewey, R., *Das Wieder Erstehende Babylon* (Leipzig, 1913)
Oates, J., *Babylon* (rev. ed., London & New York, 2008)
Unger, E., *Babylon: Die Heilige Stadt* (Berlin, 1931)

## NINEVEH

Layard, A. H., *Nineveh and Its Remains*
(Eastbourne, 2007)
Parrot, A., *Nineveh and the Old Testament*
(New York, 1955)
Reade, J., *Assyrian Sculpture* (2nd ed., London,
1996)
Russell, J. M., *The Final Sack at Nineveh: The
Discovery, Documentation, and Destruction of King
Sennacherib's Throne Room* (New Haven, 1998)

## CARTHAGE

Brown, S., *Late Carthaginian Child Sacrifice and
Sacrificial Monuments in their Mediterranean
Context* (Sheffield, 1991)
Harden, D., *The Phoenicians* (Harmondsworth,
1980)
Lancel, S., *Carthage: A History* (Oxford, 1995)
Rakob, F., 'The making of Augustan Carthage', in
E. Fentress (ed.), *Romanization and the City*
(Portsmouth, 2000) 73–82
Raven, S., *Rome in Africa* (London, 1993)
Rives, J., *Religion and Authority in Roman Carthage
from Augustus to Constantine* (Oxford, 1995)

## ATHENS

Boardman, J., *The Parthenon and its Sculptures*
(London, 1985)
Camp, J. M., *The Athenian Agora. Excavations in
the Heart of the Athenian Agora* (London & New
York, 1986)
Camp, J. M., *The Archaeology of Athens* (New Haven
& London, 2001)
Harris, D., *The Treasures of the Parthenon and the
Erechtheion* (Oxford, 1995)
Roberts, J. W., *City of Sokrates: An Introduction to
Classical Athens* (London, 1998)
Waterfield, R., *Athens, A History – From Ancient
Ideal to Modern City* (London, 2004)

## LINZI & WARRING STATES CHINA

Qiyun Zhang & Dongfang Li, *China's Cultural
Achievements During the Warring States Period*
(Taiwan, 1983)
Sun Tzu, *The Art of War*, translated by J. Minford
(London & New York, 2002)
Wu Hung, 'Rethinking Warring States cities: an
historical and methodological proposal', *Journal
of East Asian Archaeology 3.1–2* (2001) 237–57
Yu Weichao (ed.), *A Journey into China's Antiquity*,
vol. 2, *Warring States Period – Northern and
Southern Dynasties* (Beijing, 1997)

## ALEXANDRIA

Bernand, A., *Alexandrie la grande* (Paris, 1998)
Fraser, P. M., *Ptolemaic Alexandria*, 3 vols
(Oxford, 1972)
Goddio, F. & A. Bernand, *Sunken Egypt: Alexandria*
(London, 2004)
Walker, S. & P. Higgs, *Cleopatra of Egypt from
History to Myth* (London, 2001)

## MEROË

Lehner, M., *The Complete Pyramids* (London & New
York, 1997) 197–99
O'Connor, D., *Ancient Nubia: Egypt's Rival in Africa*
(Pennsylvania, 1993)
Welsby, D. A., *Kingdom of Kush: The Napatan and
Meroitic Empires* (London, 1996)

## JERUSALEM

Avigad, N., *Discovering Jerusalem* (Oxford, 1984)
Goldhill, S., *Jerusalem: City of Longing* (Cambridge,
MA, 2010)
Goodman, M., *Rome and Jerusalem: The Clash of
Ancient Civilizations* (London, 2007)
Jeremias, J., *Jerusalem in the Time of Jesus* (London,
1969)
Sebag Montefiore, S., *Jerusalem: The Biography*
(London, 2012)

## ROME

Aicher, P. J., *Rome Alive. A Source-Guide to the
Ancient City*, vol. 1 (Wauconda, IL, 2004)
Claridge, A., *Rome* (Oxford Archaeological Guides,
Oxford, 1998)
Coulston, J. C. & H. Dodge (eds), *Ancient Rome: The
Archaeology of the Eternal City* (Oxford, 2000)
*Res Gestae Divi Augusti: The Achievements of the
Divine Augustus*, P. A. Brunt & J. M. Moore (eds)
(Oxford, 1967)
Scarre, C., *Chronicle of the Roman Emperors*
(London & New York, 1995)
Wallace-Hadrill, A., *Augustan Rome* (Bristol, 1998)
Zanker, P., *The Power of Images in the Age of
Augustus* (Ann Arbor, 1990)

## The First Millennium AD

### TEOTIHUACAN

Berrin, K. & E. Pasztory (eds), *Teotihuacan: Art from the City of the Gods* (New York, 1993)

Headrick, A., *The Teotihuacan Trinity* (Austin, 2007)

Millon, R. (ed.), *Urbanization at Teotihuacan, Mexico* (Austin, TX, 1973)

Pasztory, E., *Teotihuacan: An Experiment in Living* (Norman, OK, 1997)

Sahagún, F. B. de, *The Origin of the Gods*, Book 3 of the Florentine Codex, trans. A. J. O. Anderson & C. E. Dibble (Santa Fe, 1978)

Sempowski, M. L. & W. S. Michael, *Mortuary Practices and Skeletal Remains at Teotihuacan*, with an addendum by R. Storey (Salt Lake City, 1994)

Storey, R., *Life and Death in the Ancient City of Teotihuacan: A Paleodemographic Synthesis* (Tuscaloosa, AL, 1992)

Sugiyama, S., *Human Sacrifice, Militarism, and Rulership: Materialization of State Ideology at the Feathered Serpent Pyramid, Teotihuacan* (Cambridge, 2005)

### TIKAL

Avendaño y Loyola, F. A., *Relation of Two Trips to Peten*, trans. by C. P. Bowditch & G. Rivera (Culver City, 1987)

Harrison, P. D., *The Lords of Tikal: Rulers of an Ancient Maya City* (London & New York, 1999)

Martin, S., 'In Line of the Founder: A View of Dynastic Politics at Tikal', in A. J. Sabloff (ed.), *Tikal: Dynasties, Foreigners, and Affairs of State* (Santa Fe & Oxford, 2003) 3–45

Martin, S. & Grube, N., *Chronicle of the Maya Kings and Queens: Deciphering the Dynasties of the Ancient Maya* (2nd ed., London & New York, 2008)

Sabloff, J. A. (ed.), *Tikal: Dynasties, Foreigners, and Affairs of State* (Santa Fe & Oxford, 2003)

Webster, D. et al., 'The Great Tikal Earthwork Revisited', *Journal of Field Archaeology* 32 (2007) 41–64

### CONSTANTINOPLE

Aimov, I., *Constantinople: The Forgotten Empire* (Boston, 1970)

Cormack, R. & M. Vassilaki, *Byzantium* (London, 2008)

Harris, J., *Constantinople: Capitol of Byzantium* (London, 2007)

Nicolle, D., et al., *The Fall of Constantinople: The Ottoman Conquest of Byzantium* (Oxford, 2007)

Norwich, J. J., *Byzantium: The Early Centuries* (London & New York, 1988)

Norwich, J. J., *Byzantium: The Apogee* (London & New York, 1991)

Norwich, J. J., *Byzantium: Decline and Fall* (London & New York, 1995)

### MECCA

Creswell, K. A. C., *Early Muslim Architecture* (rev. ed., Oxford, 1969)

Ibn Jubayr, *The Travels of Ibn Jubayr*, translated by R. J. C. Broadhurst (London, 1952)

Watt, M. W. & R. B. Winder, R. B., 'Makka' in *Encyclopaedia of Islam*, 2nd ed., vol. VI (Leiden, 1991) 144b–150b

### DAMASCUS

Burns, R., *Syria. An Historical Guide* (London & New York, 1999)

Burns, R., *Damascus: A History* (London & New York, 2005)

Degeorge, G., *Damascus* (Paris, 2004)

Keenan, B. & T. Beddow, *Damascus: Hidden Treasures of the Old City* (London & New York, 2000)

Kociejowski, M. (ed.), *Syria: Through Writers' Eyes* (London, 2006)

Thubron, C., *Mirror to Damascus* (London & Boston, 1967)

### CHANG'AN

Chye Kiang Heng, *Cities of Aristocrats and Bureaucrats: The Development of Medieval Chinese Cityscapes* (Honolulu, 1999)

Steinhardt, N. S., *Chinese Imperial City Planning* (Honolulu, 1999)

Wright, A. F., 'The Cosmology of the Chinese City' in G. W. Skinner (ed.), *The City in Late Imperial China* (Stanford, 1977)

Xiong, V. C., *Sui-Tang Chang'an: A Study in the Urban History of Medieval China* (Ann Arbor, MI, 2000)

## BAGHDAD

Duri, A. A., 'Baghdad' in *Encyclopaedia of Islam*, 2nd ed., vol. I (Leiden, 1986), 921a–926a

Lassner, J., *The Topography of Baghdad in the Early Middle Ages* (Detroit, 1970)

Le Strange, G., *Baghdad during the Abbasid Caliphate* (Oxford, 1900, repr. London & Dublin, 1972)

Micheau, F., 'Bagdad', in J. Garcin (ed.), *Grandes Villes Méditerranéennes du Monde Musulman Médiéval* (Rome, 2000) 87–116

## CÓRDOBA

Arberry, A. J., 'Muslim Córdoba', in A. J. Toynbee (ed.), *Cities of Destiny* (London, 1967) 166–77

Hillenbrand, R., '"The Ornament of the World" Medieval Cordoba as a Cultural Centre', in S. K. Jayyushi (ed.), *The Legacy of Muslim Spain* (Leiden & New York, 1994) 112–35

Manuel, A. A. & A. V. Triano, 'Cordoue', in J. Garcin (ed.), *Grandes Villes Méditerranéennes du Monde Musulman Médiéval* (Rome, 2000) 117–34

Seybold, C. F. & M. O. Jimenez, 'Kurtuba', in *Encyclopaedia of Islam* (2nd ed., Leiden, 1986) 509b–512a

### The Medieval World

## ANGKOR

Coe, M. D., *Angkor and the Khmer Civilization* (London & New York, 2003)

Dagens, B., *Angkor: Heart of an Asian Empire* (London, 1995)

Groslier, B. P., *Angkor: Art and Civilization* (New York, 1966)

Groslier, B. P., *Angkor and Cambodia in the Sixteenth Century. According to Portuguese and Spanish Sources*, trans. M. Smithies (Bangkok, 2006)

Jacques, C. & M. Freeman, *Angkor: Cities and Temples* (London & New York, 1997)

Jessup, H. I., *Art & Architecture of Cambodia* (London & New York, 2004)

Stierlin, H., *The Cultural History of Angkor* (London, 1984)

## PALERMO

Angeli, L., *Palermo: City of Art* (Mistretta, 1986)

Grube, E. J. & J. Johns, *The Painted Ceilings of the Cappella Palatina* (London, 2005)

Matthew, D., *The Norman Kingdom of Sicily* (Cambridge, 1992)

Norwich, J. J., *The Normans in the South 1016–1130* (London, 1967)

Norwich, J. J. *The Kingdom in the Sun 1130–1194* (London, 1970)

Norwich, J. J., *The Middle Sea. A History of the Mediterranean* (London & New York, 2006)

Runciman, S., *The Sicilian Vespers: A History of the Mediterranean World in the Later Thirteenth Century* (new ed., Cambridge, 1992)

## CAIRO

André, R., *Cairo*, trans. W. Wood (Cambridge, MA, & London, 2000)

Behrens-Abouseif, D., *Cairo of the Mamluks: A History of the Architecture and Its Culture* (London, 2007)

## SAMARKAND

Chuvin, P., *Samarkand, Bukhara, Khiva* (Paris & London, 2003)

Nedvetsky, A. G., *Samarkand* (Reading, 1992)

Robinson, F., *The Mughal Emperors and the Islamic Dynasties of India, Iran and Central Asia 1206–1925* (London & New York, 2007) 42–51

Thubron, C., *Shadow of the Silk Road* (London & New York, 2006)

## PARIS

Cazelles, R., *Nouvelle Histoire de Paris de la Fin du Règne de Philippe Auguste à la Mort de Charles V 1223–1380* (Paris, 1972)

Favier, J., *Paris: Deux Mille Ans d'Histoire* (Paris, 1997)

Hallam, E. M. & J. Everard, *Capetian France*, 2nd ed. (Harlow, 2001) 987–1328

Hussey, A., *Paris: The Secret History* (London, 2006)

Jones, C., *Paris: Biography of a City* (London, 2004)

## LÜBECK

Dollinger, P., *The German Hansa*, trans. and ed. D. S. Ault & S. H. Steinberg (Stanford, 1970)

Enns, A. B., *Lübeck: A Guide to the Architecture and Art Treasures of the Hanseatic Town* (Lübeck, 1974)

King, W., *Chronicles of Three Free Cities: Hamburg Bremen, Lübeck* (New York, 1914)

Rodnick, D., *A Portrait of Two German Cities: Lübeck and Hamburg* (Lubbock, TX, 1980)

Schildhauer, J., *The Hansa: History and Culture*, trans. K. Vanovitch (New York, 1988)

## KRAKÓW

Davies, N., *God's Playground: A History of Poland*, 2 vols (Oxford, 1981)

Jasienica, P., *Jagiellonian Poland* (Miami, 1978)

Knox, B., *The Architecture of Poland* (London, 1971)

Kozakiewicz, H., *The Renaissance in Poland* (Warsaw, 1976)

Zamoyski, A., *The Polish Way: A Thousand-Year History of the Poles and their Culture* (London, 1987)

Zamoyski, A., *Poland: A History* (London, 2009)

## VENICE

Chambers, D., *The Imperial Age of Venice: 1380–1580* (London, 1970)

Morris, J., *Venice* (3rd ed., London, 2004)

Norwich, J. J., *A History of Venice* (London & New York, 1982)

Wills, G., *Venice: Lion City: The Religion of Empire* (New York, 2001)

## FLORENCE

Cronin, V., *The Florentine Renaissance* (London, 1967)

Hibbert, C., *Florence: The Biography of a City* (London, 1993)

Hibbert, C., *The Rise and Fall of the House of Medici* (London, 1974)

Turner, R., *The Renaissance in Florence* (London, 1997)

Unger, M. *Magnifico: The Brilliant Life and Violent Times of Lorenzo de' Medici* (New York, 2008)

Vasari, G., *The Lives of the Artists* (Oxford, 1971)

## BENIN

Bradbury, R. E., *The Benin-Kingdom and the Edo-Speaking Peoples of South-Western Nigeria* (London, 1957)

Connah, G. E., *The Archaeology of Benin* (Oxford, 1975)

Darling, P. J., *Archaeology and History in Southern Nigeria: The Ancient Linear Earthworks of Benin and Ishan* (Oxford, 1984)

Egharevba, J. U., *A Short History of Benin* (Ibadan, 1968)

Johnson, S., *The History of the Yorubas* (Lagos, 1956)

McClelland, E. M., *The Kingdom of Benin in the Sixteenth Century* (Oxford, 1971)

Ryder, A. F. C., *Benin and the Europeans 1485–1897* (London, 1969)

Shaw, T., *Nigeria: Its Archaeology and Early History* (London, 1978)

Willett, F., 'Ife and its Archaeology', *Journal of African History* 1, 2 (1960) 231–48

## TIMBUKTU

Abun-Nasr, J., *History of the Maghreb in the Islamic Period* (Cambridge, 1987)

Barth, H., *Travels and Discoveries in North and Central Africa*, 3 vols (repr. London, 1965)

Bovill, E. V., *The Golden Trade of the Moors* (London & New York, 1958)

Hunwick, J. O. & A. J. Boye, *The Hidden Treasures of Timbuktu: Historic City of Islamic Africa* (London & New York, 2008)

Norris, H. T., *The Tuaregs, their Islamic Legacy and its Diffusion in the Sahel* (Warminster, 1975)

Rogerson, B., *A Traveller's History of North Africa: From Carthage to Casablanca* (new ed., Moreton-in-the-Marsh, 2008)

## CUZCO

Bauer, B. S., *The Sacred Landscape of the Inca: The Cuzco Ceque System* (Austin, TX, 1998)

Bauer, B. S., *Ancient Cuzco: Heartland of the Inca* (Austin, TX, 2004)

## TENOCHTITLAN

Berdan F. F. & P. R. Anawalt (eds), *Codex Mendoza, III: A Facsimile Reproduction* (Berkeley, 1992)

Carrasco, P., *The Tenochca Empire of Ancient Mexico: The Triple Alliance of Tenochtitlan, Tetzcoco, and Tlacopan* (Norman, OK, 1999)

Cortés, H., *Letters from Mexico*, trans. & ed. A. Pagden (New Haven, 1986)

Díaz del Castillo, B., *The Discovery and Conquest of Mexico* (c. 1560s), ed. G. García, trans. A. P. Maudslay, intro. I. A. Leonard (New York, 1956)

López Luján, L., *The Offerings of the Templo Mayor of Tenochtitlan*, trans. B. R. & T. Ortiz de Montellano (Albuquerque, NM, 2005)

Matos Moctezuma, E., *The Great Temple of the Aztecs: Treasures of Tenochtitlan*, trans. D. Heyden (London & New York, 1994)

Wolf, E. R. (ed.), *Hispanic Ecology and Society* (Albuquerque, 1976) 287–302

## The Early Modern World

### LISBON

Couto, D., *Histoire de Lisbonne* (Paris, 2000)

Góis, D. de, *Lisbon in the Renaissance*, trans. J. S. Ruth (New York, 1996)

Jack, M., *Lisbon: City of the Sea* (London, 2007)

Laidlar, J., *Lisbon*, World Bibliographical Series Vol. 199 (Oxford, 1997)

Oliveira Marques, A. H. de , *History of Portugal* (New York, 1972)

Saunders, A. C. de C. M., *A Social History of Black Slaves and Freedmen in Portugal 1441–1555* (Cambridge, 1982)

### ROME

Hibbert, C., *Rome: The Biography of a City* (Harmondsworth, 1985)

King, R., *Michelangelo and the Pope's Ceiling* (New York, 2003)

Noel, G., *The Renaissance Popes* (London, 2006)

Partridge, L., *The Art of Renaissance Rome* (New York, 1996)

Vasari, G., *The Lives of the Artists* (Oxford, 1971)

### ISTANBUL

Crowley, R., *Constantinople: The Last Great Siege 1453* (New York, 2005)

Freely, J., *Istanbul: The Imperial City* (London & New York, 1996)

Goodwin, J., *Lords of the Horizons: A History of the Ottoman Empire* (London, 1998)

Kleiterp, M. & C, Huygens, *Istanbul: The City and the Sultan* (Amsterdam, 2006)

Mansel, P., *Constantinople: City of the World's Desire 1453–1924* (London, 1995)

Orga, I., *Portrait of a Turkish Family* (London, 1988)

### AGRA

Gupta, I. P., *Urban Glimpses of Mughal India: Agra, The Imperial Capital, 16th & 17th Centuries* (Delhi, 1986)

Koch, E., *The Complete Taj Mahal and the Riverfront Gardens of Agra* (London & New York, 2006)

Peck, L., *Agra: The Architectural Heritage* (New Delhi, 2008)

### ISFAHAN

Blake, S. P., *Half the World: The Social Architecture of Safavid Isfahan, 1590–1722* (Costa Mesa, CA, 1999)

Canby, S. R., *Shah 'Abbas. The Remaking of Iran* (London, 2009)

Hillenbrand, R., 'Safavid Architecture', in P. Jackson et al. (eds), *The Cambridge History of Iran*, Vol. 6: *The Timurid and Safavid Periods* (Cambridge, 1986) 759–842

Lambton, A. K. S, 'Isfahan' in *Encyclopaedia of Islam*, 2nd ed., vol. V (Leiden, 1991)

Newman, A., *Safavid Iran: Rebirth of a Persian Empire* (London, 2006)

### BEIJING

Abru, H., *A Persian Embassy to China: being an extract from Zubdatu't Twarikh of Hafiz Abru*, trans. K. M. Maitra (Lahore, 1934)

Arlington, L. C., & W. Lewisohn, *In Search of Old Peking* (Peking, 1935)

Naquin, S., *Peking: Temples and City Life 1400–1900* (Berkeley, 2000)

### KYOTO

Downer, L., *Geisha: The Secret History of a Vanishing World* (London, 2000)

Hibbett, H., *The Floating World in Japanese Fiction* (Boston, 2001)

Kaempfer, E., *Kaempfer's Japan: Tokugawa Culture Observed*, ed., trans. & annotated B. M. Bodart-Bailey (Honolulu, 1999)

Keene, D., *World Within Walls: Japanese Literature of the Pre-Modern Era, 1600–1867* (New York, 1999)

Morris, I., *The World of the Shining Prince: Court Life in Ancient Japan* (London, 1997)

Mosher, G., *Kyoto: A Contemplative Guide* (Rutland, VT, 1964)

Varley, H. P., *Japanese Culture* (Tokyo, 1974)

### PRAGUE

Fucikova, E. (ed.), *Rudolf II and Prague: The Court and the City* (London & New York, 1997)

Lau, J. M., *Prague: Then and Now* (San Diego, 2006)

Marshall, P. H., *The Mercurial Emperor: The Magic Circle of Rudolf II in Renaissance Prague* (London & New York, 2007)

Sugliano, C., *Prague: Past and Present* (New York, 2003)

## AMSTERDAM

Kistemaker, R., *Amsterdam: The Golden Age, 1275–1795* (New York, 1983)

Prak, M. A., *The Dutch Republic in the Seventeenth Century: The Golden Age* (Cambridge, 2005)

Schama, S., *Embarrassment of Riches* (London & New York, 2004)

## MEXICO CITY

Caistor, N. & E. Poniatowska, *Mexico City: A Cultural and Literary Companion* (Oxford, 1999)

Lombardo de Ruiz, S. (ed.), *Atlas histórico de la ciudad de México* (Mexico City, 1966)

## LONDON

Campbell, J. W. P., *Building St Paul's* (London & New York, 2008)

Hollis, L., *The Phoenix: St Paul's Cathedral* (London, 2008)

Wilson, A. N., *London: A Short History* (London, 2001)

## STOCKHOLM

Buckley, V., *Christina: Queen of Sweden* (London, 2004)

Kent, N., *A Concise History of Sweden* (Cambridge, 2008)

Lockhart, P. D., *Sweden in the Seventeenth Century* (New York, 2004)

Peterson, G. D., The Warrior Kings of Sweden (Jefferson, NC & London, 2007)

Roberts, M., *Gustavus Adolphus and the Rise of Sweden* (London, 1973)

Roberts, M. *From Oxenstierna to Charles XII* (Cambridge, 1991)

## DUBLIN

Casey, C. (ed.), *Dublin. The Buildings of Ireland* (London, 2005)

Craig, M. (ed. S. O'Keefe), *Dublin 1660–1860* (repr. Dublin, 2006)

Guinness, D., *Georgian Dublin* (London, 1993)

Longford, C., *A Biography of Dublin* (London, 1936)

McParland, E., *Public Architecture in Ireland, 1680–1760* (London, 2001)

Malton, J., *A Picturesque and Descriptive View of the City of Dublin* (1799, repr. Dublin, 1978)

O'Brien, G. & F. O'Kane (eds), *Georgian Dublin* (Dublin & Portland, OR, 2008)

Pakenham, V. & T., *Dublin: A Traveller's Companion* (repr. London, 2003)

## COPENHAGEN

Berman, P. G., *In Another Light. Danish Painting in the Nineteenth Century* (London & New York, 2007)

Bukdahl, E. M. & M. Bogh, *The Roots of Neo-Classicism: Wiedewelt, Thorvaldsen and Danish Sculpture of our Time* (Copenhagen, 2004)

Raabyemagel, H. & C. M. Smidt (eds), *Classicism in Copenhagen: Architecture in the Age of C. F. Hansen* (Copenhagen, 1998)

Woodward, C., *Copenhagen. The Buildings of Europe,* (Manchester, 1998)

## ST PETERSBURG

Amery, C. & B. Curran, *St Petersburg* (London, 2006)

Hughes, L., *Peter the Great: A Biography* (New Haven & London, 2004)

Iroshikov, M., *Before the Revolution: St Petersburg in Photographs, 1890–1914* (New York, 1992)

Lincoln, W. B., *Sunlight at Midnight: St Petersburg and the Rise of Modern Russia* (New York, 2002)

Shvidkovsky, D. & A. Orloff, *St Petersburg: Architecture of the Tsars* (New York, 1995)

Volkov, S., *St Petersburg: A Cultural History* (New York, 1995)

## VIENNA

Brandstatter, C. (ed.), *Vienna 1900 and the Heroes of Modernism* (London, 2006)

Oechslin, W., *Otto Wagner, Adolf Loos and the Road to Modern Architecture* (Cambridge, 2002)

Salm-Salm, M.-A. zu, *Klimt, Schiele, Moser, Kokoschka. Vienna 1900* (London, 2005)

Schorske, C. E., *Fin-de-Siècle Vienna: Politics and Culture* (New York, 1993)

Varnedoe, K., *Vienna, 1900: Art, Architecture and Design* (New York, 1986)

## EDINBURGH

Boswell, J. *Boswell's Edinburgh Journals 1767–1786*, edited by H. M. Milne (Edinburgh, 2001)
Buchan, J., *Crowded with Genius: The Scottish Englightenment* (London, 2003)
Dudley Edwards, O. & G. Richardson, (eds), *Edinburgh* (Edinburgh, 1983)
Edwards, B. & P. Jenkins, *Edinburgh: The Making of a Capital City* (Edinburgh, 2005)
Gifford, J. et al., *Edinburgh. The Buildings of Scotland* (London, 1984)
Linklater, E., *Edinburgh* (London, 1960)
Massie, A., *Edinburgh* (London, 1994)
Scott-Moncrieff, G., *Edinburgh* (London, 1947)
Youngson, A. J., *The Making of Classical Edinburgh*, (Edinburgh, 2002)

## The Age of the Modern City

## MOSCOW

Allenov, M. M., *Moscow: Treasures and Traditions* (Washington, 1990)
Figes, O., *Natasha's Dance: A Cultural History of Russia* (London & New York, 2002)
Kelly, L. (ed.), *Moscow: A Travellers' Companion* (London, 1983)

## PARIS

Carmona, M., *Haussmann* (Paris, 2000)
Girard, L., *Napoléon III* (Paris, 1983)
de Goncourt, E. L. A. H., & J. A. H., *The Journal of the Goncourts: Pages From A Great Diary* (London, c. 1930)
Kurtz, H., *The Empress Eugénie* (London, 1964)
Mansel, P., *Paris Between Empires* (London, 2001; New York, 2003)
Mérimée, P., *Letters to an Unknown*, I & II (New York, 1906)

## LONDON

Inwood, S., *A History of London* (London, 1998)
Mayhew, H., *London Labour and the London Poor*, 4 vols (repr. New York, 1968)
Olsen, D., *The Growth of Victorian London* (London, 1983)
Owen, D., *The Government of Victorian London* (Cambridge, MA, 1982)
Wilson, A. N., *The Victorians* (London, 2007)

## BUDAPEST

Lukacs, J., *Budapest 1900: A Historical Portrait of a City and its Culture* (New York, 1988)
Sauer, W., 'Austria-Hungary: The Making of Central Europe', in R. Aldrich (ed.), *The Age of Empires* (London & New York, 2007)
Török, A., *Budapest: A Critical Guide* (rev. ed., London, 1998)

## MONTREAL

Beauchemin, Y., *The Alley Cat: A Novel* (New York, 1988)
Havard, G., *The Great Peace of Montreal of 1701: French-Native Diplomacy in the Seventeenth Century* (Montreal, 2003)
MacLean, R., *The Oatmeal Ark* (London, 2008)
Morris, J., *O Canada!* (London, 1992)
Richler, M., *The Apprenticeship of Duddy Kravitz* (New York, 1991)
Tremblay, M., *Les Belles-Soeurs* (Vancouver, 1991)
Woodcock, G., *Social History Of Canada* (Markham, ON, 1988)

## WASHINGTON DC

Berg, S. W., *Grand Avenues. The Story of the French Visionary Who Designed Washington, D.C.* (New York, 2007)
Bordewich, F., *Washington. The Making of the American Capital* (New York, 2008)
Gutheim, F. & A. J. Lee, *Worthy of the Nation, Washington, D.C., from L'Enfant to the National Capital Planning Commission* (2nd ed. Baltimore, MD, 2006)
Schama, S., *American History: The Future* (London, 2008)
Standiford, L., *Washington Burning: How a Frenchman's Vision for Our Nation's Capital Survived Congress, the Founding Fathers, and the Invading British Army* (New York, 2008)

## BARCELONA

Fernandez-Armesto, F., *Barcelona: A Thousand Years of the City's Past* (London, 1991)
Hensbergen, G. van, *Gaudi. A Biography* (London & New York, 2001)
Hughes, R., *Barcelona* (new ed. London, 2001)

## NEW DELHI

Dalrymple, W., *City of Djinns* (London, 1995; New York, 2003)

Hussey, C., *The Life of Sir Edwin Lutyens* (London, 1950)

Irving, R. G., *Indian Summer: Lutyens, Baker and Imperial Delhi* (London, 1981)

Nath, A., *Dome Over India* (Mumbai, 2002)

Ridley, J., *The Architect and his Wife: A Life of Edwin Lutyens* (London, 2002)

http://www.india-seminar.com

## BERLIN

Döblin, A., *Berlin Alexanderplatz* (London & New York, 2004)

Gaddis, J. L., *The Cold War* (London, 2006)

Isherwood, C., *Goodbye to Berlin* (London, 2003)

Kempowski, W., *Das Echolot: ein Kollektives Tagebuch* (München, 1993)

Ladd, B., *The Ghosts of Berlin: Confronting German History in the Urban Landscape* (Chicago, 1997)

Mann, H., *The Blue Angel* (New York, 1979)

Metzger, R., *Berlin in the Twenties* (London, 2007)

Richie, A., *Faust's Metropolis* (New York, 1998)

## CHICAGO

Grossman, J. R. et al., *The Encyclopedia of Chicago* (Chicago, 2004)

Mayer, H. M. & R. C. Wade, *Chicago: Growth of a Metropolis* (Chicago, 1969)

Sinkevitch, A. (ed.), *AIA Guide to Chicago* (New York, 2004)

## LOS ANGELES

Banham, R., *Los Angeles: The Architecture of Four Ecologies* (New York, 1971)

Davis, M., *City of Quartz: Excavating the Future in Los Angeles* (London & New York, 1990)

Ulin, D. L. (ed.), *Writing Los Angeles: A Literary Anthology* (New York, 2002)

## BUENOS AIRES

Collier, S. et al., *Tango. The Dance, the Song, the Story* (London & New York, 1995)

Podalsky, L., *Specular City: Transforming Culture, Consumption, and Space in Buenos Aires, 1955–1973* (Philadelphia, 2004)

Wilson, J., *Buenos Aires: A Cultural and Literary History* (Oxford, 1999)

## SINGAPORE

Barber, N., *Sinister Twilight: The Fall and Rise Again of Singapore* (London, 1968)

Jayapal, M., *Old Singapore* (Singapore, 1992)

Keay, J., *Last Post: The End of Empire in the Far East* (London, 1997)

Liu, G., *Singapore: A Pictorial History, 1819–2000* (Singapore, 1999)

Turnbull, C. M., *A History of Singapore, 1819–1975* (Kuala Lumpur, 1977)

## NEW YORK

Bloom, A., *Prodigal Sons: The New York Intellectuals and Their World* (New York, 1986)

Broyard, A., *Kafka Was the Rage. A Greenwich Village Memoir* (New York, 1993)

Homberger, E., *The Historical Atlas of New York City: A Visual Celebration of nearly 400 Years of New York City's History* (New York, 1994)

Jackson, K. T. & D. S. Dunbar, *Empire City: New York Through the Centuries* (New York, 2002)

Morris, J., *Manhattan '45* (London & New York, 1987)

Morris, J., *The Great Port:A Passage Through New York* (2nd ed., London, 1987)

Wallock, L. (ed.), *New York: Culture Capital of the World, 1940–1965* (New York, 1988)

White, E. B., *Here is New York*, intro. by R. Angell (New York, 2000)

## SÃO PAULO

Andrews, G. R., *Blacks and Whites in São Paulo, Brazil, 1888–1988* (Madison, WI, 1991)

Caldeira, T., *City of Walls: Crime, Segregation, and Citizenship in São Paulo* (Berkeley, CA, 2001)

Luna F. V. & H. S. Klein, *Slavery and the Economy of São Paulo 1750–1850* (Stanford, CA, 2003)

Morse, R. M., *From Community to Metropolis: A Biography of São Paulo, Brazil* (Gainesville, FL, 1958)

Woodard, J. P., *A Place in Politics: São Paulo, Brazil, from Seigneurial Republicanism to Regionalist Revolt* (Durham, NC, 2009)

## TOKYO

Akira Naito, *Edo, The City that Became Tokyo: An Illustrated History* (Tokyo, London & New York, 2003)

Downer, L., *The Brothers: The Hidden World of Japan's Richest Family* (London, 1994)

Richie, D., *A Lateral View: Essays on Contemporary Japan* (Tokyo, 1991)

Richie, D., *Tokyo: A View of the City* (London, 1999)

Seidensticker, E., *Low City, High City: Tokyo from Edo to the Earthquake* (New York, 1983)

Seidensticker, E., *Tokyo Rising: The City Since the Great Earthquake* (New York, 1990)

Waley, P., *Tokyo Now and Then: An Explorer's Guide* (New York & Tokyo, 1984)

## SYDNEY

Ashton, P., *The Accidental City, Planning Sydney Since 1788* (Sydney, 1993)

Birmingham, J., *Leviathan, The Unauthorised Biography of Sydney* (Sydney, 1999)

Drew, P., *The Masterpiece. Jørn Utzon, A Secret Life* (Melbourne, 1999)

Emmett, P., *Sydney. Metropolis, Suburb, Harbour* (Sydney, 2000)

Golder, H., *Sacked: Removing and Remaking the Sydney City Council* (Sydney, 2004)

Morris, J., *Sydney* (new ed. London, 1993)

Spearritt, P., *Sydney's Century: A History* (Sydney, 1999)

Watson, A. (ed.), *Building a Masterpiece: The Sydney Opera House* (Sydney, 2006)

Webber, P., *The Design of Sydney, Three Decades of Change in the City Centre* (Sydney, 1988)

## SHANGHAI

Baker, B., *Shanghai: Electric and Lurid City: An Anthology* (Oxford, 1998)

Ballard, J. G., *Empire of the Sun* (London & New York, 1984)

Nien Cheng, *Life and Death in Shanghai* (London, 1987)

Yatsko, P., *New Shanghai: The Rocky Rebirth of China's Legendary City* (New York, 2001)

# Sources of Illustrations

a = above, b = below, l = left, r = right

TEXT COPYRIGHT *The following serves as an extension of the information on p. 4:*
pp. 43–47 © 2009 Bettany Hughes; pp. 48–50 © 2009 W. J. F. Jenner; pp. 217–21, 276–79 © 2009 Simon Schama; pp. 222–25, 280 and 289–91, 313–15 © 2009 Felipe Fernandez-Armesto; pp. 261–64 © 2009 Philip Mansel

# Sources of Quotations

p. 15 A. R. George, *The Epic of Gilgamesh* (London, 1999); p. 18 Sir John Marshall, *Illustrated London News*, 20 September 1924; p. 21 Herodotus *Histories*, II: 99; p. 26 A. H. Rhind, *Thebes; its tombs and their tenants* (London, 1862); p. 30 quoted in T. Bryce *Life and Society in the Hittite World* (Oxford, 2002); p. 43 Thucydides, *History of the Peloponnesian War*, 2.38.1; p. 46 Plutarch, *Life of Perikles* 13; p. 51 Strabo, *Geography*, 17.1.8, trans. H. L. Jones (Cambridge, 1930) and Ammianus Marcellinus, History, 22.16; p. 55 Herodotus, *Histories*, II: 29, trans. G. Rawlinson (New York, 1862); p. 58 Pliny the Elder, *Natural History*, 5. 70; p. 62 Suetonius, *The Twelve Caesars, Augustus*, 28, trans. Robert Graves (London, 1957); p. 70 Sahagún, Fray Bernardino de, *The Origin of the Gods. Book 3 of the Florentine Codex*, trans. and notes by A. J. O. Anderson and C. E. Dibble (Santa Fe, 1978 [1569]): 1; p. 75 Avendaño y Loyola, Fray Andrés, *Relation of Two Trips to Peten*, trans. Charles P. Bowditch and Guillermo Rivera (Culver City 1987); p. 79 Edward Gibbon, *The Decline and Fall of the Roman Empire*, chap. 17, p. 224 (1776–89); p. 91, The Koran, 14, translated by N. J. Dawood (London 1990); p. 94 Mark Twain, *Innocents Abroad* (Hartford, 1869); p. 99 translation after Arthur Waley, *The Life and Times of Po Chü-I, 772-846 A.D.* (New York, 1949); p. 103 Yaqut al-Hamawi, *Dictionary of Countries*, 1224, from W. S. Davis (ed.) *Readings in Ancient History: Illustrative Extracts from the Sources*, 2 vols (Boston: 1912–13), vol. II, 365; p. 107 quoted in Robert Hillenbrand, '"The Ornament of the World": Medieval Córdoba as a Cultural Centre', *The Legacy of Muslim Spain*, Salmia Khadra Jayyusi (ed.) (Leiden & New York, 1992), p. 18; p. 112 H. Mouhot, *Travels in the central parts of Indo-China* (London, 1864); p. 116 Ibn Jubayr *Travels*; p. 120 Meshulam of Volterra, *Massa*, ed. A. Yaari (Jerusalem, 1948), p. 50; p. 128 after 'Song of the Peace with England', in T. Wright, *The Political Songs of England from the Reign of John to that of Edward II* (new ed., Cambridge 1996); p. 131 Jean de Jandun, 'A Treatise of the Praises of Paris', ed. & trans. by Robert. W. Berger, in *Old Paris: An Anthology of Source Descriptions, 1323–1790* (New York, 2002); p. 149, quoted in M. F. Rosenthal, *The Honest Courtesan* (Chicago, 1992), p. 31; p. 153 Scipio Ammirato, *Istorie de Firenze*; p. 158 Henry Ling Roth, *Great Benin* (Halifax, 1903); p. 165 *Narratives of the rites and laws of the Yncas*, trans C. R. Markham (New York, [1571] 1964); p. 169 Díaz, Bernal del Castillo, B. *The Discovery and Conquest of Mexico*, trans. A. P. Maudslay (New York, [1560s] 1956); p. 176 Francisco Sá de Miranda, in Rodrigues Lapa (ed.), *Obras Completas* (Lisbon, 1977); p. 188 Abu Talib Kalim, *Diwan*, ed. Partau Bayza'i (Tehran, 1957), p. 341, verse 24; p. 189 Kanbo, Bahar-sukhan, fols. 248a & 248b, as trans. in E. Koch, 'The Mughal Waterfront Garden', in A. Petruccioli (ed.), *Gardens in the Time of the Great Muslim Empires: Theory and Design, Muqarnas Supplements* (Leiden/New York/Cologne, 1997), p. 143; p. 189 F. Bernier, *Travels in the Mogul Empire: A.D. 1656–1668*, trans. A. Constable (1891, repr. New Delhi, 1972), p. 285; p. 192 J.-B. Tavernier, *Travels in India*, 2 vols. trans. V. Ball, 2nd ed. W. Crooke (1925, repr. New Delhi, 1977); p. 193 Iskandar Munshi, *Tarikh-i Alam-ara-yi-Abbasi*, Iraj Afshar (ed.) (Tehran, 1955) 1:544; p. 197 *The Voyages and Adventures of Fernão Mendes Pinto*, trans. H. Cogan (C. D. Ley (ed.), *Portuguese Voyages 1498–1663* (London, 1947), p. 154, 156; p. 197 Hafiz Abru, *A Persian Embassy to China*, trans. K. M. Maitra (Lahore, 1934), pp. 49–50; p. 201 Ihara Saikaku, trans. in H. Hibbett, *The Floating World in Japanese Fiction* (London, 1959); p. 217 Franz Kafka, *Letters to Friends, Family and Editors*, trans. R. & C. Winston (London, 1978); p. 217 Andrew Marvell, *The Character of Holland*, 1653; p. 222 J. E. Pacheco, *Vecindades del centro*, 1976; p. 226 H. H. Milman, *Annals of St Paul's Cathedral* (London, 1868); p. 235 Richard Stanyhurst *The Description of Ireland*, (1577); p. 239 Hans Christian Andersen, *The Biography* (1855); p. 242 A. Pushkin, *The Bronze Horseman* (1833), trans. Waclaw Lednicki, *Pushkin's Bronze Horseman* (Berkeley, CA 1955); p. 246 Robert Musil, *The Man Without Qualities*, trans. S. Wilkins (London, 1995); p. 251 R. L. Stevenson, *Edinburgh Picturesque Notes* (London, 1878); p. 256 F. F. Vigel *Memoirs (Zapiski)* (Moscow, 1928); p. 257 Marquis de Custine, *Empire of the Czar* (London, 1843); p. 265 C. Dickens, *Dombey and Son* (London, 1848); p. 270 Gyorgy Ligeti, interview by Dorle J. Soria, in *Musical America*, vol. 107, no. 4, September 1987; p. 276 C. Dickens, *American Notes for General Circulation* (Paris, 1842); p. 280 K. Marx & F. Engels, *Revolution in Spain* (1854, pub. London, 1939); p. 292 R. Byron, *Country Life* (1931); p. 297 quoted in O. Friedrich, *Before the Deluge: A Portrait of Berlin in the 1920s* (New York, 1963); T. Dreiser, *The Titan* (New York, 1914); p. 307 J. Fante, *Ask* the Dust (New York, 1939); p. 313 J. L. Borges, *The Mythical Founding of Buenos Aires* (1929); p. 316 Stamford Raffles to Col. Addenbrook, 10 June 1819, in V. Harlow & F. Madden, *British Colonial Developments 1774–1834* (Oxford, 1953); p. 320 T. Wolfe, *The Web and the Rock* (New York, 1939); p. 323 A. Broyard, *Kafka Was the Rage. A Greenwich Village Memoir* (New York, 1993); D. Wakefield, *New York in the Fifties* (Boston, 1992); p. 324 F. W. and G. S. McDarrah, *Beat Generation: Glory Days in Greenwich Village* (New York, 1996); p. 325 quoted in R. A. Gorman, *Michael Harrington – Speaking American* (New York, 1995); p. 330 P. Tonkin, 'City of Dionysus' in P. Emmett, *Sydney. Metropolis, Suburb, Harbour* (Sydney, 2000); p. 334 D. Richie, *A Lateral View. Essays on Contemporary Japan* (Tokyo, 1987); p. 338 J. G. Ballard, *Empire of the Sun* (London, 1984).

# Index

Numbers in *italics* indicate illustrations

Lübeck 9, 110, 133–36; guilds 134; merchants and trade 133–35
Lufthansa 136
Luftwaffe 265, 269
Lund, battle of 233
Luoyang 50, 100
Lutfallah, Sheikh 195
Luther, Martin 182
Lutheran Reformation 231
Lutyens, Edwin 255, 293, 294, 295
Lutzen, battle of 232
Luxor *see* Thebes

McCarthy, Joseph 323
Macchiavelli, Niccoló 156–7
McCoy, Horace 310
Macedon 29
Macedonia 46, 53
al-Madina al-Zahira 109
Madinat al-Zahra 109
Madrid 290, 306
Mahdi (Twelfth Imam) 196
Malaysian Federation 317
Mali (Mandingo) 163
Malmö 241
Mamet, David 304
Mamluks 88, 93, 120–23, 140
Mamontov family 259
Man Ray 310
Mandingo empire 161, 163
Mann, Heinrich 299
Mann, Thomas 136, 310
Mannerism 156
Mansa Musa 161, 163
al-Mansur, Caliph 103, 104
al-Mansur, vizier 109
Mantua 150
Manuel I, King 177
Manzoni, Alessandro 262
Mao Zedong 340
Maragall, Joan 289
Mareotis, Lake 52
Margrethe II, Queen of Denmark 239
Maria Theresa, Empress 246
Marie Antoinette, Queen 262
Marie de' Medici, Queen 218
markets and trade 21, 88, 108, 122, 123, 125, 135, 140, 145, 159, 185, 186, 218–19, 327
Marmara, Sea of (Propontis) 79–80
Martin, John 37
Martin V (Colonna), Pope 180
Mary I (Tudor), Queen 146

Masaccio 154
Masaryk, Jan 206
Maudslay, Alfred Percival 85
Maximilian, Emperor of Mexico 263
Maximilian II, Holy Roman Emperor 207
Maya 70, 71, 74, 75–6
Mayhew, Henry 267
Mecca 69, 86, 95, 96, 97, 120, 161, 186; Ka'ba 87, 91, 92, 93
Medes 40
Medici, Alessandro de' 156
Medici, Grand Duchess Anna Maria de' 157
Medici, Cosimo I de', Grand Duke of Tuscany 154–55, 156
Medici, Giuliano de' 155
Medici, Lorenzo de' (the Magnificent) 147, 155–56
Medici family 150, *see also* Leo X (de' Medici), Pope; Marie de' Medici, Queen
Medina 92, 96, 120
Medina Sidonia, Alonso, Duke of 179
Mediterranean sea 13, 41, 51, 92, 120, 149, 174, 186
Mehmet II, Sultan 184–85, 186
Meigs, Montgomery 278–89
Memphis 13, 21–24, 26, 120; Kom Qala 23; Serapeum 23
Men-nefer 23
Mendes Pinto, Ferno 197, 199–200
Menes 22
Menzel, Adolf 282
Menzies, Robert 331
merchants 115, 131, 133, 171, 178, 203, 218, 258
Merenptah, King 23
Meroé 11, 13, 55–57; Nymphaeum 56; pyramid cemeteries 55, 56, 83; 'Royal City' 56–57; temple of Amun 56
Meru, Mount 113
Mesopotamia 15–16, 20, 33, 34, 37, 95
Metternich, Klemens, Prince von 248, 249
Mexico 261, 307; conquest of 172, 223
Mexico City 10, 71, 110, 169, 175, 222–25; cathedral 223–24; Central Square (Zócalo) 215, 222
Michelangelo Buonarroti 137, 156, 181, 182, 183, 209, 279
Michelozzo 155
Mies van der Rohe, Ludwig 290, 300, 304
migration 92, 158, 183, 269, 305, *see also* immigration
Milan 26, 79, 149, 150, 260; Duke of 154
Miller, Arthur 321
Milton, John 226, 228
Ming dynasty 175, 197
Mishima, Yukio 336
Mississippi, river 273, 301, 306